ADVANCED TEXTS IN ECONOMETRICS

General Editors

C. W. J. Granger G. E. Mizon

WORKBOOK ON COINTEGRATION

PETER REINHARD HANSEN
SØREN JOHANSEN

OXFORD UNIVERSITY PRESS
1998

Oxford University Press, Great Clarendon Street, Oxford OX2 6DP
Oxford New York
Athens Auckland Bangkok Bogota Buenos Aires Calcutta
Cape Town Chennai Dar es Salaam Delhi Florence Hong Kong Istanbul
Karachi Kuala Lumpur Madrid Melbourne Mexico City Mumbai
Nairobi Paris São Paolo Singapore Taipei Tokyo Toronto Warsaw
and associated companies in
Berlin Ibadan

Oxford is a registered trade mark of Oxford University Press

Published in the United States by
Oxford University Press Inc., New York

First published 1998

British Library Cataloguing in Publication Data
Data available

Library of Congress Cataloging in Publication Data
Data available

ISBN 0–19–877608–X (Hbk)
ISBN 0–19–877607–1 (Pbk)

1 3 5 7 9 10 8 6 4 2

Printed in Great Britain
on acid-free paper by
Bookcraft (Bath) Ltd,
Midsomer Norton, Somerset

Preface

This *Workbook on Cointegration* is a companion to the monograph by S. Johansen, *Likelihood-Based Inference in Cointegrated Vector Autoregressive Models,* 2nd edn, Oxford University Press (1996), referred to in the following as SJ. The workbook contains exercises and solutions concerned with the analysis of the cointegrated vector autoregressive model. The monograph has been used for a course on cointegration at the University of Copenhagen and the majority of the exercises have been set either as training exercises or as exam questions. A few have been added. Many of them are difficult and we feel that it is appropriate to have complete solutions, so that students will know that they are on the right track when trying to solve them. We have marked some exercises with a $*$ to indicate that they illustrate a point that may be worth remembering and with $**$ if we find that they are difficult.

The exercises are divided into chapters as in SJ and each chapter starts with a brief overview of the main results obtained there, so that it is apparent what the exercises should illustrate or extend.

We refer to formula j in Chapter i of SJ by $(i.j)$ and to equation i in an exercise by (i).

It is our hope that the reader who manages to get through all these exercises will share our wonder at the richness of structure these models seem to have.

The authors would like to thank the Danish Social Sciences Research Council and Danish Science Research Council for their continuing support of our work on the development of statistical methods for econometrics.

Peter Reinhard Hansen
University of San Diego
California

Søren Johansen
European University Institute
Florence

Contents

1

Introduction

The exercises presented with solutions in this Workbook treat the theory of cointegration in the framework of the vector autoregressive model. As an introduction we give a brief summary of the most important results from the theory as presented in SJ.

The vector autoregressive model is a simple and useful econometric model for analyzing the stochastic variation of economic time series. We use the model in the error correction form

$$\Delta X_t = \Pi X_{t-1} + \sum_{i=1}^{k-1} \Gamma_i \Delta X_{t-i} + \Phi D_t + \varepsilon_t, \qquad t = 1, \ldots, T, \tag{1.1}$$

where the error term ε_t is i.i.d. and the deterministic terms D_t can be a constant, a linear term, seasonal dummies or other deterministic terms; see (4.1).

The results on cointegration in the vector autoregressive model are naturally divided into three topics. The first topic is defined by the structure theory, where the solution of the equation (1.1) is given a convenient representation; see (1.2). The next topic consists of the statistical theory, where many submodels are formulated and related to economic interpretations, and where the likelihood function is analysed with the purpose of deriving estimators and test statistics. The final topic deals with the asymptotic theory, where limit distributions of the estimators and test statistics are derived, based upon the theory of weak convergence towards Brownian motion.

1.1 The structure theory.

Equation (1.1) can be solved for X_t as a function of initial values, deterministic terms and the ε. The properties of X_t depend on the stochastic properties of ε, the choice of the parameters and the initial values of the process. The dynamic features of the process are conveniently described by the roots of the characteristic polynomial

$$A(z) = (1-z)I - \Pi z - \sum_{i=1}^{k-1} (1-z) z^i \Gamma_i.$$

If the parameters of the model are chosen such that the roots are outside the unit disc, then the initial values can be given their invariant stationary distribution and X_t becomes stationary and $I(0)$. If one or more of the roots are at $z = 1$, such that $\Pi = \alpha\beta'$, the process is said to have unit roots, and the process X_t cannot be made stationary by any choice of the initial distribution.

Granger's representation theorem (SJ, Theorems 4.2 and 4.6) clarifies how parameters and initial values should be chosen to give processes that are either $I(1)$ or $I(2)$. It is, therefore, fundamental for the analysis of the structure of the processes and is used repeatedly in the exercises. Under the assumption that the process is $I(1)$ the representation is given by:

$$X_t = C\sum_{i=1}^{t}(\varepsilon_i + \Phi D_i) + \sum_{i=0}^{\infty} C_i(\varepsilon_{t-i} + \Phi D_{t-i}) + A, \tag{1.2}$$

where

$$C = \beta_\perp(\alpha'_\perp(I - \sum_{i=1}^{k-1}\Gamma_i)\beta_\perp)^{-1}\alpha'_\perp,$$

and the coefficients C_i decrease exponentially, and A depends on initial values such that $\beta' A = 0$.

Based on such a representation one can calculate the means and variances of components of the process and derive the cointegrating. The representation theorem is also useful for discussing how the deterministic terms influence the process. Finally, it is the main tool for deriving the asymptotic properties of the process and, hence, of the derived estimators and test statistics.

The representation theorem shows explicitly the impulse response function given by the coefficients C_i, and the long-run effect of a shock to the system is given by C; see SJ, Theorem 4.2.

The exercises in Chapters 2, 3 and 4, are chosen to illustrate various types of processes that can be generated by equation (1.1). They also demonstrate how one can find parameter values that determine specific properties of the process.

1.2 The statistical theory

The possibility of interpreting cointegration vectors as economic long-run relations is the main reason why the vector autoregressive model has become widely used in the empirical analysis of economic data. The statistical concept of cointegration in the $I(1)$ model, involving linear combination of levels of the variables, corresponds to the economic concept of a long-run static steady-state relation. In a similar way, the statistical concept of multicointegration or polynomial cointegration, involving linear combinations of both levels and differences, corresponds to the economic concept of a long-run dynamic steady-state relation.

A useful aspect of the model is that it gives a framework for modelling both short- and long-run reactions in the same model. The $I(1)$ model describes the short-run adjustment in growth rates when the economy is no longer on its steady-state position, i.e. how the correction towards the equilibrium takes place.

An important aspect of the statistical analysis is the large number of misspecification tests that have been developed to detect whether the model is well specified or not. Unless the model assumptions correspond to the behaviour of the data, the statistical tests will not be valid and, therefore, render invalid inference. Thus a misspecified model requires a new model to be formulated. Used in this way one can gradually learn more about reality by analysing the data. The popularity and the widespread use of the cointegration models also lies in the availability of user friendly software producing parameter estimates in few seconds.

The exercises in Chapter 5 illustrate an important aspect of the statistical analysis, in formulating long-run economic relations as parameter restrictions on the cointegrating relations. Of special interest is the discussion and illustration of the identification problem for cointegrating vectors.

The exercises of Chapters 6 to 9 show that many submodels of the general vector autoregressive model can be solved by the reduced rank technique based on suitable modifications and reformulations. In fact important developments of the theory originate from studying various models with this property.

The formal statistical theory is developed from the Gaussian likelihood function, and includes the derivation of maximum likelihood estimators under various restrictions on the cointegrating relations β and their adjustment coefficients α. The main tool for calculating the maximum likelihood estimators and likelihood ratio tests is the algorithm for reduced rank regression which calculates eigenvalues of certain product moment matrices; see SJ, Theorems 6.1 and 6.2.

1.3 The asymptotic theory

The asymptotic theory of the estimators and test statistics in the cointegrated model relies heavily on the theory of the Brownian motion and the notion of weak convergence on function space. The basic result is that under general conditions the cumulated errors, suitably normalized, converge to a Brownian motion. This implies that the various limit distributions derived for the test for cointegrating rank and the estimator of β can be expressed in terms of Brownian motion. Thus, the test for cointegrating rank has a limit distribution given by the generalized Dickey-Fuller distribution of the form

$$tr\left\{\int_0^1 (dB)F' \left(\int_0^1 FF'du\right) \int_0^1 F(dB)'\right\}.$$

Here B is a Brownian motion given by the weak limit of the common trends, and F is defined in terms of B and the deterministic terms in the model; see SJ Chapter 11.

The limit distribution of $T(\hat{\beta} - \beta)$ is given by a mixed Gaussian distribution. The basic result is that, whereas the test statistic for determination of the rank has a limit distribution that depends on the common trends of the model, asymptotic inference on β can be conducted in the Gaussian distribution conditional on the common trends.

The exercises to Chapters 10 to 14 illustrate the asymptotic techniques by applying them to various modifications of the results given in the book.

1.4 Conclusion

What is fascinating about the cointegrated vector autoregression is the very rich structure it has. The simple linear structure in the conditional mean leads, via Granger's representation theorem, to a surprisingly rich class of processes. The many models that can be formulated as submodels of the vector autoregressive model make it an efficient framework that allows one to analyse a variety of economic phenomena. The model is used to discuss a number of important concepts like cointegration, common trends, impulse responses, identification issues, weak exogeneity etc., all of which can be treated rigorously in the same framework.

The amount of insight that one needs in order to apply these models clearly depends on what one wants to do with them. It is our impression that often when they are applied to the analysis of real data, the methods need a small modification, either the variances are not constant, or there is a structural break in the middle of the period, or perhaps some non-linearity is needed in the modelling.

If one wants to be able to modify the methods due to the changed assumptions, then one needs quite a lot of insight into the more technical aspects of the vector autoregressive model.

Granger's representation theorem for the solution of the autoregressive equations shows how variance heteroskedasticity influences inference, or what implications a dummy introduced in the model has for the process. Often the changed model assumptions imply the need to derive the maximum likelihood estimator again using some variant of the reduced rank regression, or some other optimizing technique. Similarly there is a need to modify the asymptotic results, and the techniques for doing so build upon the theory of Brownian motion. Thus, when the models are applied seriously in practice, one will have to know not only the results of the simple models, as described in SJ, but also the theory behind them.

The cointegrated vector autoregressive model is an example of an econometric model which is so simple, that it can be analysed in detail. The more one analyses the model, the more results one can obtain. It has been very interesting to see how the model has given the possibility to ask precise questions and find the natural answers.

The only way to learn the theory is to use it, and that is why the exercises provided here are useful. Complete solutions are provided and indicate many interesting aspects of the model and some potentially useful extensions. It is hoped, that by insisting on a very thorough analysis of this particular model it can serve as an example of what type of analysis one should make, if possible, of other models in econometrics.

2

The Vector Autoregressive Model

In Chapter 2 of SJ the basic facts about the vector autoregressive model with unrestricted parameters are given, and the asymptotics of the statistical theory is given in the stationary case. The p-dimensional process X_t considered throughout the book is generated by the autoregressive equations

$$X_t = \Pi_1 X_{t-1} + \cdots + \Pi_k X_{t-k} + \Phi D_t + \varepsilon_t, \qquad t = 1, \ldots, T, \tag{2.1}$$

where $X_{-k+1}, \ldots, X_0$, are fixed initial values and the ε are i.i.d. $N_p(0, \Omega)$. The deterministic terms D_t contain constants, linear terms or seasonal dummies.

The characteristic polynomial is defined as the matrix-valued polynomial

$$A(z) = I - \Pi_1 z - \cdots - \Pi_k z^k,$$

and the determinant is $|A(z)|$. In Theorem 2.1 the solution of the autoregressive equations is given as a function of initial values and the random errors ε. It is assumed throughout the book that the roots of the equation

$$|A(z)| = 0,$$

are either outside the unit disc or equal to one (see SJ, Assumption 1, p. 14), and it is then shown how the process can be made stationary by a suitable choice of the distribution of the initial values, thus representing the process as an infinite sum of past discounted errors. In section 2.2 we consider the autoregressive model generated by (2.1). The parameters are

$$(\Pi_1, \ldots, \Pi_k, \Phi, \Omega)$$

which vary freely, such that Ω is positive definite symmetric. It is shown that the maximum likelihood estimator can be found by regression and in Theorem 2.3 it is shown that the asymptotic distribution of the estimators is Gaussian if the parameters are chosen such that the process is stationary. The methods are illustrated by the analysis of two data sets, which are available on the Internet at http://www.math.ku.dk/~sjo/. Various misspecification tests are given to check that the model has been chosen reasonably well. The roots of the characteristic polynomial are calculated as a check for stationarity.

The book has no exercises for this chapter but we include two here to illustrate the concepts.

2.1

Consider the model

$$X_t = \Pi_1 X_{t-1} + \varepsilon_t, \qquad t = 1,\ 2,\ \ldots$$

where $\Pi_1 = \begin{pmatrix} \frac{1}{2} & 0 \\ 1 & \frac{1}{4} \end{pmatrix}$.

1. Show that the roots of the characteristic polynomial $A(z)$ are the reciprocal of the eigenvalues of the matrix Π_1.

2. Show that X_t can be made stationary by a suitable choice of initial conditions.

Solution to exercise 2.1

1. The characteristic polynomial $A(z)$ is given by

$$A(z) = I - \Pi_1 z = \begin{pmatrix} 1 - \frac{1}{2}z & 0 \\ -z & 1 - \frac{1}{4}z \end{pmatrix}.$$

The roots are found by solving $|A(z)| = (1 - \frac{1}{2}z)(1 - \frac{1}{4}z) = 0$ which implies $z = 2$ or $z = 4$.

The eigenvalues of Π_1 are found by solving

$$|\Pi_1 - \lambda I| = \left| \begin{pmatrix} \frac{1}{2} - \lambda & 0 \\ 1 & \frac{1}{4} - \lambda \end{pmatrix} \right| = 0,$$

which has the solutions $\lambda = \frac{1}{2}$ and $\lambda = \frac{1}{4}$.

This relation between roots of the characteristic polynomial and eigenvalues of the companion matrix (see SJ, p. 15) holds in general for all non-zero eigenvalues.

2. Since

$$|A(1)| = \left| \begin{pmatrix} \frac{1}{2} & 0 \\ -1 & \frac{3}{4} \end{pmatrix} \right| = \frac{3}{8} \neq 0,$$

Theorem 2.2 tells us that $X_t - E(X_t)$ can be made stationary by giving the initial value X_0 a suitable distribution. In this case $E(X_t) = 0$, and the stationary distribution of X_t is Gaussian with mean zero and variance given by

$$\sum_{i=0}^{\infty} \Pi_1^i \Omega \Pi_1'^i,$$

such that

$$\mathrm{Var}(X_t) = \Pi_1 \mathrm{Var}(X_t)\Pi_1' + \Omega,$$

see also exercise 4.12.

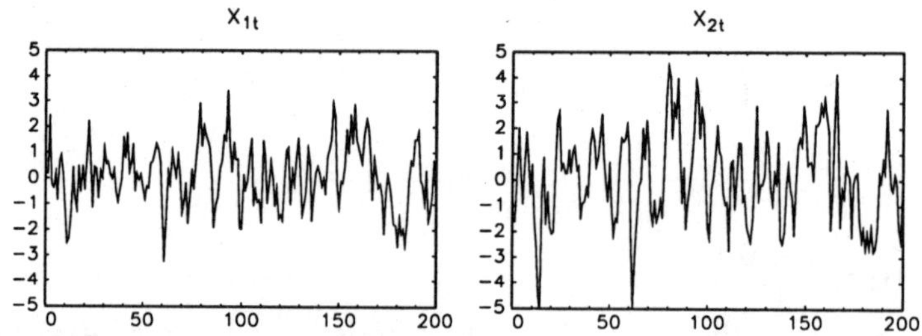

Fig. 2.1: Exercise 2.1. The variables X_{1t} and X_{2t} simulated with variance matrix $\Omega = I$ and $X_0 = (0,0)'$.

2.2

Consider a stationary autoregressive process $A(L)X_t = \varepsilon_t$ and the corresponding moving average representation

$$X_t = C(L)\varepsilon_t,$$

where $C(z) = \sum_{i=0}^{\infty} C_i z^i$.

1. Find the moving average coefficients for an AR(1) process.
2. Show that the moving average coefficients for an AR(2) can be found recursively by

$$C_0 = I, \quad C_1 = \Pi_1,$$

and

$$C_i = \Pi_1 C_{i-1} + \Pi_2 C_{i-2}, \qquad i = 2, \ldots$$

Solution to exercise 2.2

1. The characteristic polynomial $A(L)$ of an AR(1) process

$$X_t = \Pi_1 X_{t-1} + \varepsilon_t$$

is given by $A(z) = I - \Pi_1 z$. The moving average parameters are found by inverting the characteristic polynomial, which is possible for all stationary vector autoregressive processes. We find the generating function

$$C(z) = A(z)^{-1} = (I - \Pi_1 z)^{-1} = \sum_{i=0}^{\infty} \Pi_1^i z^i,$$

where we have used the formula for the sum of a geometric series. Hence, the coefficients are given by $C_i = \Pi_1^i$.

2. A stationary AR(2) process

$$X_t = \Pi_1 X_{t-1} + \Pi_2 X_{t-2} + \varepsilon_t \tag{1}$$

has a moving average representation

$$X_t = \sum_{i=0}^{\infty} C_i \varepsilon_{t-i}. \tag{2}$$

By inserting (2) into (1) we find

$$\sum_{i=0}^{\infty} C_i \varepsilon_{t-i} = \Pi_1 \sum_{i=0}^{\infty} C_i \varepsilon_{t-i-1} + \Pi_2 \sum_{i=0}^{\infty} C_i \varepsilon_{t-i-2} + \varepsilon_t,$$

which can be rewritten as

$$0 = (C_0 - I)\varepsilon_t + (C_1 - \Pi_1 C_0)\varepsilon_{t-1} + (C_2 - \Pi_1 C_1 - \Pi_2 C_0)\varepsilon_{t-2} + \cdots$$

which gives us the coefficients for each of the epsilons.

Since the epsilons can take any value in $\mathbf{R}^p$, each of these coefficients must equal zero. Hence $C_0 = I$, $C_1 = \Pi_1$ and

$$C_t = \Pi_1 C_{t-1} + \Pi_2 C_{t-2}, \qquad t = 2, 3, \ldots,$$

as claimed in the exercise; see also SJ, Theorem 2.1.

3

Basic Definitions and Concepts

A multivariate linear process is defined by

$$Y_t = \sum_{i=0}^{\infty} C_i \varepsilon_{t-i}, \qquad t = 0, 1, \ldots,$$

where the coefficient matrices C_i decrease to zero exponentially fast, so that the function $C(z) = \sum_{i=0}^{\infty} C_i z^i$ is convergent for the complex argument satisfying $|z| < 1 + \delta$ for some $\delta > 0$; see SJ, Definition 3.1. The basic idea is to define an $I(0)$ process as a multivariate linear process where the sum of the matrix coefficients is non-zero, that is, $C(1) = \sum_{i=0}^{\infty} C_i \neq 0$. The class of $I(1)$ processes is defined as those that become $I(0)$ after taking the difference, and similarly a process is $I(2)$ if the difference is $I(1)$.

An $I(1)$ process with the property that a linear combination $\beta' X_t$ is stationary, is called cointegrated and the vector β is a cointegrating vector; see SJ, Definition 3.4. The cointegrating rank is the number of such independent vectors. Such processes can be generated from a moving average representation or as the solution to autoregressive equations. The moving average representation naturally focuses on the common stochastic trends, which are random walks, $\alpha'_\perp \sum_{i=1}^{t} \varepsilon_i$; the autoregressive representation gives rise to the interpretation of cointegrating relations $\beta' X_t$ as disequilibrium errors, and the coefficients α as describing the adjustment to deviation from equilibrium. The exercises illustrate these concepts.

3.1

Let

$$X_{1t} = \textstyle\sum_{i=1}^{t} \varepsilon_{1i} + \varepsilon_{2t},$$

$$X_{2t} = \tfrac{1}{2} \textstyle\sum_{i=1}^{t} \varepsilon_{1i} + \varepsilon_{3t},$$

$$X_{3t} = \varepsilon_{2t}.$$

Show that (1, −2, 0) and (0, 0, 1) are cointegrating vectors for the $I(1)$ process X_t.

Solution to exercise 3.1

It is seen immediately that

$$(1,-2,0)X_t = X_{1t} - 2X_{2t} = \varepsilon_{2t} - 2\varepsilon_{3t} \text{ and } (0,0,1)X_t = X_{3t} = \varepsilon_{2t}$$

are stationary processes. It only remains to see that X_t is $I(1)$. We show this by defining the process Y_t as the difference of X_t

$$Y_t = \Delta X_t = \begin{pmatrix} \varepsilon_{1t} + (\varepsilon_{2t} - \varepsilon_{2t-1}) \\ \frac{1}{2}\varepsilon_{1t} + (\varepsilon_{3t} - \varepsilon_{3t-1}) \\ \varepsilon_{2t} - \varepsilon_{2t-1} \end{pmatrix} = \begin{pmatrix} 1 & 1 & 0 \\ \frac{1}{2} & 0 & 1 \\ 0 & 1 & 0 \end{pmatrix} \varepsilon_t + \begin{pmatrix} 0 & -1 & 0 \\ 0 & 0 & -1 \\ 0 & -1 & 0 \end{pmatrix} \varepsilon_{t-1}$$
$$= C_0\varepsilon_t + C_1\varepsilon_{t-1},$$

and seeing that the moving average coefficients of the process Y_t are zero apart from the first and second, C_0 and C_1.

Since the sum of the moving average coefficients

$$\sum_{i=0}^{\infty} C_i = C_0 + C_1 = \begin{pmatrix} 1 & 0 & 0 \\ \frac{1}{2} & 0 & 0 \\ 0 & 0 & 0 \end{pmatrix} \neq 0,$$

it follows, by Definition 3.2, that Y_t is $I(0)$ and hence X_t is $I(1)$; see Definition 3.3.

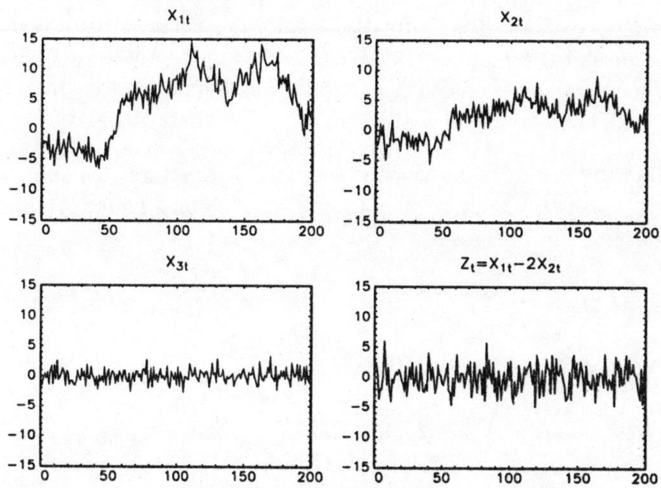

Fig. 3.1: Exercise 3.1. The figure shows the variables and the cointegrating relations. The process is simulated with $X_0 = 0$, $T = 200$ and $\Omega = I$.

3.2

Let

$$X_{1t} = \sum_{i=1}^{t}\sum_{j=1}^{i} \varepsilon_{1j} + \sum_{i=1}^{t} \varepsilon_{2i} + \varepsilon_{3t},$$

$$X_{2t} = \sum_{i=1}^{t}\sum_{j=1}^{i} \varepsilon_{1j} - \sum_{i=1}^{t} \varepsilon_{2i} + \varepsilon_{3t},$$

$$X_{3t} = \sum_{i=1}^{t} \varepsilon_{1i} + \sum_{i=1}^{t} \varepsilon_{2i} + \varepsilon_{3t}.$$

Show that X_t is $I(2)$ and that $X_{1t} - X_{2t}$ is $I(1)$, $X_{1t} - X_{2t} - 2X_{3t}$ is $I(1)$, while $X_{1t} - X_{2t} - 2X_{3t} + 2\Delta X_{1t}$ is stationary.

Answer to exercise 3.2

By defining

$$\begin{aligned} Y_t &= \Delta^2 X_t \\ &= \begin{pmatrix} 1 & 1 & 1 \\ 1 & -1 & 1 \\ 1 & 1 & 1 \end{pmatrix} \varepsilon_t + \begin{pmatrix} 0 & -1 & -2 \\ 0 & 1 & -2 \\ -1 & -1 & -2 \end{pmatrix} \varepsilon_{t-1} + \begin{pmatrix} 0 & 0 & 1 \\ 0 & 0 & 1 \\ 0 & 0 & 1 \end{pmatrix} \varepsilon_{t-2} \\ &= C_0 \varepsilon_t + C_1 \varepsilon_{t-1} + C_2 \varepsilon_{t-2}, \end{aligned}$$

we see that the sum of the moving average parameters $(C_0 + C_1 + C_2)$ is different from zero, which implies that Y_t is $I(0)$ and hence X_t is $I(2)$.

By defining the processes

$$\begin{aligned} Z_{1t} &= X_{1t} - X_{2t} &&= 2\textstyle\sum_{i=1}^{t} \varepsilon_{2i} \\ Z_{2t} &= X_{1t} - X_{2t} - 2X_{3t} &&= -2\textstyle\sum_{i=1}^{t} \varepsilon_{1t} - 2\varepsilon_{3t} \\ Z_{3t} &= X_{1t} - X_{2t} - 2X_{3t} + 2\Delta X_{1t} &&= 2\varepsilon_{2t} - 2\varepsilon_{3,t-1} \end{aligned}$$

we find the sum of the moving average parameters, corresponding to the processes ΔZ_{1t}, ΔZ_{2t} and Z_{3t}, to be $(0, 2, 0)$, $(-2, 0, 0)$ and $(0, 2, -2)$ respectively. This proves that Z_{1t} and Z_{2t} are $I(1)$ and that Z_{3t} is $I(0)$ and stationary.

3.3*

Consider the simple process $X_t = \varepsilon_t$.

1. Show that X_t is $I(0)$.

Define $Y_t = \Delta X_t$.

2. Show that Y_t is stationary but that it is not $I(0)$.

3. Show now in general that if X_t is $I(0)$, then ΔX_t is not $I(0)$, and neither is $\Delta^d X_t$, $d = 1, 2, \dots$.

One could in this case call $\Delta^d X_t$ an $I(-d)$ process.

Note that we have shown that if X_t is $I(d_1)$ and $I(d_2)$ then $d_1 = d_2$, and further that $I(0)$ does not include all the stationary processes. The processes in the union of $I(-d)$, $d = 1, 2, \dots$ are also stationary.

Answer to exercise 3.3

1. The moving average representation of X_t is given by $C(z) = I$. Hence $C(1) = I \neq 0$, which implies that X_t is $I(0)$.

2. First we note that the distribution of $Y_t = \varepsilon_t - \varepsilon_{t-1}$ is Gaussian with mean 0 and variance 2Ω, and covariance function

$$v(h) = \text{Cov}(Y_t, Y_{t+h}) = \begin{cases} 2\Omega, & h = 0, \\ -\Omega, & |h| = 1, \\ 0, & |h| = 2, 3, \dots \end{cases}$$

and hence, Y_t is stationary. The sum of the moving average parameters is $I - I = 0$, which shows that Y_t is not $I(0)$.

3. When $X_t = \sum_{i=0}^{\infty} C_i \varepsilon_{t-i}$ is $I(0)$ its difference

$$\begin{aligned} \Delta X_t &= X_t - X_{t-1} \\ &= \sum_{i=0}^{\infty} C_i \varepsilon_{t-i} - \sum_{i=0}^{\infty} C_i \varepsilon_{t-i-1} \\ &= \sum_{i=0}^{\infty} (C_i - C_{i-1}) \varepsilon_{t-i}, \end{aligned}$$

is also a linear process, where we define $C_{-1} = 0$. But the difference is not $I(0)$ since its moving average parameters sum to zero:

$$\begin{aligned} \sum_{i=0}^{\infty} (C_i - C_{i-1}) &= \sum_{i=0}^{\infty} C_i - \sum_{i=-1}^{\infty} C_i \\ &= \sum_{i=0}^{\infty} C_i - \sum_{i=0}^{\infty} C_i = 0. \end{aligned}$$

The general case, that $\Delta^d X_t$ is not $I(0)$, is easily shown by induction.

3.4*

Let $Z_{1t} = \sum_{i=1}^{t} \varepsilon_{1i}$ and $Z_{2t} = \varepsilon_{2t}$.

1. Show that Z_{2t} is $I(0)$ and that Z_{1t} and $Z_t = Z_{1t} + Z_{2t}$ are $I(1)$.

2. Show now in general that if X_t is $I(d_1)$ and Y_t is $I(d_2)$, where $d_1 = 0, 1, \ldots, d_2 = 0, 1, \ldots,$ and $d_1 \neq d_2$, then $X_t + Y_t$ is $I(d)$, where $d = \max(d_1, d_2)$.

Answer to exercise 3.4

1. The processes $Z_{2t} = \varepsilon_{2t}$, $\Delta Z_{1t} = \varepsilon_{1t}$ and $\Delta Z_t = \varepsilon_{1t} + \varepsilon_{2t} - \varepsilon_{2t-1}$ are all $I(0)$ since the moving average parameters sum to something different from zero. Hence, Z_{2t} is $I(0)$ and the processes Z_{1t} and Z_t are $I(1)$.

2. Assume (without loss of generality) that $d_1 > d_2$, and define $Z_t = \Delta^{d_1}(X_t + Y_t)$. Since $\Delta^{d_1} X_t$ is $I(0)$ we know that $\Delta^{d_1} X_t = \sum_{i=0}^{\infty} C_i^x \varepsilon_{x,t-i}$ with $C^x = \sum_{i=0}^{\infty} C_i^x \neq 0$, and from exercise 3.3 we know that $\Delta^{d_1} Y_t = \sum_{i=0}^{\infty} C_i^y \varepsilon_{y,t-i}$ with $C^y = \sum_{i=0}^{\infty} C_i^y = 0$. Hence

$$Z_t = \sum_{i=0}^{\infty} (C_i^x, C_i^y) \begin{pmatrix} \varepsilon_{x,t-i} \\ \varepsilon_{y,t-i} \end{pmatrix} \equiv \sum_{i=0}^{\infty} C_i^z \tilde{\varepsilon}_{t-i},$$

where $\sum_{i=0}^{\infty} C_i^z = (C^x, C^y) = (C^x, 0) \neq 0$. This shows that $(X_t + Y_t)$ is $I(d_1)$. The important point here is that it is not possible for two variables that are integrated of different order to cointegrate. For example, if X_t is $I(2)$ and Y_t is $I(1)$ (both one-dimensional) there is no linear combination of the two processes that is stationary, the linear combination $aX_t + bY_t$ will be $I(2)$ for any choice of (a, b) with $a \neq 0$, but ΔX_t and Y_t might cointegrate.

3.5

Consider the autoregressive process X_t defined by

$$\Delta X_{1t} = -\tfrac{1}{2}(X_{1t-1} - X_{2t-1}) + \varepsilon_{1t},$$

$$\Delta X_{2t} = \varepsilon_{2t}.$$

Find an expression for X_t as a function of $X_0, \varepsilon_1, \ldots, \varepsilon_t$. Show that $X_{1t} - X_{2t}$ can be given an initial distribution such that it becomes stationary.

Answer to exercise 3.5

1. Summing the second equation for $i = 1, \ldots, t$ we find

$$X_{2t} = X_{20} + \sum_{i=1}^{t} \varepsilon_{2i},$$

which gives X_{2t} as a function of the ε's and the initial values. By subtracting the equations we find

$$\Delta(X_{1t} - X_{2t}) = -\frac{1}{2}(X_{1t-1} - X_{2t-1}) + \varepsilon_{1t} - \varepsilon_{2t},$$

which gives

$$X_{1t} - X_{2t} = \sum_{i=0}^{t-1} \frac{1}{2^i}(\varepsilon_{1t-i} - \varepsilon_{2t-i}) + \frac{1}{2^t}(X_{10} - X_{20}).$$

Hence

$$X_{1t} = \sum_{i=1}^{t} \varepsilon_{2i} + \sum_{i=0}^{t-1} \frac{1}{2^i}(\varepsilon_{1t-i} - \varepsilon_{2t-i}) + \frac{1}{2^t}(X_{10} - X_{20}) + X_{20},$$

which gives X_{1t} as a function of the initial values and the ε's.

If we choose

$$X_{10} - X_{20} = \sum_{i=0}^{\infty} \frac{1}{2^i}(\varepsilon_{1,-i} - \varepsilon_{2,-i}),$$

we make $X_{1t} - X_{2t}$ stationary, and its distribution is Gaussian with mean zero and variance $\frac{4}{3}\mathrm{Var}(\varepsilon_{1t} - \varepsilon_{2t})$.

3.6*

Consider the equations

$$\Delta X_{1t} = -\tfrac{1}{2}\,(X_{1t-1} - X_{2t-1}) + \varepsilon_{1t},$$

$$\Delta X_{2t} = \ \tfrac{1}{4}\,(X_{1t-1} - X_{2t-1}) + \varepsilon_{2t}.$$

Solve the equations for X_{1t} and X_{2t}, and show by direct calculation that $X_{1t} - X_{2t}$ is stationary, while the processes X_{1t} and X_{2t} are non-stationary. (Hint: find an equation for $X_{1t} - X_{2t}$ and another for $X_{1t} + 2X_{2t}$.)

What happens if you replace $\frac{1}{4}$ by $-\frac{1}{4}$?

Answer to exercise 3.6

Define the processes $Z_t = X_{1t} - X_{2t}$ and $Y_t = X_{1t} + 2X_{2t}$. These will satisfy $Z_t = \frac{1}{4}Z_{t-1} + (\varepsilon_{1t} - \varepsilon_{2t})$ and $Y_t = Y_{t-1} + (\varepsilon_{1t} + 2\varepsilon_{2t})$, showing that Z_t is $I(0)$ while the random walk Y_t is $I(1)$.

So $X_{1t} = \frac{2}{3}Z_t + \frac{1}{3}Y_t$ and $X_{2t} = -\frac{1}{3}Z_t + \frac{1}{3}Y_t$ are both $I(1)$, because a linear combination of an $I(0)$ process and an $I(1)$ process is $I(1)$; see exercise 3.4. If we replace $\frac{1}{4}$ by $-\frac{1}{4}$ we can redefine Y_t to be $Y_t = X_{1t} - 2X_{2t}$. Then we find the representation $Z_t = \frac{3}{4}Z_{t-1} + \varepsilon_{zt}$ and $Y_t = Y_{t-1} + \varepsilon_{yt}$. Hence Z_t is still $I(0)$ and Y_t is still $I(1)$.

One might say that X_{2t} is "corrected" in the wrong direction away from the stationary relation $X_{1t} - X_{2t}$, since the coefficient of X_{2t-1} in the equation for ΔX_{2t} is positive ($\Pi_{22} = \frac{1}{4}$). The stationarity, however, is saved by the stronger "proper" correction of X_{1t}.

If we instead had replaced $\frac{1}{4}$ by $-\frac{1}{2}$, $(X_{1t} - X_{2t})$ would no longer be stationary, and the process X_t would be integrated of order 2 with no cointegration; see Figures 3.3, 3.4 and 3.5. Figure 3.2 displays how the process is corrected for disequilibrium in $\beta' X_t = X_{1t} - X_{2t}$.

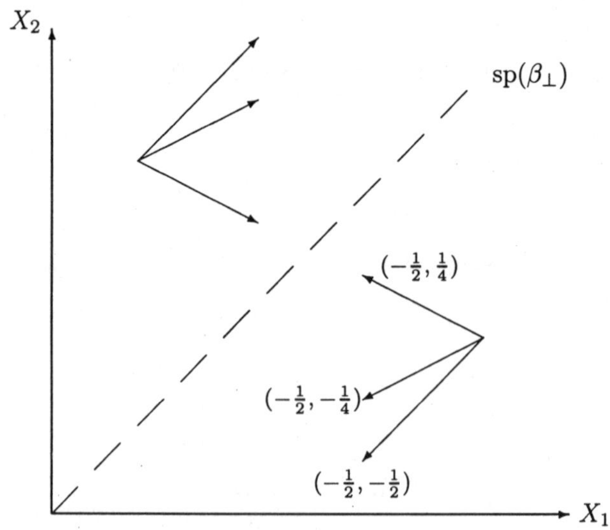

Fig. 3.2: Exercise 3.6. The process X_t is pulled by the adjustment coefficients. For $\alpha = (-\frac{1}{2}, \frac{1}{4})$ and $\alpha = (-\frac{1}{2}, -\frac{1}{4})$, we see that X_t is pulled towards the attractor sp($\beta_\perp$), while for $\alpha = (-\frac{1}{2}, -\frac{1}{2})$ it is pulled parallel to the attractor, so the stability is lost.

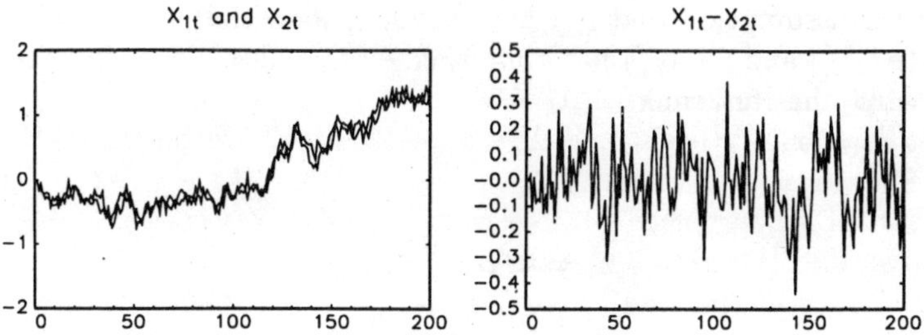

Fig. 3.3: Exercise 3.6. The process simulated with $\alpha = (-\frac{1}{2}, \frac{1}{4})$, Gaussian errors, variance matrix $\frac{1}{10}I$ and $X_0 = (0,0)'$.

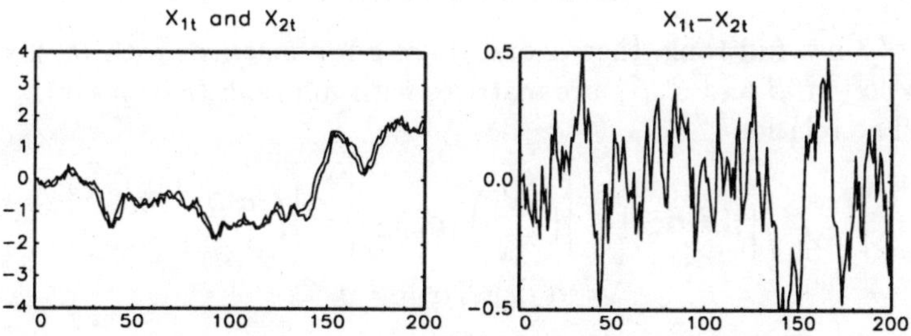

Fig. 3.4: Exercise 3.6. The process simulated with $\alpha = (-\frac{1}{2}, -\frac{1}{4})$, Gaussian errors, variance matrix $\frac{1}{10}I$ and $X_0 = (0,0)'$.

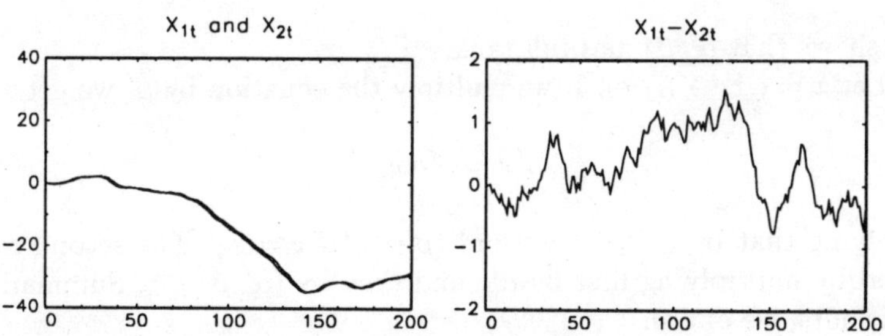

Fig. 3.5: Exercise 3.6. The process simulated with $\alpha = (-\frac{1}{2}, -\frac{1}{2})$, Gaussian errors, variance matrix $\frac{1}{10}I$ and $X_0 = (0,0)'$.

3.7

Under the assumption that $\beta'\alpha$ has full rank, show that:

1. $(\alpha, \beta_\perp)$ and $(\beta, \alpha_\perp)$ have full rank.
2. $\alpha'_\perp\beta_\perp$ has full rank.

Let $x = \alpha x_1 + \beta_\perp x_2$

3. Show that

$$x_1 = (\beta'\alpha)^{-1}\beta' x,$$
$$x_2 = (\alpha'_\perp\beta_\perp)^{-1}\alpha'_\perp x,$$

and hence

$$I = \alpha(\beta'\alpha)^{-1}\beta' + \beta_\perp(\alpha'_\perp\beta_\perp)^{-1}\alpha'_\perp.$$

Answer to exercise 3.7

Since $\alpha'\beta$ has full rank, then α and β are $p \times r$ matrices with rank r and $\alpha'\alpha$, $\alpha'_\perp\alpha_\perp$, $\beta'\beta$ and $\beta'_\perp\beta_\perp$ are matrices with full rank (r or $p - r$).

1. The relation

$$\left|\begin{pmatrix}\alpha' \\ \alpha'_\perp\end{pmatrix}\right| |(\beta, \alpha_\perp)| = \left|\begin{pmatrix}\alpha' \\ \alpha'_\perp\end{pmatrix}(\beta, \alpha_\perp)\right| = \left|\begin{pmatrix}\alpha'\beta & 0 \\ \alpha'_\perp\beta & \alpha'_\perp\alpha_\perp\end{pmatrix}\right|$$
$$= |\alpha'\beta|\,|\alpha'_\perp\alpha_\perp| \neq 0$$

shows that $(\beta, \alpha_\perp)$ has full rank. By interchanging α and β we have also proved that $(\alpha, \beta_\perp)$ has full rank.

2. We apply the same type of identity as in 1.

$$0 \neq \left|\begin{pmatrix}\alpha' \\ \alpha'_\perp\end{pmatrix}(\alpha, \beta_\perp)\right| = \left|\begin{pmatrix}\alpha'\alpha & \alpha'\beta_\perp \\ 0 & \alpha'_\perp\beta_\perp\end{pmatrix}\right| = |\alpha'\alpha|\,|\alpha'_\perp\beta_\perp|,$$

which shows that $\alpha'_\perp\beta_\perp$ has full rank.

3. Let $x = \alpha x_1 + \beta_\perp x_2$. If we multiply the equation by β' we get

$$\beta' x = \beta'\alpha x_1.$$

Multiplying that by $(\beta'\alpha)^{-1}$ we find $(\beta'\alpha)^{-1}\beta' x = x_1$. The second result is found by multiplying first by $\alpha'_\perp$ and then by $(\alpha'_\perp\beta_\perp)^{-1}$. Summarizing these results, we obtain

$$\begin{aligned} x &= \alpha x_1 + \beta_\perp x_2 \\ &= \alpha(\beta'\alpha)^{-1}\beta' x + \beta_\perp(\alpha'_\perp\beta_\perp)^{-1}\alpha'_\perp x \\ &= [\alpha(\beta'\alpha)^{-1}\beta' + \beta_\perp(\alpha'_\perp\beta_\perp)^{-1}\alpha'_\perp]x, \end{aligned}$$

which proves that

$$I = \alpha(\beta'\alpha)^{-1}\beta' + \beta_\perp(\alpha'_\perp\beta_\perp)^{-1}\alpha'_\perp.$$

3.8**

Consider the model

$$\Delta X_t = \alpha\beta' X_{t-1} + \mu + \varepsilon_t, \qquad t = 1, \ldots, T. \tag{3.4}$$

Show that if $|\text{eig}(I + \beta'\alpha)| < 1$, then X_t has the representation

$$X_t = \left(I - \alpha(\beta'\alpha)^{-1}\beta'\right)\left(X_0 + \sum_{i=1}^{t}\varepsilon_i + \mu t\right) + Y_t,$$

where Y_t is a stationary process. (Hint: multiply (3.4) by β' and solve for $\beta' X_t$, then insert the expression for $\beta' X_{t-1}$ into (3.4) and sum over t.)

Answer to exercise 3.8

The assumption that the eigenvalues of $(I + \beta'\alpha)$ are smaller than one in absolute value implies that $\beta'\alpha$ has full rank. This is proved by assuming that $\beta'\alpha$ has reduced rank such that it has a zero eigenvalue and a corresponding eigenvector v. Multiplying $(I + \beta'\alpha)$ by v shows that $(I + \beta'\alpha)$ has one as eigenvalue which contradicts the assumption. Hence we conclude that $\beta'\alpha$ has full rank.

Summation of

$$\Delta X_i = \alpha\beta' X_{i-1} + \mu + \varepsilon_i \tag{1}$$

for $i = 1, \ldots, t$ gives

$$X_t = X_0 + \alpha\sum_{i=0}^{t-1}\beta' X_i + \mu t + \sum_{i=1}^{t}\varepsilon_i. \tag{2}$$

If we multiply (2) by β', we find

$$\beta' X_t = \beta' X_0 + \beta'\alpha\sum_{i=0}^{t-1}\beta' X_i + \beta'\mu t + \beta'\sum_{i=1}^{t}\varepsilon_i,$$

such that

$$\sum_{i=0}^{t-1}\beta' X_i = (\beta'\alpha)^{-1}\left(\beta' X_t - \beta' X_0 - \beta'\mu t - \beta'\sum_{i=1}^{t}\varepsilon_i\right).$$

If we insert this into (2), we get

$$X_t = X_0 + \alpha\left(\beta'\alpha\right)^{-1}\left(\beta' X_t - \beta' X_0 - \beta'\mu t - \beta' \sum_{i=1}^{t} \varepsilon_i\right) + \mu t + \sum_{i=1}^{t} \varepsilon_i$$

$$= \left(I - \alpha\left(\beta'\alpha\right)^{-1}\beta'\right)\left(X_0 + \sum_{i=1}^{t} \varepsilon_i + \mu t\right) + \alpha\left(\beta'\alpha\right)^{-1}\beta' X_t. \tag{3}$$

We define the process

$$Y_t = \alpha\left(\beta'\alpha\right)^{-1}\beta' X_t$$

with the stationary representation

$$Y_t = \alpha\left(\beta'\alpha\right)^{-1}\sum_{i=0}^{\infty}(I + \beta'\alpha)^i \beta'(\mu + \varepsilon_{t-i}).$$

If we define $C = \beta_\perp(\alpha'_\perp\beta_\perp)^{-1}\alpha'_\perp$ and apply the result from exercise 3.7 we see that (3) can be written

$$X_t = CX_0 + C\sum_{i=1}^{t} \varepsilon_i + C\mu t + Y_t,$$

which is a special case of the Granger representation theorem. The representation shows that the constant μ in equation (1) gives rise to a deterministic linear trend unless $C\mu = 0$.

4

Cointegration and Representation of Integrated Variables

This is the most substantial chapter devoted to understanding the behaviour of the type of non-stationary processes that are discussed here, namely $I(1)$ and $I(2)$. The equations are formulated in the error correction form

$$\Delta X_t = \Pi X_{t-1} + \sum_{i=1}^{k-1} \Gamma_i \Delta X_{t-i} + \Phi D_t + \varepsilon_t, \qquad t = 1, \ldots, T,$$

where $\Pi = -A(1) = I - \sum_{i=1}^{k} \Pi_i$, $\Gamma_i = -\sum_{j=i+1}^{k} \Pi_j$. For the processes considered, non-stationarity implies that $z = 1$ is a root, that is, $|A(1)| = 0$. In this case we can find matrices α and β of dimension $p \times r$, such that $\Pi = \alpha\beta'$ and the autoregressive equation becomes

$$\Delta X_t = \alpha\beta' X_{t-1} + \sum_{i=1}^{k-1} \Gamma_i \Delta X_{t-i} + \Phi D_t + \varepsilon_t, \qquad t = 1, \ldots, T. \qquad (1)$$

The main result is Granger's representation theorem, Theorem 4.2, which gives the probability properties of the solution of the autoregressive equations (1) provided Assumption 1 (SJ, p. 14) is satisfied. A necessary and sufficient condition for the process X_t to be an $I(1)$ process is that

$$|\alpha'_\perp \Gamma \beta_\perp| \neq 0.$$

Under these conditions we have Granger's representation

$$X_t = C \sum_{i=1}^{t} (\varepsilon_i + \Phi D_i) + C(L)(\varepsilon_t + \Phi D_t) + A,$$

where A depends on initial conditions and $\beta' A = 0$. We define the matrices Γ and C by

$$\Gamma = I - \sum_{i=1}^{k-1} \Gamma_i = \Pi + \sum_{j=1}^{k} j\Pi_j,$$

$$C = \beta_\perp(\alpha'_\perp \Gamma \beta_\perp)^{-1}\alpha'_\perp.$$

In Theorem 4.6 similar conditions are found for the process to be $I(2)$, and a Granger representation is given.

Another formulation of the conditions for $I(1)$ is that $A(1)$ has reduced rank, such that $A(1) = -\alpha\beta'$, but also that $\alpha'_\perp \dot{A}(1)\beta_\perp$ has full rank, where $\dot{A}(1)$ is the derivative of $A(z)$ at the point $z = 1$.

The exercises extend some of the concepts and exemplify the general results obtained. Note in particular exercise 4.3 which shows that the interpretation of the adjustment coefficients is not so easy. In exercise 4.7 we discuss what the cointegrating relations look like in the companion form, thereby giving a proof of the Granger representation for two lags using the result for one lag. Exercise 4.8 extends the Granger representation to seasonal cointegration.

4.1*

Consider the system

$$\Delta X_{1t} = \alpha_1 (X_{1t-1} - \beta_2 X_{2t-1}) + \mu_1 + \varepsilon_{1t}, \quad (4.30)$$
$$\Delta X_{2t} = \mu_2 + \varepsilon_{2t}. \quad (4.31)$$

1. Find the matrices α, β, Π, C and Γ expressed in terms of the parameters α_1, β_2 and μ. Note the two cases, $\alpha_1 = 0$ and $\alpha_1 \neq 0$.

2. Find the representation of X_t in terms of ε_i, $i = 1, \ldots, t$ and find $E(X_t|X_0)$ and $\mathrm{Var}(X_t|X_0)$.

3. Calculate the roots of the characteristic polynomial. Under what condition on the parameters is the process X_t an $I(1)$ process? If the process is not $I(1)$ what is it then?

4. Show explicitly from (4.30) and (4.31) without using Granger's representation that $\beta' X_t$ is stationary if $-2 < \alpha_1 < 0$.

5. Under what condition on the parameters is there no linear trend?

6. If we add a linear term $\eta_1 t$ and $\eta_2 t$ to (4.30) and (4.31) respectively, show that X_t has a quadratic trend.

7. Under what condition does the quadratic trend disappear?

Solution to exercise 4.1

1. We rewrite the process in the vector formulation

$$\Delta X_t = \begin{pmatrix} \alpha_1 \\ 0 \end{pmatrix} (1, -\beta_2) X_{t-1} + \begin{pmatrix} \mu_1 \\ \mu_2 \end{pmatrix} + \varepsilon_t. \quad (1)$$

If $\alpha_1 \neq 0$ we find

$$\alpha = \begin{pmatrix} \alpha_1 \\ 0 \end{pmatrix}, \ \beta = \begin{pmatrix} 1 \\ -\beta_2 \end{pmatrix}, \ \Pi = \begin{pmatrix} \alpha_1 & -\alpha_1\beta_2 \\ 0 & 0 \end{pmatrix}, \ \Gamma = I$$

and hence $\alpha_\perp = (0,1)$, $\beta_\perp = (\beta_2, 1)$, $\alpha'_\perp \Gamma \beta_\perp = 1$ and

$$C = \beta_\perp \left(\alpha'_\perp \Gamma \beta_\perp\right)^{-1} \alpha'_\perp = \begin{pmatrix} 0 & \beta_2 \\ 0 & 1 \end{pmatrix}.$$

In the case where $\alpha_1 = 0$ we have $\alpha = 0$, $\beta = 0$ and $\Gamma = \alpha_\perp = \beta_\perp = C = I$.

2. By rewriting the process as

$$\begin{aligned} X_t &= (I + \Pi)X_{t-1} + \mu + \varepsilon_t \\ &= (I + \Pi)^t X_0 + \sum_{i=0}^{t-1} (I + \Pi)^i (\varepsilon_{t-i} + \mu), \end{aligned}$$

we can calculate the mean and variance of X_t given X_0:

$$\begin{aligned} E(X_t|X_0) &= (I + \Pi)^t X_0 + \sum_{i=0}^{t-1} (I + \Pi)^i \mu \\ \operatorname{Var}(X_t|X_0) &= \operatorname{Var}\left(\sum_{i=0}^{t-1} (I + \Pi)^i \varepsilon_{t-i}\right) \\ &= \sum_{i=0}^{t-1} (I + \Pi)^i \Omega (I + \Pi)'^i. \end{aligned}$$

3. The characteristic polynomial is given by

$$\begin{aligned} A(z) &= I(1 - z) - \begin{pmatrix} \alpha_1 \\ 0 \end{pmatrix} (1, -\beta_2) z \\ &= \begin{pmatrix} 1 - (1 + \alpha_1)z & \alpha_1 \beta_2 z \\ 0 & 1 - z \end{pmatrix}, \end{aligned}$$

such that $|A(z)| = (1 - (1 + \alpha_1)z)(1 - z) = 0$ if and only if

$$z = \begin{cases} 1 \text{ or } 1/(1 + \alpha_1), & \text{if } \alpha_1 \neq -1, \\ 1, & \text{if } \alpha_1 = -1. \end{cases}$$

Hence, for the process X_t to fulfil the root assumption (see SJ, p. 14, Assumption 1), α_1 has to be in the interval $]-2, 0]$. The other conditions of Granger's representation theorem are fulfilled, so we conclude that X_t is $I(1)$ when $-2 < \alpha_1 \leq 0$. In the case $\alpha_1 = 0$, the process is a pure $I(1)$ process which does not cointegrate. For α_1 less than -2 or greater than zero, the process X_t is explosive and for $\alpha_1 = -2$ the process is seasonally cointegrated; see exercise 4.8.

4. By multiplying (1) by β' we find the equation

$$(X_{1t} - \beta_2 X_{2t}) = (1+\alpha_1)(X_{1t-1} - \beta_2 X_{2t-1}) + (\mu_1 - \beta_2\mu_2) + \tilde{\varepsilon}_t.$$

Hence $(X_{1t} - \beta_2 X_{2t})$ is a simple AR(1) process, which has a stationary representation if and only if $|(1+\alpha_1)| < 1$ or equivalently $-2 < \alpha_1 < 0$.

5. By applying Granger's representation theorem we find the representation of X_t:

$$X_t = C\sum_{i=1}^{t} \varepsilon_i + C\mu t + C(L)(\varepsilon_t + \mu) + A.$$

Hence X_t has a linear trend if and only if $C\mu \neq 0$. The process X_t has no linear trend if $C\mu = 0$, which is equivalent to $\alpha_\perp'\mu = 0$ which again is equivalent to $\mu \in \text{sp}(\alpha)$. Hence X_t has no linear trend if and only if $\mu = \begin{pmatrix}\alpha_1 \\ 0\end{pmatrix}\varphi$ for some $\varphi \in \mathbf{R}$, that is, $\mu_2 = 0$.

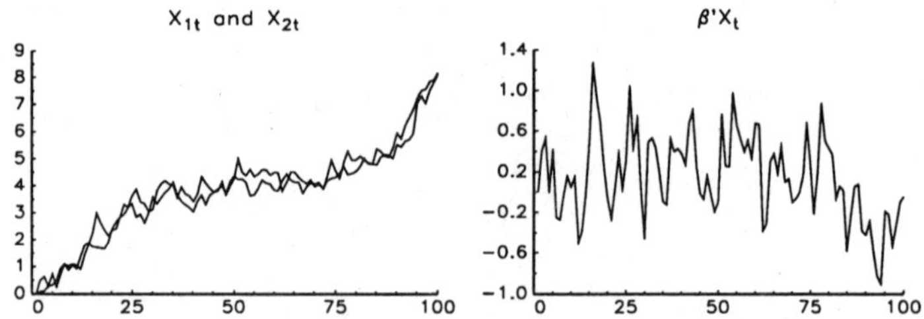

Fig. 4.1: Exercise 4.1. The process simulated with $\alpha_1 = -\frac{1}{2}$, $\beta_2 = 1$ and constant $\mu = (\frac{1}{5}, \frac{1}{10})'$.

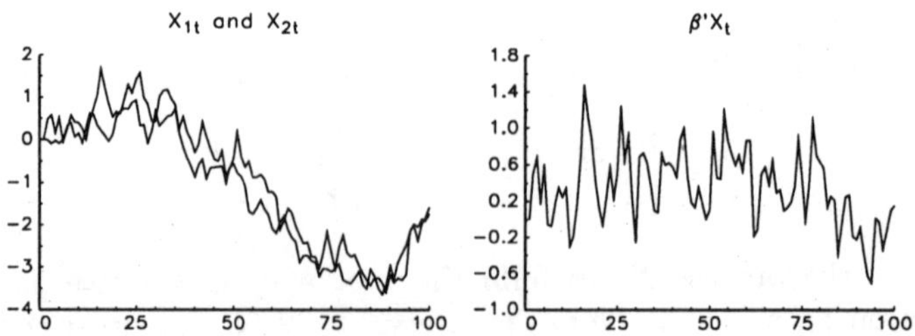

Fig. 4.2: Exercise 4.1. The process simulated with $\alpha_1 = -\frac{1}{2}$, $\beta_2 = 1$ and constant $\mu = (\frac{1}{5}, 0)'$.

6. The process is now given by the equation

$$\Delta X_t = \begin{pmatrix} \alpha_1 \\ 0 \end{pmatrix} (1, -\beta_2) X_{t-1} + \mu + \eta t + \varepsilon_t.$$

We apply Granger's representation theorem:

$$\begin{aligned} X_t &= C \sum_{i=1}^{t} (\varepsilon_i + \mu + \eta i) + C(L)(\varepsilon_t + \mu + \eta t) + A \\ &= C \sum_{i=1}^{t} \varepsilon_i + \left(C\mu + \frac{1}{2} C\eta + C(1)\eta \right) t + \frac{1}{2} C\eta t^2 \\ &+ C(1)\mu - \sum_{i=0}^{\infty} i C_i \eta + C(L)\varepsilon_t + A. \end{aligned}$$

Hence the process has the quadratic trend given by $\frac{1}{2}C\eta t^2$, which disappears in $\beta' X_t$, since $\beta' C = 0$.

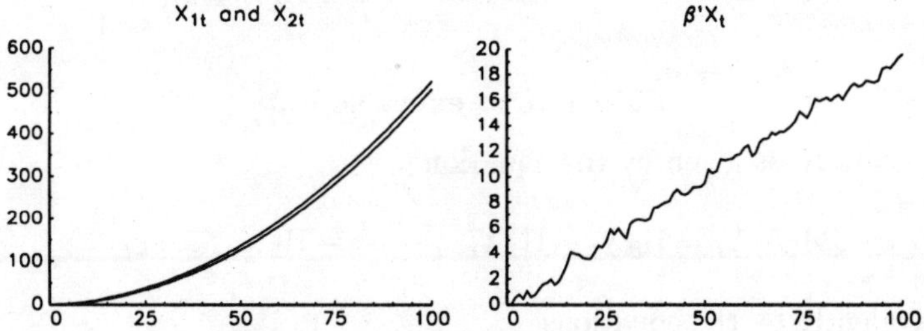

Fig. 4.3: Exercise 4.1. The process simulated with $\alpha_1 = -\frac{1}{2}$, $\beta_2 = 1$, constant $\mu = (0,0)'$ and linear term $\eta = (\frac{1}{5}, \frac{1}{10})'$.

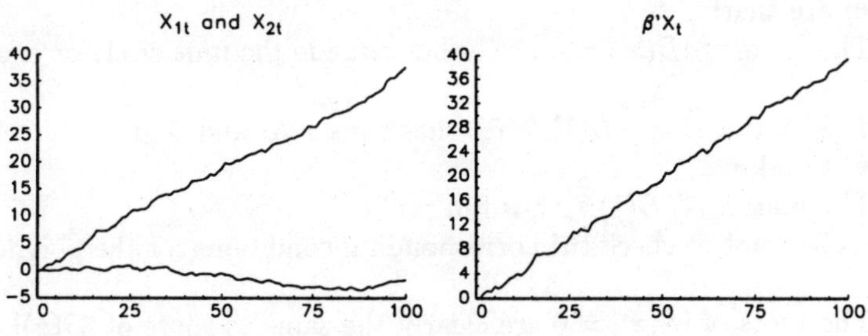

Fig. 4.4: Exercise 4.1. The process simulated with $\alpha_1 = -\frac{1}{2}$, $\beta_2 = 1$, constant $\mu = (0,0)'$ and linear term $\eta = (\frac{1}{5}, 0)'$.

7. The quadratic trend will disappear if $C\eta = 0$ or, equivalently, if

$$\eta = \begin{pmatrix} \alpha_1 \\ 0 \end{pmatrix} \vartheta$$

for some $\vartheta \in \mathbf{R}$, that is, $\eta_2 = 0$.

We saw that a constant in an error correction model can give rise to a linear deterministic trend, and that a linear term can give rise to a quadratic deterministic trend in the variables. But in the stationary relations, $\beta' X_t$, a constant will only give rise to a mean different from zero, and a linear term will only give rise to a linear deterministic trend. This is seen by multiplying the Granger representation by β, which shows that the deterministic terms are not cumulated in $\beta' X_t$, since $\beta' C = 0$.

4.2*

Granger's theorem is formulated for a characteristic polynomial $A(z)$ with $A(0) = I$.

Find the conditions for the process to be $I(1)$ as expressed by $A(0)$, $A(1)$, and $\dot{A}(1)$ when $A(0)$ has full rank even if $A(0) \neq I$.

Solution to exercise 4.2

The process X_t is given by the equation

$$A(L)X_t = \Pi_0 X_t - \Pi_1 X_{t-1} - \cdots - \Pi_k X_{t-k} = \varepsilon_t,$$

or equivalently by the equations

$$X_t - \Pi_0^{-1}\Pi_1 X_{t-1} - \cdots - \Pi_0^{-1}\Pi_k X_{t-k} = \Pi_0^{-1}\varepsilon_t,$$

since $A(0) = \Pi_0$ has full rank. Define the characteristic polynomial $B(z) = A(0)^{-1}A(z)$, such that $B(L)X_t = \Pi_0^{-1}\varepsilon_t$. The conditions for Granger's theorem are that:

1. The roots of $|B(z)| = 0$ are either outside the unit circle or equal to 1.

2. The matrix $\tilde{\Pi} = -B(1) = \tilde{\alpha}\tilde{\beta}'$ has rank r ($\tilde{\alpha}$ and $\tilde{\beta}$ are of dimension $p \times r$ and rank r).

3. The matrix $\tilde{\alpha}'_\perp \dot{B}(1)\tilde{\beta}_\perp$ has full rank.

We now want to check the corresponding conditions for the polynomial $A(z)$.

1. The roots of $|A(z)| = 0$ are clearly the same as those of $|B(z)| = 0$.

2. The matrix $\Pi = -A(1) = -A(0)B(1) = A(0)\tilde{\alpha}\tilde{\beta}' = \alpha\beta'$, where $\alpha = A(0)\tilde{\alpha}$ and $\beta = \tilde{\beta}$. These matrices are of dimension $p \times r$ and rank r since $A(0)$ has full rank.

3. We find that $\alpha_\perp = (A(0)^{-1})'\tilde{\alpha}_\perp$ and $\beta_\perp = \tilde{\beta}_\perp$, such that $\alpha'_\perp \dot{A}(1)\beta_\perp = \tilde{\alpha}'_\perp A(0)^{-1}A(0)\dot{B}(1)\tilde{\beta}_\perp = \tilde{\alpha}'_\perp \dot{B}(1)\tilde{\beta}_\perp$, which has full rank.

4.3

Under the assumptions of Theorem 4.2, show that for the model

$$\Delta X_t = \alpha\beta' X_{t-1} + \varepsilon_t,$$

the matrix $\beta'\alpha$ has full rank, and has eigenvalues contained in the circle $\{z : |z+1| < 1\}$. Show that $\alpha'_\perp X_t$ is non-stationary. Next consider the example

$$\Delta X_{1t} = -\tfrac{1}{4}(X_{1,t-1} - X_{2,t-1}) + \Delta X_{2,t-1} + \varepsilon_{1t},$$

$$\Delta X_{2t} = -\tfrac{1}{4}(X_{1,t-1} - X_{2,t-1}) + \varepsilon_{2t}.$$

Show that in this case $\alpha_\perp = \beta$, such that $\alpha'_\perp X_t$ is stationary.

Solution to exercise 4.3

Multiplying

$$\Delta X_t = \alpha\beta' X_{t-1} + \varepsilon_t$$

by β' gives the equation

$$\beta' X_t = (I + \beta'\alpha)\beta' X_{t-1} + \beta'\varepsilon_t.$$

Under the assumptions of Granger's representation theorem, $\beta' X_t$ can be made stationary. Hence the characteristic polynomial for the process $\beta' X_t$ will have roots outside the unit disc, which in this case is equivalent to

$$|\mathrm{eig}(I + \beta'\alpha)| < 1.$$

Since the identity $|\beta'\alpha| = 0$ implies that $(I + \beta'\alpha)$ has an eigenvalue equal to one (see exercise 3.8) we can conclude that $\beta'\alpha$ has full rank.

Multiplying by $\alpha'_\perp$ gives the equation

$$\alpha'_\perp X_t = \alpha'_\perp X_{t-1} + \alpha'_\perp \varepsilon_t,$$

such that $\alpha'_\perp X_t$ is a random walk and hence non-stationary.

In the example we find

$$\alpha = -\frac{1}{4}\begin{pmatrix}1\\1\end{pmatrix},\ \beta = \begin{pmatrix}1\\-1\end{pmatrix},\ \alpha_\perp = \begin{pmatrix}1\\-1\end{pmatrix},\ \beta_\perp = \begin{pmatrix}1\\1\end{pmatrix}$$

$$A(z) = \begin{pmatrix} 1 - z + \frac{1}{4}z & -\frac{1}{4}z - (1-z)z \\ \frac{1}{4}z & 1 - z - \frac{1}{4}z \end{pmatrix}$$

$$|A(z)| = (1-z)\left(\frac{1}{2}z - 1\right)^2$$

$$\dot{A}(1) = \frac{1}{4}\begin{pmatrix} -3 & 3 \\ 1 & -5 \end{pmatrix}, \; \alpha'_\perp \dot{A}(1)\beta_\perp = 1.$$

These results show that we have an $I(1)$ process with cointegration, and in this particular case $\alpha_\perp = \beta$.

This shows that, as a general definition of trends, it is not a good idea to define them as $\alpha'_\perp X_t$. The common trends are defined either as $\alpha'_\perp \sum_{i=1}^t \varepsilon_i$ or, if one wants to have linear combinations of the observed processes, as $\alpha'_\perp \Gamma X_t$; see SJ, p. 53.

4.4

Consider the equation

$$\begin{pmatrix} 1 & 2 \\ 2 & 4 \end{pmatrix} X_t + \begin{pmatrix} 0 & \frac{1}{2} \\ \frac{1}{2} & 2 \end{pmatrix} \Delta X_t + \begin{pmatrix} 0 & -\frac{1}{2} \\ -\frac{1}{2} & -1 \end{pmatrix} \Delta^2 X_t = \varepsilon_t, \qquad t = 0, 1, \ldots.$$

1. Define in this case the characteristic polynomial $A(z)$ as

$$A(z) = \begin{pmatrix} 1 & 2 \\ 2 & 4 \end{pmatrix} + \begin{pmatrix} 0 & \frac{1}{2} \\ \frac{1}{2} & 2 \end{pmatrix}(1-z) + \begin{pmatrix} 0 & -\frac{1}{2} \\ -\frac{1}{2} & -1 \end{pmatrix}(1-z)^2,$$

note that $A(0)$ is not the identity (see exercise 4.2), and show that

$$|A(z)| = (1-z)^2\left(1 - \frac{1}{4}z^2\right).$$

2. Show that $\Pi = -A(1)$ has reduced rank and find α and β such that $\Pi = \alpha\beta'$. Find the matrix $\Gamma = -\dot{A}(1) + A(1)$.

3. Show that $\alpha'_\perp \Gamma \beta_\perp = 0$, such that the process X_t is not $I(1)$.

4. Show that if we define

$$Y_{1t} = X_{1t} + 2X_{2t},$$

$$Y_{2t} = \Delta X_{2t},$$

then Y_t is $I(1)$.

5. Find the cointegrating relations between Y_{1t} and Y_{2t}. What are they, expressed in terms of X_{1t} and X_{2t}?

Solution to exercise 4.4

1. We can rewrite the characteristic polynomial as

$$A(z) = \begin{pmatrix} 1 & 2+\frac{1}{2}(1-z)-\frac{1}{2}(1-z)^2 \\ 2+\frac{1}{2}(1-z)-\frac{1}{2}(1-z)^2 & 4+2(1-z)-(1-z)^2 \end{pmatrix}$$

and hence the determinant is

$$\begin{aligned} |A(z)| &= \left[4+2(1-z)-(1-z)^2\right]-\left[2+\tfrac{1}{2}(1-z)-\tfrac{1}{2}(1-z)^2\right]^2 \\ &= \left[4+(1-z)(1+z)\right]-\left[2+\tfrac{1}{2}(1-z)z\right]^2 \\ &= \left[4+(1-z)(1+z)\right]-\left[4+2(1-z)z+\tfrac{1}{4}(1-z)^2z^2\right] \\ &= (1-z)\left[(1+z)-(2z+\tfrac{1}{4}(1-z)z^2)\right] \\ &= (1-z)^2\left(1-\tfrac{z^2}{4}\right). \end{aligned}$$

2. For $z=1$, we find from the characteristic polynomial that

$$\Pi = -A(1) = -\begin{pmatrix} 1 & 2 \\ 2 & 4 \end{pmatrix} = \begin{pmatrix} -1 \\ -2 \end{pmatrix}(1,2)$$

which shows that Π has reduced rank, $\alpha = (-1,-2)'$ and $\beta = (1,2)'$.

$$\dot{A}(z) = -\begin{pmatrix} 0 & \frac{1}{2} \\ \frac{1}{2} & 2 \end{pmatrix} - 2\begin{pmatrix} 0 & -\frac{1}{2} \\ -\frac{1}{2} & -1 \end{pmatrix}(1-z).$$

Hence

$$\Gamma = -\dot{A}(1) + A(1) = \begin{pmatrix} 1 & \frac{5}{2} \\ \frac{5}{2} & 6 \end{pmatrix}.$$

3. We find the orthogonal matrices to be $\alpha'_\perp = \beta'_\perp = (2,-1)$ (one can use any vector which spans the same subspace), and hence

$$\alpha'_\perp \Gamma \beta_\perp = (2,-1)\begin{pmatrix} 1 & \frac{5}{2} \\ \frac{5}{2} & 6 \end{pmatrix}\begin{pmatrix} 2 \\ -1 \end{pmatrix} = (-\tfrac{1}{2},-1)\begin{pmatrix} 2 \\ -1 \end{pmatrix} = 0.$$

4. If we express the equations for X_t in terms of Y_t we find

$$\begin{aligned} Y_{1t} + \frac{1}{2}Y_{2t} - \frac{1}{2}\Delta Y_{2t} &= \varepsilon_{1t} \\ 2Y_{1t} + Y_{2t} + \frac{1}{2}\Delta Y_{1t} - \frac{1}{2}\Delta^2 Y_{1t} &= \varepsilon_{2t}, \end{aligned}$$

with characteristic polynomial $A_y(z)$ given by

$$\begin{pmatrix} 1 & \frac{1}{2}-\frac{1}{2}(1-z) \\ 2+\frac{1}{2}(1-z)-\frac{1}{2}(1-z)^2 & 1 \end{pmatrix} = \begin{pmatrix} 1 & \frac{1}{2}z \\ 2+\frac{1}{2}z-\frac{1}{2}z^2 & 1 \end{pmatrix}.$$

We find the roots by calculating the determinant

$$|A_y(z)| = \frac{1}{4}(z-1)(z-2)(z+2),$$

which has the roots 1, −2 and 2. From

$$-A_y(1) = -\begin{pmatrix} 1 & \frac{1}{2} \\ 2 & 1 \end{pmatrix} = -\begin{pmatrix} 1 \\ 2 \end{pmatrix}(1, \tfrac{1}{2}) = \alpha\beta' = \Pi,$$

we see that the reduced rank condition is fulfilled, and the orthogonal matrices can be expressed as $\alpha'_\perp = (2,-1)$ and $\beta'_\perp = (1,-2)$. The mean lag matrix is found by calculating the derivative of $A_y(z)$ at one, changing sign and adding $A_y(1)$ $(= -\Pi)$. Hence

$$\Gamma = -\dot{A}_y(1) - \Pi = \begin{pmatrix} 0 & -\frac{1}{2} \\ \frac{1}{2} & 0 \end{pmatrix} + \begin{pmatrix} 1 & \frac{1}{2} \\ 2 & 1 \end{pmatrix} = \begin{pmatrix} 1 & 0 \\ \frac{5}{2} & 1 \end{pmatrix}$$

and $\alpha'_\perp \Gamma \beta_\perp = \frac{3}{2} \neq 0$. Thus all the conditions to ensure $I(1)$-ness are satisfied, and hence Y_t is $I(1)$.

5. The cointegrating relation for the Y-process was found to be $\beta' = (1, \frac{1}{2})$ such that

$$2Y_{1t} + Y_{2t}$$

can be given a stationary representation. In terms of X_t, this is the process

$$2X_{1t} + 4X_{2t} + \Delta X_{2t} = 2X_{1t} + 5X_{2t} - X_{2t-1}.$$

We observe here the $I(2)$ phenomenon that the levels and differences of the X_t variables cointegrate to stationarity. This type of cointegration is called polynomial cointegration (see SJ, p. 58).

4.5

1. In the context of Granger's theorem, show that for the process

$$\Delta X_t = \alpha\beta' X_{t-1} + \sum_{i=1}^{k-1} \Gamma_i \Delta X_{t-i} + \mu + \varepsilon_t,$$

the stationary process $\beta' X_t$ has mean given by

$$E(\beta' X_t) = \bar{\alpha}'(\Gamma C - I)\mu, \tag{4.32}$$

where $C = \beta_\perp(\alpha'_\perp \Gamma \beta_\perp)^{-1}\alpha'_\perp$ and $\bar{\alpha} = \alpha(\alpha'\alpha)^{-1}$.

2. Calculate $E(\beta' X_t)$ in the case where $\Gamma_1 = \Gamma_2 = \cdots = \Gamma_{k-1} = 0$.

Consider in the following the process

$$\Delta X_t = \begin{pmatrix} -\frac{1}{2} \\ \frac{1}{2} \end{pmatrix} (1, \, -1) \, X_{t-1} + \begin{pmatrix} \mu_1 \\ \mu_2 \end{pmatrix} + \varepsilon_t.$$

3. Find $E(\beta' X_t)$ as a function of μ_1 and μ_2.

4. Draw in a two-dimensional coordinate system $(X_{1t}, \, X_{2t})$ a typical example of the behaviour of the process in each of the cases $\mu' = (0, \, 0)$, $\mu' = (-1, \, 1)$ and $\mu' = (1, \, 1)$.

Comment: the decomposition

$$\alpha\beta' X_t + \mu = \alpha(\beta' X_t + (\alpha'\alpha)^{-1} \alpha'\mu) + \alpha_\perp (\alpha_\perp' \alpha_\perp)^{-1} \alpha_\perp' \mu$$

decomposes μ into two components. The first can be given the following interpretation: the agents react to a disequilibrium as measured by the deviation of

$$\beta' X_t + (\alpha'\alpha)^{-1} \alpha'\mu$$

from zero. One could call the relation

$$\beta' X + (\alpha'\alpha)^{-1} \alpha'\mu = 0$$

the revealed target. The strength of the reaction is measured by the coefficients α. The actual process $\beta' X_t$ fluctuates around its mean as given above in (4.32). Thus the actual behaviour results in a path that deviates from the target relations. The difference is given by $\bar{\alpha}'\Gamma C\mu$.

Solution to exercise 4.5

1. From the Granger representation

$$X_t = C \sum_{i=1}^{t} (\varepsilon_i + \mu) + C(L)(\varepsilon_t + \mu) + A$$

we find

$$E\Delta X_t = C\mu.$$

Taking expectations in the equation, which defines the process, and using the fact that $E(\beta' X_{t-1}) = E(\beta' X_t)$ due to stationarity, we find

$$C\mu = \alpha E(\beta' X_t) + \sum_{i=1}^{k-1} \Gamma_i C\mu + \mu.$$

Multiplying this by $\bar{\alpha}' = (\alpha'\alpha)^{-1}\alpha'$ and rearranging terms leads to

$$E(\beta' X_t) = \bar{\alpha}' \left(I - \sum_{i=1}^{k-1} \Gamma_i \right) C\mu - \bar{\alpha}'\mu \quad (1)$$
$$= \bar{\alpha}'(\Gamma C - I)\mu.$$

2. If $\Gamma_i = 0$, $i = 1, \ldots, k-1$, equation (1) reduces to

$$\begin{aligned} E(\beta' X_t) &= \bar{\alpha}'[C - I]\mu \\ &= \bar{\alpha}'[\beta_\perp(\alpha_\perp'\beta_\perp)^{-1}\alpha_\perp' - I]\mu \\ &= \bar{\alpha}'[-\alpha(\beta'\alpha)^{-1}\beta']\mu \\ &= -(\beta'\alpha)^{-1}\beta'\mu. \end{aligned}$$

3. In the specific example one finds

$$E(\beta' X_t) = -(-1)^{-1}(1, -1)\mu = \mu_1 - \mu_2.$$

4. The six graphs in Figures 4.6–4.8 have been generated from two series of Gaussian-distributed epsilons. One series was used to generate the processes to the left and the other to generate the processes to the right. The dotted line in the graphs in Figures 4.6 and 4.7 refers to the attractor line. The intercept on the X_1 axis is the expectation of $\beta' X_t = X_{1t} - X_{2t}$. Compare the graphs with Figure 4.5 and Figure 3.1 in SJ, p. 41.

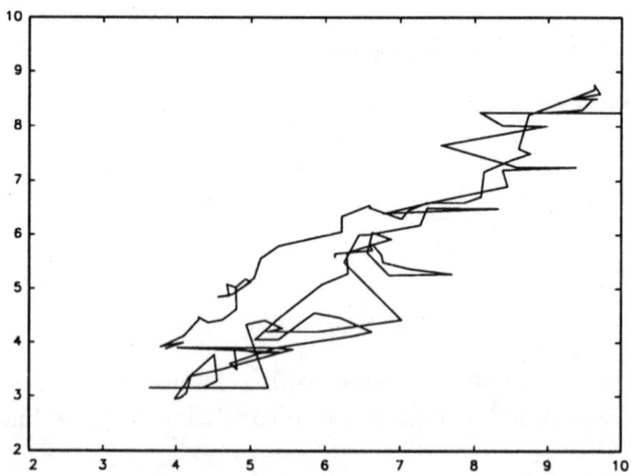

Fig. 4.5: Exercise 4.5. The German Treasury Bill Rate (3 month) plotted against the Austrian Treasury Bill Rate (3 month) from 1984:3 to 1995:11 (EcoWin database).

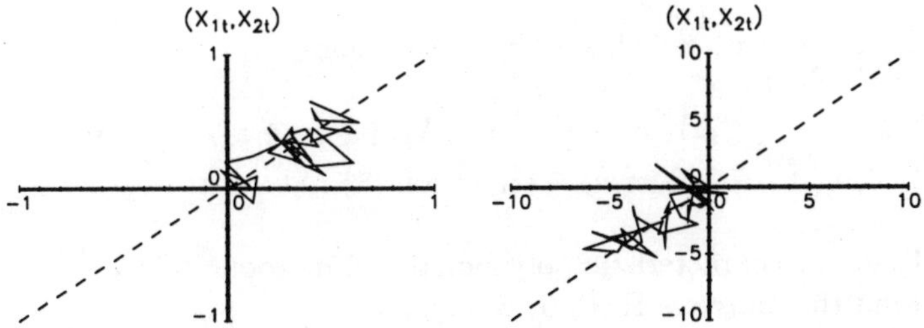

Fig. 4.6: Exercise 4.5. The process X_t is simulated with initial value $X_0 = (0,0)'$ and $\mu = (0,0)$. The process in the left panel was simulated with variance $\Omega = \frac{1}{10}I$ and the process in the right panel with variance $\Omega = I$. In this case the process has $E(\beta' X_t) = 0$ and no drift.

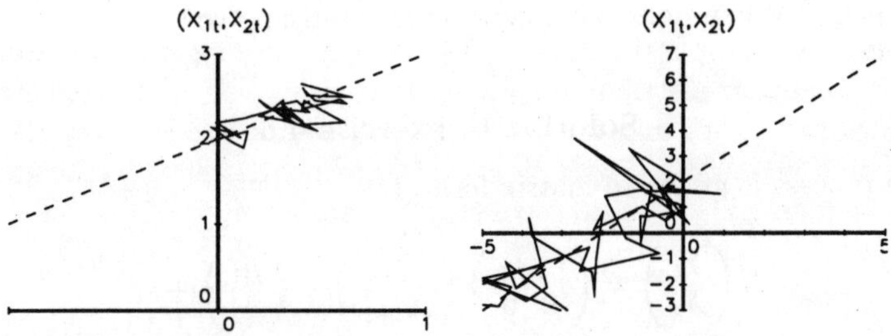

Fig. 4.7: Exercise 4.5. The process X_t is simulated with initial value $X_0 = (0,2)'$ and $\mu = (-1,1)$. The process in the left panel was simulated with variance $\Omega = \frac{1}{10}I$ and the process in the right panel with variance $\Omega = I$. In this case the process has $E(\beta' X_t) = E(X_{1t} - X_{2t}) = -2$ and no drift.

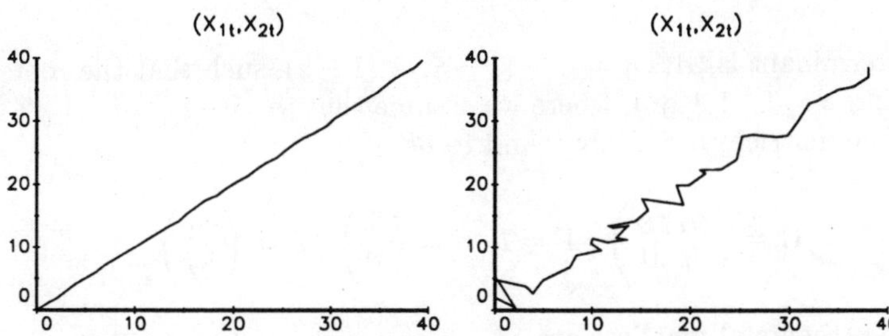

Fig. 4.8: Exercise 4.5. The process X_t is simulated with initial value $X_0 = (0,0)'$ and $\mu = (1,1)$. The process in the left panel was simulated with variance $\Omega = \frac{1}{10}I$ and the process in the right panel with variance $\Omega = I$. In this case the process has $E(\beta' X_t) = 0$ and a drift in the direction $(1,1)$.

4.6

Consider the processes defined by the equations

$$\Delta Y_t = \gamma_1 Y_{t-1} + \gamma_2 X_{t-1} + \mu_1 + \varepsilon_{1t},$$
$$\Delta X_t = \mu_2 + \varepsilon_{2t}.$$

1. Find the characteristic polynomial and its roots.
2. Find the matrices Π, Γ, α, β, $\alpha_\perp$, $\beta_\perp$.
3. Check that Π has reduced rank and find the condition for $\alpha'_\perp \Gamma \beta_\perp$ to have reduced rank.
4. Find $(\alpha, \alpha_1, \alpha_2)$ and $(\beta, \beta_1, \beta_2)$ in this case and show that

$$C_2 = \begin{pmatrix} 0 & \gamma_2 \\ 0 & 0 \end{pmatrix}$$

What is C_1? When does the quadratic trend disappear?

Solution to exercise 4.6

1. The process is given, in matrix form, by

$$\Delta \begin{pmatrix} Y_t \\ X_t \end{pmatrix} = \begin{pmatrix} \gamma_1 & \gamma_2 \\ 0 & 0 \end{pmatrix} \begin{pmatrix} Y_{t-1} \\ X_{t-1} \end{pmatrix} + \begin{pmatrix} \mu_1 \\ \mu_2 \end{pmatrix} + \varepsilon_t$$

and has characteristic polynomial

$$A(z) = I(1-z) - \begin{pmatrix} \gamma_1 & \gamma_2 \\ 0 & 0 \end{pmatrix} z$$
$$= \begin{pmatrix} 1-(1+\gamma_1)z & -\gamma_2 z \\ 0 & 1-z \end{pmatrix}.$$

The determinant is $|A(z)| = (1-(1+\gamma_1)z)(1-z)$, such that the roots are $z = 1$ and $z = 1/(1+\gamma_1)$, where we assume that $\gamma_1 \neq -1$.

2. The matrices are easily found to be

$$\Pi = \begin{pmatrix} \gamma_1 & \gamma_2 \\ 0 & 0 \end{pmatrix}, \ \Gamma = I, \ \alpha = \begin{pmatrix} 1 \\ 0 \end{pmatrix}, \ \beta = \begin{pmatrix} \gamma_1 \\ \gamma_2 \end{pmatrix},$$

and the orthogonal matrices are

$$\alpha_\perp = \begin{pmatrix} 0 \\ 1 \end{pmatrix}, \ \beta_\perp = \begin{pmatrix} \gamma_2 \\ -\gamma_1 \end{pmatrix}$$

if $(\gamma_1, \gamma_2) \neq (0, 0)$, which we assume. Finally $\alpha'_\perp \Gamma \beta_\perp = -\gamma_1$.

3. The Π matrix has clearly reduced rank since it has a row of zeros. The matrix $\alpha'_\perp \Gamma \beta_\perp = -\gamma_1$ has reduced rank if and only if $\gamma_1 = 0$. What happens in the case where $\gamma_1 = 0$ is that the difference of Y_t equals X_t multiplied by a scalar plus the stationary term $(\mu + \varepsilon_t)$. And since X_t is a random walk with drift, and hence $I(1)$, the process Y_t becomes $I(2)$ with a quadratic trend.

4. Under the conditions $\gamma_1 = 0$ and $\gamma_2 \neq 0$, we have

$$\alpha = \begin{pmatrix} 1 \\ 0 \end{pmatrix}, \ \beta = \begin{pmatrix} 0 \\ \gamma_2 \end{pmatrix}, \ \alpha_1 = \beta_1 = 0, \ \alpha_2 = \begin{pmatrix} 0 \\ 1 \end{pmatrix}, \ \beta_2 = \begin{pmatrix} 1 \\ 0 \end{pmatrix},$$

where we have applied the formulae in SJ, p. 57,

$$\alpha_1 = \bar{\alpha}_\perp \xi, \quad \alpha_2 = \alpha_\perp \xi_\perp,$$

$$\beta_1 = \bar{\beta}_\perp \eta, \quad \beta_2 = \beta_\perp \eta_\perp,$$

and used the fact that $\xi = \eta = 0$, such that $\alpha_2 = \alpha_\perp$ and $\beta_2 = \beta_\perp$. We find the parameter θ to be

$$\theta = \Gamma \bar{\beta} \bar{\alpha}' \Gamma = I \begin{pmatrix} 0 \\ 1/\gamma_2 \end{pmatrix} (1, 0) I = \begin{pmatrix} 0 & 0 \\ 1/\gamma_2 & 0 \end{pmatrix},$$

such that

$$\begin{aligned} C_2 &= \beta_2 (\alpha_2' \theta \beta_2)^{-1} \alpha_2' \\ &= \begin{pmatrix} 1 \\ 0 \end{pmatrix} \left((0, 1) \begin{pmatrix} 0 & 0 \\ 1/\gamma_2 & 0 \end{pmatrix} \begin{pmatrix} 1 \\ 0 \end{pmatrix} \right)^{-1} (0, 1) \\ &= \begin{pmatrix} 1 \\ 0 \end{pmatrix} \gamma_2 (0, 1) = \begin{pmatrix} 0 & \gamma_2 \\ 0 & 0 \end{pmatrix}. \end{aligned}$$

The C_1 matrix is found by calculating the Granger representation of X_t and Y_t. The solution for the process X_t is

$$\begin{aligned} X_t &= \sum_{i=1}^{t} (\mu_2 + \varepsilon_{2i}) + X_0 \\ &= \sum_{i=1}^{t} \varepsilon_{2i} + \mu_2 t + X_0 \end{aligned}$$

such that the representation of Y_t is

$$
\begin{aligned}
Y_t &= \sum_{s=1}^{t}(\gamma_2 X_{s-1} + \mu_1 + \varepsilon_{1s}) + Y_0 \\
&= \gamma_2 \sum_{s=1}^{t}\left(\sum_{i=1}^{s-1}\varepsilon_{2i} + \mu_2(s-1) + X_0\right) + \sum_{i=1}^{t}\varepsilon_{1i} + \mu_1 t + Y_0 \\
&= \gamma_2\left(\sum_{s=1}^{t}\sum_{i=1}^{s}\varepsilon_{2i} - \sum_{i=1}^{t}\varepsilon_{2i} + \mu_2\frac{t(t-1)}{2} + tX_0\right) + \sum_{i=1}^{t}\varepsilon_{1i} + \mu_1 t + Y_0 \\
&= \gamma_2\sum_{s=1}^{t}\sum_{i=1}^{s}\varepsilon_{2i} + \sum_{i=1}^{t}\varepsilon_{1i} - \gamma_2\sum_{i=1}^{t}\varepsilon_{2i} + \frac{1}{2}\gamma_2\mu_2 t^2 \\
&\quad + \left(-\frac{1}{2}\gamma_2\mu_2 + \gamma_2 X_0 + \mu_1\right)t + Y_0.
\end{aligned}
$$

Hence

$$
C_1 = \begin{pmatrix} 1 & -\gamma_2 \\ 0 & 1 \end{pmatrix}.
$$

From the expansion of Granger representation of an $I(2)$ process, and the expression above, it is seen that the process has a quadratic trend given by

$$
\frac{1}{2}C_2\mu t^2 = \frac{1}{2}\begin{pmatrix} 0 \\ \gamma_2\beta_2 \end{pmatrix} t^2,
$$

which disappears if $\mu_2 = 0$.

4.7*

Consider the model

$$
X_t = \Pi_1 X_{t-1} + \varepsilon_t.
$$

1. Show that the conditions from Granger's theorem, (4.4) and (4.5), are given by

$$
\Pi_1 = I + \alpha\beta', \quad \alpha'_\perp\beta_\perp \text{ full rank.} \tag{4.35}
$$

Consider next the model

$$
X_t = \Pi_1 X_{t-1} + \Pi_2 X_{t-2} + \varepsilon_t,
$$

and define $\Pi = -I + \Pi_1 + \Pi_2$ and $\Gamma = I + \Pi_2$. The conditions are now

$$
\Pi_1 + \Pi_2 = I + \alpha\beta', \quad \alpha'_\perp (I + \Pi_2)\beta_\perp \text{ full rank.} \tag{4.36}
$$

Now rewrite the model as

$$\Delta\begin{pmatrix} X_t \\ X_{t-1} \end{pmatrix} = \begin{pmatrix} \Pi_1 - I & \Pi_2 \\ I & -I \end{pmatrix}\begin{pmatrix} X_{t-1} \\ X_{t-2} \end{pmatrix} + \begin{pmatrix} \varepsilon_t \\ 0 \end{pmatrix} = \tilde{\Pi}\tilde{X}_{t-1} + \tilde{\varepsilon}_t.$$

2. Show that the matrix $\tilde{\Pi}$ has reduced rank $\tilde{\Pi} = \tilde{\alpha}\tilde{\beta}'$ and that

$$\tilde{\beta}_\perp = \begin{pmatrix} \beta_\perp \\ \beta_\perp \end{pmatrix}, \ \tilde{\alpha}_\perp = \begin{pmatrix} \alpha_\perp \\ \Pi_2'\alpha_\perp \end{pmatrix},$$

so that condition (4.36) reduces to condition (4.35) for the companion matrix.

Solution to exercise 4.7

1. The two conditions of Granger's representation theorem we must check are that Π has reduced rank (4.4), and that $\alpha_\perp'\Gamma\beta_\perp$ has full rank (4.5).

In the AR(1) model, we have the relations $\Pi = \Pi_1 - I = \alpha\beta'$ and $\Gamma = I$, such that (4.4) is equivalent to $\Pi_1 = I + \alpha\beta'$, where α and β are $p \times r$ matrices with $r < p$, and (4.5) reduces to $\alpha_\perp'\beta_\perp$ having full rank.

2. By adding the last p columns of $\tilde{\Pi}$ to the p first, we see that

$$\mathrm{sp}(\tilde{\Pi}) = \mathrm{sp}\begin{pmatrix} \alpha\beta' & \Pi_2 \\ 0 & -I \end{pmatrix},$$

which is a subspace of $\mathbf{R}^{2p}$ with dimension $p + r$. Hence $\tilde{\Pi}$ has rank $p + r$.

The identities

$$(\alpha_\perp', \alpha_\perp'\Pi_2)\begin{pmatrix} \Pi_1 - I & \Pi_2 \\ I & -I \end{pmatrix} = (\alpha_\perp'\alpha\beta', \alpha_\perp'\Pi_2 - \alpha_\perp'\Pi_2) = 0,$$

and

$$\begin{pmatrix} \Pi_1 - I & \Pi_2 \\ I & -I \end{pmatrix}\begin{pmatrix} \beta_\perp \\ \beta_\perp \end{pmatrix} = \begin{pmatrix} \alpha\beta'\beta_\perp \\ \beta_\perp - \beta_\perp \end{pmatrix} = 0,$$

show that we can express the orthogonal matrices as

$$\tilde{\alpha}_\perp = \begin{pmatrix} \alpha_\perp \\ \Pi_2'\alpha_\perp \end{pmatrix} \text{ and } \tilde{\beta}_\perp = \begin{pmatrix} \beta_\perp \\ \beta_\perp \end{pmatrix},$$

since they both have full rank $p - r$. Note that

$$\begin{aligned} \tilde{\alpha}_\perp'\tilde{\beta}_\perp &= \alpha_\perp'\beta_\perp + \alpha_\perp'\Pi_2\beta_\perp \\ &= \alpha_\perp'(I + \Pi_2)\beta_\perp = \alpha_\perp'\Gamma\beta_\perp, \end{aligned}$$

such that condition (4.35) for the companion form is equivalent to (4.36).

4.8**

The following is an extension of Granger's theorem.

Let $A(z) = I - \sum_{i=1}^{k} \Pi_i z^i$ be the characteristic polynomial of the p-dimensional autoregressive process X_t. We assume that $|A(z)| = 0$ implies that $|z| > 1$ except for the s distinct points $z = (z_1, \ldots, z_s)$, where $|z_i| \leq 1$, $i = 1, \ldots, s$, and want to find an expression for $A^{-1}(z)$. We define $z_0 = 0$ and the polynomials

$$P(z) = \prod_{m=0}^{s} (z - z_m),$$

$$P_i(z) = \prod_{m=0, m\neq i}^{s} (z - z_m),$$

$$P_{ij}(z) = \prod_{m=0, m\neq i,j}^{s} (z - z_m).$$

1. Show that

$$\frac{dP(z)}{dz} = \sum_{i=0}^{s} P_i(z),$$

$$\frac{d^2P(z)}{dz^2} = \sum_{\substack{i,j=0 \\ i\neq j}}^{s} P_{ij}(z).$$

2. Prove the representation

$$A(z) = \sum_{i=0}^{s} A(z_i) \frac{P_i(z)}{P_i(z_i)} + P(z)A^*(z), \tag{4.37}$$

where $A^*(z)$ is a polynomial, and show how this representation gives rise to an error correction formulation of the model for X_t. (Hint: consider the polynomial

$$A(z) - \sum_{i=0}^{s} A(z_i) \frac{P_i(z)}{P_i(z_i)},$$

and check the values for $z = z_0, z_1, \ldots, z_s$.)

3. Show that for $m = 0, \ldots, s$

$$\Gamma_m = \frac{dA(z)}{dz}|_{z=z_m}$$

$$= A(z_m) \sum_{\substack{j=0 \\ j\neq m}}^{s} \frac{P_{mj}(z_m)}{P_m(z_m)} + \sum_{\substack{i=0 \\ i\neq m}}^{s} A(z_i) \frac{P_{im}(z_m)}{P_i(z_i)} + P_m(z_m)A^*(z_m).$$

4. Consider the special cases where $z = 1$ is the only root with absolute value ≤ 1, and define $z_0 = 0,\ z_1 = 1$. Let $A(1) = -\alpha\beta'$, and note that $A(0) = I$. Find the error correction model for this case.

5. Consider next the case where $z = 1$ and $z = -1$ are roots and choose $z_0 = 0,\ z_1 = 1,\ z_2 = -1$. Define $A(z_1) = -\alpha_1\beta_1',\ A(z_2) = -\alpha_2\beta_2'$ and find the corresponding error correction model, and the Granger representation.

Consider again the general situation. Since $z_1, \ldots, z_s$ are roots of the equation $|A(z)| = 0$ it follows that $A(z_i) = -\alpha_i\beta_i'$ for some $p \times r_i$ matrices of full rank, $0 \leq r_i < p,\ i = 1, \ldots, s$. Assume further that for $i = 1, \ldots, s$, $\alpha_{i\perp}'\Gamma_i\beta_{i\perp}$ has full rank and define

$$C_i = \beta_{i\perp}\left(\alpha_{i\perp}'\Gamma_i\beta_{i\perp}\right)^{-1}\alpha_{i\perp}'.$$

6. Show that

$$C(z) = \sum_{i=1}^{s} C_i \frac{1}{z - z_i} + C^*(z),$$

where $C^*(z) = \sum_{i=0}^{\infty} C_i^* z^i$, can be chosen such that $C(z)A(z) = I$.

(Hint: the function $A^{-1}(z)$ is well defined for all points $|z| \leq 1$, apart from the points $z_1, \ldots, z_s$. Show that in a neighbourhood of z_i

$$A^{-1}(z) - C_i\frac{1}{z - z_i} = \left(\beta_i, \frac{1}{z - z_i}\beta_{i\perp}\right)$$
$$\times\left\{(\alpha_i, \alpha_{i\perp})'A(z)\left(\beta_i, \frac{1}{z - z_i}\beta_{i\perp}\right)\right\}^{-1}(\alpha_i, \alpha_{i\perp})' - C_i\frac{1}{z - z_i}$$

has no pole at $z = z_i$, and hence that

$$A^{-1}(z) - \sum_{i=1}^{s} C_i\frac{1}{z - z_i}$$

has a convergent power series.) See Hylleberg et al. (1990) and Johansen and Schaumburg (1998).

Solution to exercise 4.8

1. These relations follow from the usual rules for differentiation of products.

2. Consider the matrix polynomial

$$G(z) = A(z) - \sum_{i=0}^{s} A(z_i)\frac{P_i(z)}{P_i(z_i)}. \tag{1}$$

At $z = z_0$, say, we note that $P_i(z_0) = 0$, for $i = 1, \ldots, s$, such that

$$G(z_0) = A(z_0) - A(z_0)\frac{P_0(z_0)}{P_0(z_0)} = 0.$$

Thus each of the entries of G is a polynomial with the property that it is zero at $z = z_0$. Hence, each of them can be factorized as $(z - z_0)$ times a polynomial. This therefore also holds for the matrix polynomial $G(z)$. The same argument applied for each of the roots $z_0, \dots, z_s$ shows that we can factorize

$$G(z) = \prod_{i=0}^{s}(z - z_i)A^*(z) = P(z)A^*(z),$$

for some matrix polynomial $A^*(z)$.

The representation (4.37) applied to the process X_t gives the error correction formulation, using $A(0) = I$ and $A(z_i) = -\alpha_i\beta_i'$,

$$A(L)X_t = \frac{P_0(L)}{P_0(z_0)}X_t - \sum_{i=1}^{s}\alpha_i\beta_i'\frac{P_i(L)}{P_i(z_i)}X_t + P(L)A^*(L)X_t = \varepsilon_t.$$

The idea here is that under certain conditions (see below) the factor

$$\frac{P_0(L)}{P_0(z_0)} = \frac{\prod_{i=1}^{s}(L - z_i)}{\prod_{i=1}^{s}(z_0 - z_i)}$$

and the factor $P(L)$ make X_t stationary, and that the remaining terms $\frac{P_i(L)}{P_i(z_i)}X_t$ are non-stationary, but $\beta_i'\frac{P_i(L)}{P_i(z_i)}X_t$ is stationary. In order to see this one needs a version of Granger's representation theorem that holds more generally for roots with absolute value 1.

3. We find

$$\frac{dA(z)}{dz} = \sum_{i=0}^{s}A(z_i)\sum_{j\neq i}\frac{P_{ij}(z)}{P_i(z_i)} + \sum_{i=0}^{s}P_i(z)A^*(z) + P(z)\frac{dA^*(z)}{dz}.$$

At the point $z = z_m$ we find that only terms with $P_{mj}(z_m)$ or $P_{jm}(z_m)$ contribute to the first double sum, and that the last term is zero due to the factor $P(z_m) = 0$. Thus

$$\begin{aligned}\Gamma_m &= \frac{dA(z)}{dz}|_{z=z_m} \\ &= A(z_m)\sum_{\substack{j=0\\ j\neq m}}^{s}\frac{P_{mj}(z_m)}{P_m(z_m)} + \sum_{\substack{i=0\\ i\neq m}}^{s}A(z_i)\frac{P_{im}(z_m)}{P_i(z_i)} + P_m(z_m)A^*(z_m).\end{aligned}$$

Note that if $A(z_i) = -\alpha_i\beta_i'$ then

$$\alpha'_{m\perp}\Gamma_m\beta_{m\perp} = -\sum_{\substack{i=0\\ i\neq m}}^{s} \alpha'_{m\perp}\alpha_i\beta'_i\beta_{m\perp}\frac{P_{im}(z_m)}{P_i(z_i)} + P_m(z_m)\alpha'_{m\perp}A^*(z_m)\beta_{m\perp}.$$

4. We find in this case the polynomials

$$\begin{aligned} P(z) &= z(z-1), & & \\ P_0(z) &= z-1, & P_0(0) &= -1, \\ P_1(z) &= z, & P_1(1) &= \ \ 1, \end{aligned}$$

and the error correction model

$$\begin{aligned} \varepsilon_t &= \frac{P_0(L)}{P_0(0)}X_t - \alpha\beta'\frac{P_1(L)}{P_1(1)} + P(L)A^*(L)X_t \\ &= \frac{L-1}{-1}X_t - \alpha\beta'\frac{L}{1}X_t + L(1-L)A^*(L)X_t, \end{aligned}$$

such that we get the well-known error correction form

$$\Delta X_t = \alpha\beta' X_{t-1} - A^*(L)\Delta X_{t-1} + \varepsilon_t.$$

5. In this case we find the polynomials

$$\begin{aligned} P(z) &= z(z-1)(z+1) = z(z^2-1) & & \\ P_0(z) &= z^2-1, & P_0(0) &= -1 \\ P_1(z) &= z(z+1), & P_1(1) &= \ \ 2 \\ P_{-1}(z) &= z(z-1), & P_{-1}(-1) &= \ \ 2 \end{aligned}$$

and the error correction model

$$\begin{aligned} (1-L^2)X_t = \alpha_1\beta'_1 & \frac{X_{t-1}+X_{t-2}}{2} \\ & -\alpha_{-1}\beta'_{-1}\frac{X_{t-1}-X_{t-2}}{2} - A^*(L)(L^2-1)X_{t-1} + \varepsilon_t. \end{aligned}$$

The Granger representation will follow from the answers below.

6. If we express the inverse matrix using Kramer's formula we get

$$A^{-1}(z) = \frac{\text{adj}(A(z))}{\det(A(z))} = \frac{\text{adj}(A(z))}{\prod_{i=1}^N (z-z_i)/(-z_i)},$$

where $\text{adj}(A(z))$ is the adjoint matrix. This shows that $A^{-1}(z)$ has poles at all the roots of $|A(z)| = 0$.

Consider first the roots that are outside the unit circle z_i, $i = s+1, \ldots, N$. The function

$$\frac{\text{adj}(A(z))}{\prod_{i=s+1}^N (z-z_i)/(-z_i)}$$

has a convergent power series in a disc given by $|z| \leq 1+\delta$, where $\delta > 0$ is given by

$$1+\delta = \min_{\{s<i\leq N\}} |z_i|.$$

Each of the remaining roots $z_1, \ldots, z_s$ gives rise to a pole in the function on the unit circle. The conditions given ensure that no multiple poles arise, that is, that the function can be expanded as indicated. We consider the function

$$A^{-1}(z) - \sum_{i=1}^{s} C_i \frac{1}{z-z_i}$$

and want to prove that this function has no poles at the points $z_1, \ldots, z_s$, that is, that the poles in $A^{-1}(z)$ can be removed by subtracting expressions like $C_i \frac{1}{z-z_i}$. We therefore consider the function in a neighbourhood of z_i and consider first the new matrix polynomial

$$\tilde{A}(z) = (\bar{\alpha}_i, \alpha_{i\perp})' A(z) \left(\bar{\beta}_i, \beta_{i\perp}\frac{1}{z-z_i}\right).$$

It is not clear that this is a polynomial, since we introduce a pole by the third factor. We expand $A(z)$ around $z = z_i$ and find for suitable polynomials $A_2(z)$ and $A_3(z)$, and $z \neq z_i$,

$$\begin{aligned}\tilde{A}(z) &= (\bar{\alpha}_i, \alpha_{i\perp})'(-\alpha_i\beta_i' + (z-z_i)\dot{A}(z_i) + (z-z_i)^2 A_2(z)) \left(\bar{\beta}_i, \beta_{i\perp}\frac{1}{z-z_i}\right) \\ &= -\begin{pmatrix} I & 0 \\ 0 & 0 \end{pmatrix} + \begin{pmatrix} (z-z_i)\bar{\alpha}_i'\dot{A}(z_i)\bar{\beta}_i & \bar{\alpha}_i'\dot{A}(z_i)\beta_{i\perp} \\ (z-z_i)\alpha_{i\perp}'\dot{A}(z_i)\bar{\beta}_i & \alpha_{i\perp}'\dot{A}(z_i)\beta_{i\perp} \end{pmatrix} + (z-z_i)A_3(z),\end{aligned}$$

and for $z = z_i$ we get by continuity

$$\tilde{A}(z_i) = \begin{pmatrix} -I & \bar{\alpha}_i'\dot{A}(z_i)\beta_{i\perp} \\ 0 & \alpha_{i\perp}'\dot{A}(z_i)\beta_{i\perp} \end{pmatrix},$$

which is invertible by the assumptions on $\dot{A}(z_i)$. Thus the function $\tilde{A}(z)$ does not have a pole at $z = z_i$, and is in fact a polynomial. Moreover $|\tilde{A}(z)| = 0$ does not have a root at $z = z_i$ since $\tilde{A}(z_i)$ is invertible under the assumption that $|\alpha_{i\perp}'\dot{A}(z_i)\beta_{i\perp}| \neq 0$. For $z \neq z_i$ the roots of $|\tilde{A}(z)| = 0$ are exactly the same as those of $|A(z)| = 0$, as is seen from the expression for $\tilde{A}(z)$. Finally we consider the identity valid for z in a neighbourhood of z_i, $z \neq z_i$:

$$\begin{aligned}A^{-1}(z) &= \left(\bar{\beta}_i, \beta_{i\perp}\frac{1}{z-z_i}\right)\left((\bar{\alpha}_i, \alpha_{i\perp})' A(z)\left(\bar{\beta}_i, \beta_{i\perp}\frac{1}{z-z_i}\right)\right)^{-1}(\bar{\alpha}_i, \alpha_{i\perp})' \\ &= \left(\bar{\beta}_i, \beta_{i\perp}\frac{1}{z-z_i}\right)\tilde{A}(z)^{-1}(\bar{\alpha}_i, \alpha_{i\perp})'\end{aligned}$$

$$= \left(\bar{\beta}_i, \beta_{i\perp}\frac{1}{z - z_i}\right)\left(\begin{pmatrix} -I & \bar{\alpha}_i'\dot{A}(z_i)\beta_{i\perp} \\ 0 & \alpha_{i\perp}'\dot{A}(z_i)\beta_{i\perp} \end{pmatrix}^{-1} + (z - z_i)C_1(z)\right)(\bar{\alpha}_i, \alpha_{i\perp}$$

$$= \beta_{i\perp}\left(\alpha_{i\perp}'\dot{A}(z_i)\beta_{i\perp}\right)^{-1}\alpha_{i\perp}'\frac{1}{z - z_i} + C_i^*(z)$$

$$= C_i\frac{1}{z - z_i} + C_i^*(z),$$

where $C_1(z)$ and $C_i^*(z)$ have no poles at $z = z_i$. Thus by applying this transformation we expose the pole and can subtract it from $A^{-1}(z)$. By successively applying transformations we can remove the poles corresponding to the roots at $z_1, \ldots, z_s$. The remaining function $C^*(z)$ has no poles at these points and hence no poles for $|z| \leq 1 + \delta$, as was to be proved.

We can now return to the question of finding a Granger representation for the case of more than one unit root.

Consider for simplicity first the case with only one unit root at $z = 1$, that is

$$A(z)^{-1} = C_1\frac{1}{z - 1} + C^*(z),$$

where $C^*(z)$ has a convergent power series for $|z| < 1 + \delta$.

Now multiply by $(1 - z)A(z)$ and we find the relation

$$(1 - z) = (-C_1 + (1 - z)C^*(z))A(z).$$

This identity in the lag operator L is applied to the process X_t. We use the relation $A(L)X_t = \varepsilon_t$ and define $Y_t = C^*(L)\varepsilon_t$:

$$\Delta X_t = -C_1\varepsilon_t + \Delta Y_t, \qquad t = 1, \ldots, T.$$

The solution of this equation is

$$X_t = -C_1\sum_{i=1}^{t}\varepsilon_i + Y_t + X_0 - Y_0.$$

In the notation from the book we have

$$\alpha_{1\perp}'\Gamma_1\beta_{1\perp} = -\alpha_\perp'\Gamma\beta_\perp,$$

so that $C = -C_1$.

Next consider the situation with roots $z = 1$ and $z = -1$. In this case we have the formula

$$A^{-1}(z) = C_1\frac{1}{z - 1} + C_{-1}\frac{1}{z + 1} + C^*(z).$$

Now multiply by $(1 - z)(1 + z)$ and $A(z)$ and find

$$(1-z)(1+z) = [-C_1(1+z) + C_{-1}(1-z) + (1-z)(1+z)C^*(z)]A(z).$$

We now apply this to the process X_t and use the relation $A(L)X_t = \varepsilon_t$ and define $Y_t = C^*(L)\varepsilon_t$. Then

$$(1-L)(1+L)X_t = [-C_1(\varepsilon_t + \varepsilon_{t-1}) + C_{-1}(\varepsilon_t - \varepsilon_{t-1}) + (1-L)(1+L)Y_t].$$

A solution to this equation is given by

$$X_t = -C_1 \sum_{i=1}^{t} \varepsilon_i + (-1)^t C_{-1} \sum_{i=1}^{t} (-1)^i \varepsilon_i + Y_t,$$

and the complete solution to the homogeneous equation $(1-L)(1+L)X_t = 0$ is of the form

$$X_t = A_0 + (-1)^t A_1,$$

where A_0 and A_1 are determined from the initial values X_0 and X_{-1}. Thus the full solution is given by

$$X_t = -C_1 \sum_{i=1}^{t} \varepsilon_i + (-1)^t C_{-1} \sum_{i=1}^{t} (-1)^i \varepsilon_i + Y_t + A_0 + (-1)^t A_1.$$

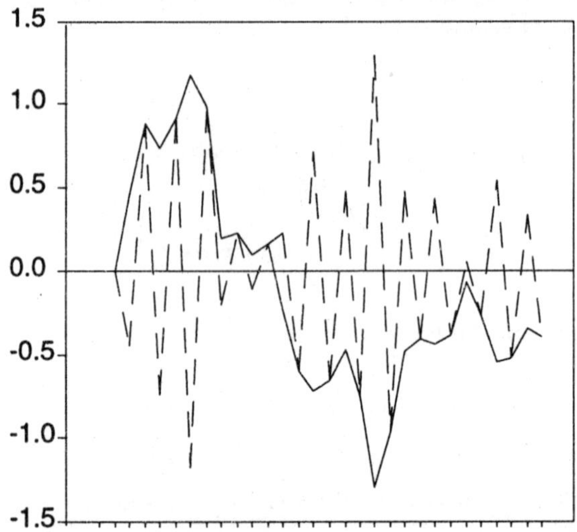

Fig. 4.9: Exercise 4.8. Plot of a random walk (solid line) and a seasonal random walk (dashed line).

4.9

Let the univariate process be defined by the equations

$$\Delta X_t = \pi X_{t-1} + \varepsilon_t,$$

for some π in the interval $-2 < \pi < 0$, and define the correlation

$$\lambda^2 = \text{Cov}\left(\Delta X_t, X_{t-1}\right)^2 / (\text{Var}\left(\Delta X_t\right) \text{Var}\left(X_{t-1}\right)).$$

Show that $\lambda^2 = -\frac{1}{2}\pi$.

Solution to exercise 4.9

Note first that X_t is stationary since $|1+\pi| < 1$ and

$$X_t = (1+\pi)X_{t-1} + \varepsilon_t.$$

The variance can be calculated from its stationary representation,

$$X_t = \sum_{i=0}^{\infty}(1+\pi)^i \varepsilon_{t-i}.$$

Hence

$$\text{Var}(X_t) = E(X_t^2) = \sigma^2 / \left[1 - (1+\pi)^2\right],$$

where $\sigma^2 = \text{Var}(\varepsilon_t)$. The covariance and variance are given by

$$\begin{aligned}
\text{Cov}(\Delta X_t, X_{t-1}) &= E(\Delta X_t X_{t-1}) \\
&= E\left[(\pi X_{t-1} + \varepsilon_t)X_{t-1}\right] \\
&= \pi E X_{t-1}^2 \\
\text{Var}(\Delta X_t) &= E(\Delta X_t)^2 \\
&= E(\pi X_{t-1} + \varepsilon_t)^2 \\
&= \pi^2 E X_{t-1}^2 + \sigma^2,
\end{aligned}$$

where we use the fact that $E(\varepsilon_t X_{t-1}) = 0$, since the processes are independent. Hence we find the identity

$$\begin{aligned}
\lambda^2 &= \frac{\text{Cov}(\Delta X_t, X_{t-1})^2}{\text{Var}(\Delta X_t)\text{Var}(X_t)} \\
&= \frac{(\pi E X_{t-1}^2)^2}{\left(\pi^2 E X_{t-1}^2 + \sigma^2\right) E X_{t-1}^2} \\
&= \frac{1}{1 + \frac{\sigma^2}{\pi^2 E X_{t-1}^2}} = \frac{1}{1 + \frac{1-(1+\pi)^2}{\pi^2}} = -\frac{\pi}{2}
\end{aligned}$$

as stated.

4.10*

Consider the usual model

$$\Delta X_t = \alpha\beta' X_{t-1} + \varepsilon_t,$$

where ε_t has variance Ω, and define the matrices

$$\begin{aligned}\Sigma_{00} &= \mathrm{Var}(\Delta X_t),\\ \Sigma_{\beta\beta} &= \mathrm{Var}(\beta' X_t),\\ \Sigma_{\beta 0} &= \mathrm{Cov}(\beta' X_{t-1}, \Delta X_t).\end{aligned}$$

1. Show that

$$\Sigma_{00} = \alpha\Sigma_{\beta 0} + \Omega, \tag{1}$$
$$\Sigma_{\beta 0} = \Sigma_{\beta\beta}\alpha', \tag{2}$$

such that

$$\Sigma_{00} = \alpha\Sigma_{\beta\beta}\alpha' + \Omega. \tag{3}$$

2. Apply these results to show that

$$(\alpha'\Sigma_{00}^{-1}\alpha)^{-1}\alpha'\Sigma_{00}^{-1} = (\alpha'\Omega^{-1}\alpha)^{-1}\alpha'\Omega^{-1}, \tag{4}$$

$$\begin{aligned}\Sigma_{00}^{-1} - \Sigma_{00}^{-1}\alpha(\alpha'\Sigma_{00}^{-1}\alpha)^{-1}\alpha'\Sigma_{00}^{-1} &= \alpha_\perp(\alpha'_\perp\Sigma_{00}\alpha_\perp)^{-1}\alpha'_\perp\\ &= \alpha_\perp(\alpha'_\perp\Omega\alpha_\perp)^{-1}\alpha'_\perp\\ &= \Omega^{-1} - \Omega^{-1}\alpha(\alpha'\Omega^{-1}\alpha)^{-1}\alpha'\Omega^{-1},\end{aligned} \tag{5}$$

$$\Sigma_{\beta\beta}(\Sigma_{\beta 0}\Sigma_{00}^{-1}\Sigma_{0\beta})^{-1}\Sigma_{\beta\beta} - \Sigma_{\beta\beta} = (\alpha'\Omega^{-1}\alpha)^{-1}. \tag{6}$$

Solution to exercise 4.10

1. Post-multiply

$$\Delta X_t = \alpha\beta' X_{t-1} + \varepsilon_t$$

by $\Delta X_t'$ and take expectations to prove (1). Equation (2) is proved similarly, by post-multiplying by $X_{t-1}'\beta$, taking expectations and transposing.

2. If we multiply (1) by $\alpha'_\perp$, we find $\alpha'_\perp\Sigma_{00} = \alpha'_\perp\Omega$ or equivalently $\Sigma_{00}\alpha_\perp = \Omega\alpha_\perp$; post-multiplying (4) by this reduces both sides to zero.

When post-multiplying by α we get the identity. Since Ω is positive definite, $(\alpha, \Omega\alpha_\perp)$ has full rank, and (4) is proved.

The first equality in (5) is found by post-multiplying by $(\alpha, \Sigma_{00}\alpha_\perp)$. The second holds from the identity $\Sigma_{00}\alpha_\perp = \Omega\alpha_\perp$. The third is proved like the first by multiplying by $(\alpha, \Omega\alpha_\perp)$.

Equation (6) is proved by first using the identity $\alpha = \Sigma_{0\beta}\Sigma_{\beta\beta}^{-1}$ which is found from (2). Equation (6) then becomes

$$\begin{aligned}\Sigma_{\beta\beta}\left(\Sigma_{\beta 0}\Sigma_{00}^{-1}\Sigma_{0\beta}\right)^{-1}\Sigma_{\beta\beta} - \Sigma_{\beta\beta} &= \Sigma_{\beta\beta}\left(\Sigma_{\beta\beta}\alpha'\Sigma_{00}^{-1}\alpha\Sigma_{\beta\beta}\right)^{-1}\Sigma_{\beta\beta} - \Sigma_{\beta\beta}\\ &= \Sigma_{\beta\beta}\Sigma_{\beta\beta}^{-1}\left(\alpha'\Sigma_{00}^{-1}\alpha\right)^{-1}\Sigma_{\beta\beta}^{-1}\Sigma_{\beta\beta} - \Sigma_{\beta\beta}\\ &= \left(\alpha'\Sigma_{00}^{-1}\alpha\right)^{-1} - \Sigma_{\beta\beta}.\end{aligned}$$

Post-multiplying (4) by $\Sigma_{00}\bar{\alpha} = \alpha\Sigma_{\beta\beta} + \Omega\bar{\alpha}$, which is found from (3) (where $\bar{\alpha} = \alpha(\alpha'\alpha)^{-1}$), gives

$$\begin{aligned}\left(\alpha'\Sigma_{00}^{-1}\alpha\right)^{-1} &= \left(\alpha'\Omega^{-1}\alpha\right)^{-1}\alpha'\Omega^{-1}(\alpha\Sigma_{\beta\beta} + \Omega\bar{\alpha})\\ &= \Sigma_{\beta\beta} + \left(\alpha'\Omega^{-1}\alpha\right)^{-1},\end{aligned}$$

which proves (6). These identities are proved in Chapter 10 and are applied in various places in the proofs of the results on asymptotic behaviour.

4.11

Consider the equation

$$|\lambda\Sigma_{\beta\beta} - \Sigma_{\beta 0}\Sigma_{00}^{-1}\Sigma_{0\beta}| = 0. \tag{4.38}$$

1. Introduce $\alpha = \Sigma_{0\beta}\Sigma_{\beta\beta}^{-1}$ and use $\Sigma_{00} = \alpha\Sigma_{\beta\beta}\alpha' + \Omega$ to reduce (4.38) to

$$|\lambda\Sigma_{\beta\beta}^{-1} - \alpha'\left(\alpha\Sigma_{\beta\beta}\alpha' + \Omega\right)^{-1}\alpha| = 0.$$

2. Show that if ρ solves

$$|\rho\Sigma_{\beta\beta}^{-1} - \alpha'\Omega^{-1}\alpha| = 0,$$

then

$$\lambda = \rho/(1+\rho).$$

Solution to exercise 4.11

1. The identity

$$\begin{aligned}\left|\lambda\Sigma_{\beta\beta}-\Sigma_{\beta0}\Sigma_{00}^{-1}\Sigma_{0\beta}\right| &= \left|\lambda\Sigma_{\beta\beta}-\Sigma_{\beta\beta}\alpha'\Sigma_{00}^{-1}\alpha\Sigma_{\beta\beta}\right| \\ &= \left|\Sigma_{\beta\beta}\right| \left|\lambda\Sigma_{\beta\beta}^{-1}-\alpha'\Sigma_{00}^{-1}\alpha\right| \left|\Sigma_{\beta\beta}\right| \\ &= \left|\lambda\Sigma_{\beta\beta}^{-1}-\alpha'\left(\alpha\Sigma_{\beta\beta}\alpha'+\Omega\right)^{-1}\alpha\right| \left|\Sigma_{\beta\beta}\right|^2\end{aligned}$$

shows that

$$\left|\lambda\Sigma_{\beta\beta}-\Sigma_{\beta0}\Sigma_{00}^{-1}\Sigma_{0\beta}\right|=0,$$

if and only if

$$\left|\lambda\Sigma_{\beta\beta}^{-1}-\alpha'\left(\alpha\Sigma_{\beta\beta}\alpha'+\Omega\right)^{-1}\alpha\right|=0,$$

since $|\Sigma_{\beta\beta}|\neq 0$.

2. In order to simplify the problem we introduce the normalized vectors $u=\Omega^{-\frac{1}{2}}\alpha\Sigma_{\beta\beta}^{\frac{1}{2}}$, such that

$$\begin{aligned}\alpha &= \Omega^{\frac{1}{2}}u\Sigma_{\beta\beta}^{-\frac{1}{2}}, \\ \alpha'\Omega^{-1}\alpha &= \Sigma_{\beta\beta}^{-\frac{1}{2}}u'u\Sigma_{\beta\beta}^{-\frac{1}{2}}.\end{aligned}$$

The roots of (4.38) solve the equation

$$|\lambda\Sigma_{\beta\beta}^{-1}-\Sigma_{\beta\beta}^{-\frac{1}{2}}u'\Omega^{\frac{1}{2}}(\Omega^{\frac{1}{2}}uu'\Omega^{\frac{1}{2}}+\Omega)^{-1}\Omega^{\frac{1}{2}}u\Sigma_{\beta\beta}^{-\frac{1}{2}}|=0,$$

or

$$|\lambda I-u'(uu'+I)^{-1}u|=0.$$

It is not difficult to see that $u'(uu'+I)^{-1}u=u'u(I+u'u)^{-1}$ such that λ solves

$$|\lambda I-u'u(u'u+I)^{-1}|=0,$$

or

$$\begin{aligned}|\lambda(u'u+I)-u'u| &= 0, \\ |\lambda I-(1-\lambda)u'u| &= 0, \\ \left|\frac{\lambda}{1-\lambda}I-u'u\right| &= 0.\end{aligned}$$

Now we let $\rho=\frac{\lambda}{1-\lambda}$, and insert $u'u=\Sigma_{\beta\beta}^{\frac{1}{2}}\alpha'\Omega^{-1}\alpha\Sigma_{\beta\beta}^{\frac{1}{2}}$ and find

$$|\rho I-\Sigma_{\beta\beta}^{\frac{1}{2}}\alpha'\Omega^{-1}\alpha\Sigma_{\beta\beta}^{\frac{1}{2}}|=0 \text{ or } |\rho\Sigma_{\beta\beta}^{-1}-\alpha'\Omega^{-1}\alpha|=0.$$

4.12**

Consider the model

$$\Delta X_t = \alpha\beta' X_{t-1} + \varepsilon_t.$$

1. Show that

$$\beta' X_t = \sum_{i=0}^{t-1} (I + \beta'\alpha)^i \beta' \varepsilon_{t-i} + (I + \beta'\alpha)^t \beta' X_0. \tag{1}$$

2. Show that if the roots of the characteristic polynomial are either greater than 1 in absolute value or equal to 1 and if $\alpha'_\perp \beta_\perp$ has full rank then $I + \beta'\alpha$ has eigenvalues in the unit circle and we can define

$$\beta' X_0 = \sum_{i=0}^{\infty} (I + \beta'\alpha)^i \beta' \varepsilon_{0-i},$$

which makes $\beta' X_t$ a stationary process.

3. Show that this relation implies that $\Delta X_t = C(L)\varepsilon_t$, where

$$C(0) = I \text{ and } C_n = \alpha (I + \beta'\alpha)^{n-1} \beta', \qquad n = 1,\ 2, \ldots ,$$

and show that

$$C = C(1) = \beta_\perp (\alpha'_\perp \beta_\perp)^{-1} \alpha'_\perp.$$

4. Define $\Sigma_{\beta\beta}$ =Var$(\beta' X_t)$ and show that

$$\begin{aligned}\Sigma_{\beta\beta} &= \sum_{i=0}^{\infty} (I + \beta'\alpha)^i \beta'\Omega\beta (I + \alpha'\beta)^i \\ &= \beta'\Omega\beta + (I + \beta'\alpha) \Sigma_{\beta\beta} (I + \alpha'\beta).\end{aligned}$$

Show that

$$\Sigma_{00} = \text{Var}(\Delta X_t) = \alpha \Sigma_{\beta\beta} \alpha' + \Omega,$$

and that

$$\begin{aligned}\Sigma_1 &= \lim_{T\to\infty} T^{-1} \sum_{t=1}^{T} E\left(\sum_{i=1}^{t-1} \Delta X_i\right) \Delta X'_t \\ &= -\alpha\Sigma_{\beta\beta} (I + \alpha'\beta)^{-1} (\alpha'\beta)^{-1} \alpha' - \Omega\beta (\alpha'\beta)^{-1} \alpha',\end{aligned}$$

and

$$\Sigma = \lim_{T\to\infty} T^{-1} E\left(\sum_{i=1}^{T} \Delta X_i\right)\left(\sum_{i=1}^{T} \Delta X_i\right)' = C\Omega C'.$$

5. Next show that

$$\Sigma = \Sigma_{00} + \Sigma_1 + \Sigma_1'.$$

(Hint: it pays to show that

$$(\beta'\alpha)^{-1}\beta'\Omega\beta(\alpha'\beta)^{-1} = -\Sigma_{\beta\beta} - \Sigma_{\beta\beta}(\alpha'\beta)^{-1} - (\beta'\alpha)^{-1}\Sigma_{\beta\beta}.)$$

Solution to exercise 4.12

1. Multiplying by β', we get

$$\Delta\beta' X_t = \beta'\alpha\beta' X_{t-1} + \beta'\varepsilon_t,$$

which represents $\beta' X_t$ as an AR(1) process with the solution

$$\beta' X_t = \sum_{i=0}^{t-1}(I + \beta'\alpha)^i \beta'\varepsilon_{t-i} + (I + \beta'\alpha)^t \beta' X_0. \tag{1}$$

2. The condition that $\alpha_\perp'\beta_\perp$ has full rank is equivalent to the condition that $\alpha'\beta$ has full rank. To see this, assume that $\alpha'\beta\xi = 0$ for some vector ξ. Then $\beta\xi$ is orthogonal to α and hence contained in the space spanned by $\alpha_\perp$. Thus $\beta\xi = \alpha_\perp\psi$ for some vector ψ. Then we find that

$$\beta_\perp'\alpha_\perp\psi = \beta_\perp'\beta\xi = 0,$$

which contradicts the assumption. Thus $\alpha'\beta$ has full rank. Hence the matrices $(\alpha, \beta_\perp)$ and $(\beta, \alpha_\perp)$ also have full rank, since the product

$$(\beta, \alpha_\perp)'(\alpha, \beta_\perp) = \begin{pmatrix} \beta'\alpha & 0 \\ 0 & \alpha_\perp'\beta_\perp \end{pmatrix}$$

has full rank; see exercise 3.7.

In order to evaluate the roots of the polynomial $A(z) = (1-z)I - \alpha\beta' z$, we multiply by $(\alpha, \beta_\perp)'$ and $(\beta, \alpha_\perp)$ and find

$$\begin{aligned} |A(z)||\beta'\alpha||\alpha_\perp'\beta_\perp| &= \left|(1-z)\begin{pmatrix} \beta'\alpha & 0 \\ 0 & \alpha_\perp'\beta_\perp \end{pmatrix} - z\begin{pmatrix} (\beta'\alpha)^2 & 0 \\ 0 & 0 \end{pmatrix}\right| \\ &= (1-z)^{p-r}|\beta'\alpha||\alpha_\perp'\beta_\perp||I - z(I + \beta'\alpha)|. \end{aligned}$$

Now $z = 1$ is not a root of the last factor since $\beta'\alpha$ has full rank, hence $z = 1$ is a root with multiplicity $p - r$ and the remaining roots are the roots of

$$|I - (I + \beta'\alpha)z| = 0,$$

which are assumed to be outside the unit disc. Thus the eigenvalues of $(I + \beta'\alpha)$ must have absolute value less than 1.

The process

$$\beta' X_0 = \sum_{i=0}^{\infty} (I + \beta'\alpha)^i \beta' \varepsilon_{0-i}$$

is thus well defined since the coefficients decrease exponentially; see Lemma A.12. This choice inserted into (1) shows that

$$\beta' X_t = \sum_{i=0}^{\infty} (I + \beta'\alpha)^i \beta' \varepsilon_{t-i}, \tag{2}$$

which is stationary.

3. If we insert this into the equation for ΔX_t, we find

$$\Delta X_t = \alpha \sum_{i=0}^{\infty} (I + \beta'\alpha)^i \beta' \varepsilon_{t-1-i} + \varepsilon_t,$$

which gives the required representation of ΔX_t. To calculate the sum of the coefficients, note that

$$\begin{aligned} C &= I + \sum_{i=1}^{\infty} \alpha (I + \beta'\alpha)^{i-1} \beta' \\ &= I - \alpha(\beta'\alpha)^{-1}\beta' \\ &= \beta_\perp (\alpha_\perp' \beta_\perp)^{-1} \alpha_\perp'; \end{aligned}$$

see exercise 3.8.

4. From the representation (2) for $\beta' X_t$, we find that

$$\begin{aligned} \Sigma_{\beta\beta} &= \sum_{i=0}^{\infty} (I + \beta'\alpha)^i \beta' \Omega \beta (I + \alpha'\beta)^i \\ &= \beta'\Omega\beta + \sum_{i=1}^{\infty} (I + \beta'\alpha)^i \beta' \Omega \beta (I + \alpha'\beta)^i \\ &= \beta'\Omega\beta + (I + \beta'\alpha) \Sigma_{\beta\beta} (I + \alpha'\beta). \end{aligned} \tag{3}$$

From the model equations we find, by taking the variance on both sides and using the independence of ε_t and X_{t-1}, that

$$\Sigma_{00} = \mathrm{Var}(\Delta X_t) = \alpha \Sigma_{\beta\beta} \alpha' + \Omega.$$

Next consider the process ΔX_t and let $\gamma(h)$ denote the autocovariance function, which, for $h = 1, \ldots,$ is given by

$$\begin{aligned}\gamma(h) &= \mathrm{Cov}(\Delta X_t, \Delta X_{t+h}) \\ &= \Omega\beta(I+\alpha'\beta)^{h-1}\alpha' + \sum_{i=0}^{\infty}\alpha(I+\beta'\alpha)^i\beta'\Omega\beta(I+\alpha'\beta)^{h+i}\alpha' \\ &= \Omega\beta(I+\alpha'\beta)^{h-1}\alpha' + \alpha\Sigma_{\beta\beta}(I+\alpha'\beta)^h\alpha'.\end{aligned}$$

Then we calculate

$$\begin{aligned}\Sigma_1 &= \lim_{T\to\infty} T^{-1}\sum_{t=1}^{T} E\left(\sum_{i=1}^{t-1}\Delta X_i\right)\Delta X_t' \\ &= \lim_{T\to\infty} T^{-1}\sum_{t=1}^{T}\sum_{i=1}^{t-1}\gamma(t-i) \\ &= \lim_{T\to\infty} T^{-1}\sum_{t=1}^{T}\sum_{i=1}^{t-1}\gamma(i) = \sum_{i=1}^{\infty}\gamma(i).\end{aligned}$$

Thus we only have to sum the autocovariances found above and we find

$$\begin{aligned}\Sigma_1 &= \sum_{h=1}^{\infty}\gamma(h) \\ &= \sum_{h=1}^{\infty}\Omega\beta(I+\alpha'\beta)^{h-1}\alpha' + \alpha\Sigma_{\beta\beta}(I+\alpha'\beta)^h\alpha' \\ &= -\Omega\beta(\alpha'\beta)^{-1}\alpha' - \alpha\Sigma_{\beta\beta}(I+\alpha'\beta)(\alpha'\beta)^{-1}\alpha'.\end{aligned}$$

Finally we consider

$$\begin{aligned}\Sigma &= \lim_{T\to\infty} T^{-1}E\left(\sum_{i=1}^{T}\Delta X_i\right)\left(\sum_{i=1}^{T}\Delta X_i\right)' \\ &= \lim_{T\to\infty} T^{-1}\sum_{i,j=1}^{T}\gamma(j-i) \\ &= \lim_{T\to\infty} T^{-1}\left(T\gamma(0) + \sum_{h=1}^{T}(T-h)\gamma(h) + \sum_{h=1}^{T}(T-h)\gamma(h)'\right) \\ &= \gamma(0) + \sum_{h=1}^{\infty}\gamma(h) + \sum_{h=1}^{\infty}\gamma(h)' \\ &= \Sigma_{00} + \Sigma_1 + \Sigma_1',\end{aligned}$$

which deals with question 5.

In order to solve question 4 we calculate Σ from this formula, and find, from the above,

$$\begin{aligned}
&\alpha\Sigma_{\beta\beta}\alpha' + \Omega - \Omega\beta(\alpha'\beta)^{-1}\alpha' - \alpha\Sigma_{\beta\beta}(I + \alpha'\beta)(\alpha'\beta)^{-1}\alpha' \\
&-\alpha(\beta'\alpha)^{-1}\beta'\Omega - \alpha(\beta'\alpha)^{-1}(I + \beta'\alpha)\Sigma_{\beta\beta}\alpha' \\
&= \Omega - \Omega\beta(\alpha'\beta)^{-1}\alpha' - \alpha(\beta'\alpha)^{-1}\beta'\Omega \\
&-\alpha(\Sigma_{\beta\beta} + \Sigma_{\beta\beta}(\alpha'\beta)^{-1} + (\beta'\alpha)^{-1}\Sigma_{\beta\beta})\alpha' \\
&= \Omega - \Omega\beta(\alpha'\beta)^{-1}\alpha' - \alpha(\beta'\alpha)^{-1}\beta'\Omega + \alpha(\beta'\alpha)^{-1}\beta'\Omega\beta(\alpha'\beta)^{-1}\alpha' \\
&= (I - \alpha(\beta'\alpha)^{-1}\beta')\Omega(I - \beta(\alpha'\beta)^{-1}\alpha') \\
&= \beta_\perp(\alpha'_\perp\beta_\perp)^{-1}\alpha'_\perp\Omega\alpha_\perp(\beta'_\perp\alpha_\perp)^{-1}\beta'_\perp = C\Omega C'.
\end{aligned}$$

Finally simply note that the hint is an easy consequence of the first relation proved in 4, equation (3), since

$$\Sigma_{\beta\beta} = \beta'\Omega\beta + (I + \beta'\alpha)\Sigma_{\beta\beta}(I + \alpha'\beta)$$

implies that

$$0 = \beta'\Omega\beta + \beta'\alpha\Sigma_{\beta\beta}\alpha'\beta + \beta'\alpha\Sigma_{\beta\beta} + \Sigma_{\beta\beta}\alpha'\beta,$$

from which the hint follows by dividing by $\beta'\alpha$ and $\alpha'\beta$.

Another way of finding the matrix Σ is to notice that from Granger's representation theorem we find that

$$X_t - X_0 = C\sum_{i=1}^{t}\varepsilon_i + Y_t - Y_0.$$

Hence

$$\begin{aligned}
&T^{-1}E\left(\sum_{i=1}^{T}\Delta X_i\right)\left(\sum_{i=1}^{T}\Delta X_i\right)' \\
&= T^{-1}E(X_T - X_0)(X_T - X_0)' \\
&= T^{-1}E\left(C\sum_{i=1}^{T}\varepsilon_i + Y_T - Y_0\right)\left(C\sum_{i=1}^{T}\varepsilon_i + Y_T - Y_0\right)' \\
&= C\Omega C' + R_T,
\end{aligned}$$

where the remainder term

$$\begin{aligned}
R_T = T^{-1}E&\left(C\sum_{i=1}^{T}\varepsilon_i\,(Y_T - Y_0)'\right) \\
&+T^{-1}E\,(Y_T - Y_0)\,(Y_T - Y_0)' + T^{-1}E\left((Y_T - Y_0)\sum_{i=1}^{T}\varepsilon'_i C'\right)
\end{aligned}$$

tends to zero as $T \to \infty$. The matrix Σ is the long-run variance for the process X_t and determines the asymptotic behaviour of the process completely.

4.13

Let

$$Y_t = B'X_t + \varepsilon_{1t},$$
$$\Delta^2 X_t = \varepsilon_{2t}.$$

1. Find the characteristic polynomial and its roots. Find Π, Γ, α, β, $\alpha_\perp$, $\beta_\perp$ and check the rank condition for $I(2)$.

2. Find $(\alpha,\ \alpha_1,\ \alpha_2)$ and $(\beta,\ \beta_1,\ \beta_2)$ and the representation of $(Y_t,\ X_t)$ as a function of the initial values and the ε's.

Solution to exercise 4.13

From the model we see directly that the process X_t is $I(2)$, since its second-order differences are $I(0)$. Hence the process Y_t is also $I(2)$ when $B \neq 0$. Moreover it is seen that Y_t and X_t cointegrate, with cointegrating vectors $(I, -B')'$.

1. The characteristic polynomial is

$$A(z) = \begin{pmatrix} I & -B' \\ 0 & 0 \end{pmatrix} + (1-z)^2 \begin{pmatrix} 0 & 0 \\ 0 & I \end{pmatrix} = \begin{pmatrix} I & -B' \\ 0 & (1-z)^2 I \end{pmatrix}$$
$$\dot{A}(z) = -2(1-z) \begin{pmatrix} 0 & 0 \\ 0 & I \end{pmatrix}$$
$$\ddot{A}(z) = 2 \begin{pmatrix} 0 & 0 \\ 0 & I \end{pmatrix},$$

with $|A(z)| = (1-z)^{2p_x}$, where p_x is the dimension of X_t.

We find the matrices

$$\Pi = -A(1) = \begin{pmatrix} -I & B' \\ 0 & 0 \end{pmatrix}$$
$$\Gamma = -\dot{A}(1) + A(1) = \begin{pmatrix} I & -B' \\ 0 & 0 \end{pmatrix}$$
$$\alpha = \begin{pmatrix} -I \\ 0 \end{pmatrix}, \beta = \begin{pmatrix} I \\ -B \end{pmatrix}, \alpha_\perp = \begin{pmatrix} 0 \\ I \end{pmatrix}, \beta_\perp = \begin{pmatrix} B' \\ I \end{pmatrix}.$$

Next we calculate

$$\alpha'_\perp \Gamma \beta_\perp = 0,$$

which shows that

$$\alpha_1 = \beta_1 = 0,$$

and hence

$$\alpha_2 = \alpha_\perp,\ \beta_2 = \beta_\perp.$$

Finally we check the $I(2)$ condition by calculating

$$\alpha_2'\left(\Gamma\bar{\alpha}\bar{\beta}'\Gamma - \frac{1}{2}\ddot{A}(1)\right)\beta_2 = -\frac{1}{2}\alpha_\perp'\ddot{A}(1)\beta_\perp$$
$$= -\alpha_\perp'\begin{pmatrix}0 & 0\\ 0 & I\end{pmatrix}\beta_\perp = -I.$$

This has full rank, so the $I(2)$ condition is satisfied.

2. The parameters (α, α_1, α_2) and (β, β_1, β_2) were found in question 1. We want the representation of the process as a function of the initial values and the ε's.

The second equation gives

$$\Delta X_t = \sum_{i=1}^{t} \varepsilon_{2i} + \Delta X_0,$$

and

$$X_t = \sum_{i=1}^{t}\sum_{j=1}^{i} \varepsilon_{2j} + t\Delta X_0 + X_0.$$

Hence we find

$$Y_t = B'\sum_{i=1}^{t}\sum_{j=1}^{i} \varepsilon_{2j} + t\Delta B'X_0 + B'X_0 + \varepsilon_{1t}.$$

Note that the initial values give rise to a linear trend.

4.14

Consider the four economic variables

$$\begin{aligned} m_t &= \text{ log of nominal money} \\ y_t &= \text{ log of nominal income} \\ p_t &= \text{ log of price index} \\ i_t &= \text{ log of } (1 + r_t), \end{aligned}$$

where r_t is the percentage interest rate. We would like to formulate the hypothesis that money m_t, income y_t and prices p_t are $I(2)$, while real money $m_t - p_t$, real income $y_t - p_t$ and the interest rate are $I(1)$, and that inflation minus the interest rate $\Delta p_t - i_t$ and real money measured with respect to real income $(m_t - p_t) - (y_t - p_t) = m_t - y_t$ are stationary. The order of integration of the variables and relations is as displayed below.

	Variables	Differences	Cointegrating relations
$I(2)$	$m_t,\ y_t,\ p_t$		
$I(1)$	i_t	$\Delta m_t,\ \Delta y_t,\ \Delta p_t$	$m_t - p_t,\ y_t - p_t$
$I(0)$		Δi_t	$\Delta p_t - i_t,\ m_t - y_t.$

Define the vector of variables $X_t = (m_t, y_t, p_t, i_t)$, and assume that X_t is a vector autoregressive process of order 2.

1. Give the number of unit roots of the characteristic polynomial under the hypothesis. Give also the values of $r = \text{rank}(\Pi)$ and $s = \text{rank}(\alpha'_\perp \Gamma \beta_\perp)$.

The VAR(2) model can be rewritten as

$$\Delta^2 X_t = \Pi X_{t-1} - \Gamma \Delta X_{t-1} + \varepsilon_t,$$

which is convenient when X_t is $I(2)$. The parameters Π and Γ will then be in accordance with their definitions; see SJ, p. 45.

We consider the model with the simplified structure

$$\begin{aligned}
\Delta^2 m_t &= -\frac{1}{2}(m_{t-1} - y_{t-1}) - \frac{1}{2}(\Delta m_{t-1} - \Delta p_{t-1}) + \varepsilon_{1t} \\
\Delta^2 y_t &= \frac{1}{2}(m_{t-1} - y_{t-1}) - \frac{1}{2}(\Delta y_{t-1} - \Delta p_{t-1}) + \varepsilon_{2t} \\
\Delta^2 p_t &= a(m_{t-1} - y_{t-1}) + \frac{1}{2}(i_{t-1} - \Delta p_{t-1}) + \frac{1}{2}(\Delta m_{t-1} - \Delta p_{t-1}) + \varepsilon_{3t} \\
\Delta^2 i_t &= -b(m_{t-1} - y_{t-1}) - \frac{1}{2}(i_{t-1} - \Delta p_{t-1}) \\
&\quad -c\Delta i_{t-1} + \frac{1}{2}(\Delta y_{t-1} - \Delta p_{t-1}) + \varepsilon_{4t}
\end{aligned}$$

where a, b and c are constants to be specified below. That is,

$$\Pi = \begin{pmatrix} -\frac{1}{2} & \frac{1}{2} & 0 & 0 \\ \frac{1}{2} & -\frac{1}{2} & 0 & 0 \\ a & -a & 0 & \frac{1}{2} \\ -b & b & 0 & -\frac{1}{2} \end{pmatrix} \text{ and } \Gamma = \begin{pmatrix} \frac{1}{2} & 0 & -\frac{1}{2} & 0 \\ 0 & \frac{1}{2} & -\frac{1}{2} & 0 \\ -\frac{1}{2} & 0 & 1 & 0 \\ 0 & -\frac{1}{2} & 0 & c \end{pmatrix}.$$

2. Calculate β, β_1, β_2 and $\bar{\alpha}'\Gamma\bar{\beta}_2\beta'_2$ and check if the cointegrating relations are in accordance with the hypothesis, when

a) $a = b = 0$, and $c = \frac{1}{2}$, such that

$$\Pi = \begin{pmatrix} -\frac{1}{2} & \frac{1}{2} & 0 & 0 \\ \frac{1}{2} & -\frac{1}{2} & 0 & 0 \\ 0 & 0 & 0 & \frac{1}{2} \\ 0 & 0 & 0 & -\frac{1}{2} \end{pmatrix} \text{ and } \Gamma = \begin{pmatrix} \frac{1}{2} & 0 & -\frac{1}{2} & 0 \\ 0 & \frac{1}{2} & -\frac{1}{2} & 0 \\ -\frac{1}{2} & 0 & 1 & 0 \\ 0 & -\frac{1}{2} & 0 & \frac{1}{2} \end{pmatrix};$$

b) $a = b = 1$ and $c = \frac{1}{2}$, such that

$$\Pi = \begin{pmatrix} -\frac{1}{2} & \frac{1}{2} & 0 & 0 \\ \frac{1}{2} & -\frac{1}{2} & 0 & 0 \\ 1 & -1 & 0 & \frac{1}{2} \\ -1 & 1 & 0 & -\frac{1}{2} \end{pmatrix} \text{ and } \Gamma = \begin{pmatrix} \frac{1}{2} & 0 & -\frac{1}{2} & 0 \\ 0 & \frac{1}{2} & -\frac{1}{2} & 0 \\ -\frac{1}{2} & 0 & 1 & 0 \\ 0 & -\frac{1}{2} & 0 & \frac{1}{2} \end{pmatrix};$$

c) $a = b = 0$ and $c = 0$, such that

$$\Pi = \begin{pmatrix} -\frac{1}{2} & \frac{1}{2} & 0 & 0 \\ \frac{1}{2} & -\frac{1}{2} & 0 & 0 \\ 0 & 0 & 0 & \frac{1}{2} \\ 0 & 0 & 0 & -\frac{1}{2} \end{pmatrix} \text{ and } \Gamma = \begin{pmatrix} \frac{1}{2} & 0 & -\frac{1}{2} & 0 \\ 0 & \frac{1}{2} & -\frac{1}{2} & 0 \\ -\frac{1}{2} & 0 & 1 & 0 \\ 0 & -\frac{1}{2} & 0 & 0 \end{pmatrix}.$$

Solution to 4.14

1. Expressed in a notation like that in Theorem 4.6, the hypothesis is that

$$\begin{pmatrix} 1 & -1 & 0 & 0 \\ 0 & 0 & 0 & 1 \end{pmatrix} X_t - \begin{pmatrix} 0 & 0 & 0 & 0 \\ 0 & 0 & 1 & 0 \end{pmatrix} \Delta X_t$$

and

$$\beta_1' \Delta X_t = (1, 1, -2, 0)\, \Delta X_t$$

can be made $I(0)$. Hence $r = 2$ and $s = 1$. So the characteristic polynomial has $s + 2(p - r - s) = 3$ unit roots.

More heuristically, the number of unit roots can be determined as follows. Since m_t, y_t and p_t are $I(2)$ and there are exactly two linear independent relations ($m_t - p_t$ and $y_t - p_t$) among these three variables that cointegrate, we can conclude that there is only one $I(2)$ trend, hence $p - r - s = 1$. The matrix β contains those cointegrating relations (from order 2 to order 1 or 0) that cointegrate with linear combinations of differences (the part of ΔX_t that is $I(1)$). The variable i_t cointegrates with Δp_t and $m_t - y_t$ cointegrates to stationarity. Thus β contains two linear independent relations so that $r = 2$. Since $p = 4$ we have $s = 1$ and hence $2 + 1 = 3$ unit roots.

2. a) The parameters are found to be

$$\beta = \begin{pmatrix} 1 & 0 \\ -1 & 0 \\ 0 & 0 \\ 0 & 1 \end{pmatrix}, \ \beta_1 = \begin{pmatrix} \frac{1}{2} \\ \frac{1}{2} \\ -1 \\ 0 \end{pmatrix}, \ \beta_2 = \begin{pmatrix} 1 \\ 1 \\ 1 \\ 0 \end{pmatrix}, \ \bar{\alpha}' \Gamma \bar{\beta}_2 \beta_2' = \begin{pmatrix} 0 & \frac{1}{3} \\ 0 & \frac{1}{3} \\ 0 & \frac{1}{3} \\ 0 & 0 \end{pmatrix}'.$$

Thus stationarity of

$$\beta' X_{t-1} + \bar{\alpha}'\Gamma\bar{\beta}_2\beta_2'\Delta X_t = \begin{pmatrix} m_t - y_t \\ i_t - \frac{1}{3}(\Delta m_t + \Delta y_t + \Delta p_t) \end{pmatrix}$$

is consistent with the hypotheses, since the stationarity of

$$\beta_1'\Delta X_t = \frac{1}{2}(\Delta m_t + \Delta y_t) - \Delta p_t$$

implies that also $i_t - \Delta p_t$ is stationary.

b) The parameters are now

$$\beta = \begin{pmatrix} 1 & 0 \\ -1 & 0 \\ 0 & 0 \\ 0 & 1 \end{pmatrix}, \beta_1 = \begin{pmatrix} 0 \\ 0 \\ 1 \\ 0 \end{pmatrix}, \beta_2 = \begin{pmatrix} 1 \\ 1 \\ 0 \\ 0 \end{pmatrix}, \bar{\alpha}'\Gamma\bar{\beta}_2\beta_2' = \begin{pmatrix} 0 & 0 \\ 0 & 0 \\ 0 & 0 \\ 0 & 0 \end{pmatrix}',$$

implying that

$$\beta' X_t = \begin{pmatrix} m_t - y_t \\ i_t \end{pmatrix}$$

$$\beta_1'\Delta X_t = \Delta p_t$$

are stationary, which is not in accordance with the hypotheses.

c) The four parameters are here the same as in a), and hence still in accordance with the hypothesis. Hence Δi_t has a stationary representation even though $\Gamma_{i4} = 0$, $i = 1, \ldots, 4$. If we expressed the system with first order differences rather than second order differences, Δi_{t-1} would only appear in the equation for Δi_t

$$\Delta i_t = \Delta i_{t-1} - \frac{1}{2}(i_{t-1} - \Delta p_{t-1}) + \frac{1}{2}(\Delta y_{t-1} - \Delta p_{t-1}) + \varepsilon_{4t},$$

and even though its coefficient is one, Δi_t is not behaving like a random walk. This emphasizes the importance of considering the full system of equations when properties of variables are investigated.

5

The $I(1)$ Models and Their Interpretation

One of the main points of SJ is to emphasize that the important aspect of model building is the formulation and analysis of the model, which include the formulation of economically relevant hypotheses as restrictions on the parameters in the model. This chapter discusses the interpretation of the error correction models, how they are nested, what type of questions we can ask about the coefficients, and what these questions mean. If $H(r)$ is the error correction model with cointegrating rank $\leq r$ we have the relations

$$H(0) \subset \cdots \subset H(r) \subset \cdots \subset H(p).$$

Linear hypotheses on β are formulated as

$$\beta = H\varphi,$$

for some φ, where H is a known matrix, or equivalently as restrictions on the parameters

$$R'\beta = 0,$$

where $R = H_{\perp}$, that is, R is orthogonal to H. The identification problem is formulated for the cointegrating relations in section 5.3, and linear hypotheses on α are formulated in section 5.4.

An important sequence of models defined by restrictions on the constant term is given in section 5.7. If $\mu_t = \Phi D_t$ denotes the deterministic term in the equation, we define a sequence of models by various restrictions

$$\begin{aligned} H(r) &: \mu_t = \mu_0 + \mu_1 t, \\ H^*(r) &: \mu_t = \mu_0 + \alpha\rho_1 t, \\ H_1(r) &: \mu_t = \mu_0, \\ H_1^*(r) &: \mu_t = \alpha\rho_0, \\ H_2(r) &: \mu_t = 0. \end{aligned}$$

The exercises illustrate the concepts and give various examples of models and questions that can be formulated in the autoregressive framework.

5.1

A statistical model for a p-dimensional autoregressive process with an intercept can be formulated as the solution of the equation

$$\Delta(X_t - m) = \alpha\beta'(X_{t-1} - m) + \varepsilon_t,$$

where α and β are $p \times r$ and m is $p \times 1$.

1. Show that this model is a submodel of

$$\Delta X_t = \alpha\beta' X_{t-1} + \mu + \varepsilon_t,$$

where α, β are $p \times r$ and μ is $p \times 1$, with the constraint $\alpha'_\perp \mu = 0$, and find μ as a function of m.

2. Show that m is not identified unless α and β are of rank p.

Solution to exercise 5.1

1. The model can be written

$$X_t = m + Y_t,$$

where

$$\Delta Y_t = \alpha\beta' Y_{t-1} + \varepsilon_t.$$

Thus the deterministic and stochastic components are modelled separately. In order to relate the model to the usual formulation we write the equations as

$$\Delta X_t = \alpha\beta' X_{t-1} - \alpha\beta' m + \varepsilon_t \tag{1}$$

So the model is a submodel of the model with an unrestricted constant

$$\Delta X_t = \alpha\beta' X_{t-1} + \mu + \varepsilon_t.$$

The restriction on μ is $\alpha'_\perp \mu = 0$.

2. Even though the formulation $X_t = m + Y_t$ is convenient as a model formulation, it has the consequence of introducing an unidentified parameter. In order to show that m is not identified we have to find two different values of m, say m' and m'', which give rise to the same probability measure and are therefore observationally equivalent. It is clear that if we take

$$m'' = m' + \beta_\perp b$$

for some vector b, then $\beta' m'' = \beta' m'$, and since only $\beta' m$ appears in equation (1), which defines the process X_t, the parameters m'' and m' are observationally equivalent, which means that m is not identified.

5.2

A model for a p-dimensional autoregressive process with an intercept and trend can be formulated as the solution of the equation

$$\Delta(X_t - m_0 - m_1 t) = \alpha\beta'(X_{t-1} - m_0 - m_1(t-1)) + \varepsilon_t,$$

where α and β are $p \times r$ and m_0 and m_1 are $p \times 1$.

1. Show that this model is a submodel of

$$\Delta X_t = \alpha\beta' X_{t-1} + \mu_0 + \mu_1 t + \varepsilon_t,$$

where α and β are $p \times r$ and μ_0 and μ_1 are $p \times 1$ with the constraint $\alpha_\perp'\mu_1 = 0$, and express μ_0 and μ_1 as functions of m_0 and m_1.

2. Show that m_0 is not identified unless α and β are of rank p.

Solution to exercise 5.2

1. The model can be expressed as

$$X_t = m_0 + m_1 t + Y_t,$$

where

$$\Delta Y_t = \alpha\beta' Y_{t-1} + \varepsilon_t.$$

In order to write it in the usual way we eliminate Y_t, and find

$$\Delta X_t = \alpha\beta' X_{t-1} + (\alpha\beta'(m_1 - m_0) + m_1) - \alpha\beta' m_1 t + \varepsilon_t,$$

which is a submodel of the model with the unrestricted parameters

$$\Delta X_t = \alpha\beta' X_{t-1} + \mu_0 + \mu_1 t + \varepsilon_t,$$

where

$$\mu_0 = \alpha\beta'(m_1 - m_0) + m_1, \quad \mu_1 = -\alpha\beta' m_1.$$

From the relation $\mu_1 = -\alpha\beta' m_1$ we get the restriction $\alpha_\perp'\mu_1 = 0$.

2. The parameters m_0 and m_1 are identified if they are uniquely given as functions of the identified parameters μ_0 and μ_1. From the identities

$$\bar{\alpha}_\perp'\mu_0 = \bar{\alpha}_\perp' m_1$$

and

$$\begin{aligned}\bar{\alpha}'\mu_1 &= -\beta' m_1 \\ &= -\beta'(\alpha\bar{\alpha}' m_1 + \alpha_\perp\bar{\alpha}_\perp' m_1) \\ &= -\beta'\alpha\bar{\alpha}' m_1 - \beta'\alpha_\perp\bar{\alpha}_\perp'\mu_0,\end{aligned}$$

we find

$$\bar{\alpha}' m_1 = -(\beta'\alpha)^{-1} (\bar{\alpha}'\mu_1 + \beta'\alpha_\perp \bar{\alpha}'_\perp \mu_0),$$

such that

$$\begin{aligned} m_1 &= \alpha\bar{\alpha}' m_1 + \alpha_\perp \bar{\alpha}'_\perp m_1 \\ &= -\alpha(\beta'\alpha)^{-1} (\bar{\alpha}'\mu_1 + \beta'\alpha_\perp \bar{\alpha}'_\perp \mu_0) + \bar{\alpha}'_\perp \mu_0, \end{aligned}$$

and hence m_1 is identified. As in the previous exercise it is seen that if we take

$$m_0'' = m_0' + \beta_\perp b,$$

for some value of b, then these two values of m_0 give rise to the same equations and hence they are observationally equivalent. Thus, m_0 is not identified. However, the parameter function $\beta' m_0$ can be estimated.

5.3

Consider the four variables m_t, y_t, i_{1t}, and i_{2t}, that is, money, income and two interests rates. We think of the money relation

$$m_t = y_t + c\,(i_{1t} - i_{2t}) + \mu_1$$

and the interest relation

$$i_{1t} = i_{2t} + \mu_2$$

as describing stable economic relations.

This hypothesis is formulated in a vector autoregressive model as the statement that the vectors

$$\begin{aligned} \beta_1 &= (1, -1, -c, c)', \\ \beta_2 &= (0, 0, 1, -1)', \end{aligned}$$

are cointegrating vectors.

Let us assume that the cointegrating rank is $r = 2$, and that, in order to check the restrictions implicit in the above relations, we first formulate the hypothesis

$$\begin{aligned} \beta_1 &= (a_1, a_2, a_3, a_4)', \\ \beta_2 &= (0, 0, a_5, a_6)'. \end{aligned}$$

1. Formulate this hypothesis in the form

$$\beta = (H_1\varphi_1, H_2\varphi_2),$$

and check whether this hypothesis is a restriction on the cointegrating space. Are the equations identified?

2. Consider the same questions for

$$\beta_1 = (a_1, -a_1, a_3, a_4)',$$
$$\beta_2 = (0, 0, a_5, a_6)'.$$

3. Consider the same questions for

$$\beta_1 = (a_1, -a_1, a_3, -a_3)',$$
$$\beta_2 = (0, 0, a_5, a_6)'.$$

4. Consider the same questions for

$$\beta_1 = (a_1, -a_1, a_3, -a_3)',$$
$$\beta_2 = (0, 0, a_5, -a_5)'.$$

Solution to exercise 5.3

For every hypothesis we give the H matrices as well as their orthogonal complements (the R matrices) which we need to check identification of the equations. One should note that the matrices are not uniquely given, since one can use any other matrix which spans the same subspace.

1. The hypothesis $\beta_1 = (a_1, a_2, a_3, a_4)'$ and $\beta_2 = (0, 0, a_5, a_6)'$ can be formulated as

$$H_1 = I, H_2 = \begin{pmatrix} 0 & 0 \\ 0 & 0 \\ 1 & 0 \\ 0 & 1 \end{pmatrix}, R_1 = 0, R_2 = \begin{pmatrix} 1 & 0 \\ 0 & 1 \\ 0 & 0 \\ 0 & 0 \end{pmatrix}.$$

The first equation is not identified since $\text{rank}(R_1' H_2) = 0 < 1$, while the second is identified since $\text{rank}(R_2' H_1) = 2 \geq 1$. The reason why the first is not identified is that one can add some of β_2 to β_1, and then have a different β which spans the same subspace and fulfils the restrictions on β. Note that the hypothesis can be tested even though the equations are not identified – but only estimates of identified equations can be interpreted.

2. The hypothesis $\beta_1 = (a_1, -a_1, a_3, a_4)'$ and $\beta_2 = (0, 0, a_5, a_6)'$ can be formulated in terms of the matrices

$$H_1 = \begin{pmatrix} 1 & 0 & 0 \\ -1 & 0 & 0 \\ 0 & 1 & 0 \\ 0 & 0 & 1 \end{pmatrix}, H_2 = \begin{pmatrix} 0 & 0 \\ 0 & 0 \\ 1 & 0 \\ 0 & 1 \end{pmatrix}, R_2 = \begin{pmatrix} 1 \\ 1 \\ 0 \\ 0 \end{pmatrix}, R_2 = \begin{pmatrix} 1 & 0 \\ 0 & 1 \\ 0 & 0 \\ 0 & 0 \end{pmatrix}.$$

The first equation is not identified, while the second is.

3. The hypothesis $\beta_1 = (a_1, -a_1, a_3, -a_3)'$ and $\beta_2 = (0, 0, a_5, a_6)'$ can be formulated in terms of the matrices

$$H_1 = \begin{pmatrix} 1 & 0 \\ -1 & 0 \\ 0 & 1 \\ 0 & -1 \end{pmatrix}, H_2 = \begin{pmatrix} 0 & 0 \\ 0 & 0 \\ 1 & 0 \\ 0 & 1 \end{pmatrix}, R_2 = \begin{pmatrix} 1 & 0 \\ 1 & 0 \\ 0 & 1 \\ 0 & 1 \end{pmatrix}, R_2 = \begin{pmatrix} 1 & 0 \\ 0 & 1 \\ 0 & 0 \\ 0 & 0 \end{pmatrix}.$$

Both equations are identified.

4. The hypothesis $\beta_1 = (a_1, -a_1, a_3, -a_3)'$ and $\beta_2 = (0, 0, a_5, -a_5)'$ can be formulated in terms of the matrices

$$H_1 = \begin{pmatrix} 1 & 0 \\ -1 & 0 \\ 0 & 1 \\ 0 & -1 \end{pmatrix}, H_2 = \begin{pmatrix} 0 \\ 0 \\ 1 \\ -1 \end{pmatrix}, R_2 = \begin{pmatrix} 1 & 0 \\ 1 & 0 \\ 0 & 1 \\ 0 & 1 \end{pmatrix}, R_2 = \begin{pmatrix} 1 & 0 & 0 \\ 0 & 1 & 0 \\ 0 & 0 & 1 \\ 0 & 0 & 1 \end{pmatrix}.$$

The first equation is not identified, while the second is.

It is worth noticing that hypotheses 2, 3 and 4 could be formulated in the form

$$\beta = H\varphi,$$

since only the subspace $\text{sp}(\beta)$ is identified (when α is unrestricted). Hypothesis 2 could be formulated as

$$\beta = \begin{pmatrix} 1 & 0 & 0 \\ -1 & 0 & 0 \\ 0 & 1 & 0 \\ 0 & 0 & 1 \end{pmatrix} \varphi_{3\times 2},$$

since for two such vectors, one can always find a linear combination with zeroes at the first two positions.

The restrictions on β under hypothesis 3 are identical to the restrictions on β under hypothesis 2, since one can always (assuming $a_5 \neq -a_6$) achieve $a_3 + a_4 = 0$ for a suitable linear combination.

The restrictions on β under hypothesis 4 can be formulated as

$$\beta = \begin{pmatrix} 1 & 0 \\ -1 & 0 \\ 0 & 1 \\ 0 & -1 \end{pmatrix} \varphi_{2\times 2}.$$

The advantage of this formulation is that estimates of the parameters can be found explicitly, and no iterative algorithm has to be applied. See SJ, pp. 110–111.

5.4

Consider the model

$$\Delta X_t = \alpha\beta' X_{t-1} + \Gamma_1 \Delta X_{t-1} + \varepsilon_t,$$

and assume that all parameters vary freely except for $\alpha = A\psi$. Show that $A'_\perp X_t$ is weakly exogenous for (ψ, β).

The combinations $\alpha'_\perp \sum_{i=1}^t \varepsilon_i$ are the common trends. The hypothesis that the shocks from a given equation, a price equation say, cumulate to a common trend can be formulated as $\alpha_\perp = (a_0, \varphi)$, for a suitable unit vector a_0. Show that in this case $a'_0 X_t$ is weakly exogenous for (ψ, β); see SJ, Chapter 8.

Solution to exercise 5.4

Assume, without loss of generality, that A has full rank, say s, such that $A_\perp$ is defined, and define the two variables

$$Y_t = A'X_t,$$
$$Z_t = A'_\perp X_t.$$

We have to show that Z_t is weakly exogenous for (ψ, β). Hence we have to show that we can split the likelihood function into the product of a partial likelihood and a marginal likelihood

$$\begin{aligned} L_{full}(\theta) &= L_{part}(\theta_c) L_{marg}(\theta_m) \\ &= \prod_{t=1}^T g_t(Y_t | X_1, \ldots, X_{t-1}, Z_t, \theta_c) \prod_{t=1}^T h_t(Z_t | X_1, \ldots, X_{t-1}, \theta_m), \end{aligned}$$

where the parameters (θ_m, θ_c) vary in a product space $\Theta_m \times \Theta_c$, and $(\psi, \beta) = f(\theta_c)$.

Hence we split the joint model

$$\Delta X_t = A\psi\beta' X_{t-1} + \Gamma_1 \Delta X_{t-1} + \varepsilon_t,$$

into a marginal model

$$\Delta Z_t = A'_\perp \Gamma_1 \Delta X_{t-1} + \varepsilon_{a_\perp t}$$

and a partial model

$$\begin{aligned} \Delta Y_t &= A'A\psi\beta' X_{t-1} + A'\Gamma_1 \Delta X_{t-1} + \omega(\Delta Z_t - A'_\perp \Gamma_1 \Delta X_{t-1}) + \varepsilon_{aa.a_\perp t} \\ &= (A'A)\psi\beta' X_{t-1} + (A' - \omega A'_\perp)\Gamma_1 \Delta X_{t-1} + \omega \Delta Z_t + \varepsilon_{aa.a_\perp t} \\ &= (A'A)\theta_{c1}\theta'_{c2} X_{t-1} + \theta_{c3} \Delta X_{t-1} + \theta_{c4} \Delta Z_t + \varepsilon_{aa.a_\perp t}, \end{aligned}$$

where the joint model has parameters $(\psi, \beta, \Gamma_1, \Omega)$ in the parameter space

$\Theta = \mathbf{R}^{s\times r} \times \mathbf{R}^{p\times r} \times \mathbf{R}^{p\times p} \times \mathbf{D}(p)$ ($\mathbf{D}(p)$ is the space of symmetric positive definite $p \times p$ matrices), the marginal model has parameters $(\theta_{m1}, \theta_{m2}) = (A_\perp'\Gamma_1, \Omega_{a_\perp a_\perp})$ in $\Theta_m = \mathbf{R}^{(p-s)\times p} \times \mathbf{D}(p-s)$ and the partial model has parameters $(\theta_{c1}, \theta_{c2}, \theta_{c3}, \theta_{c4}, \theta_{c5}) = (\psi, \beta, (A' - \omega A_\perp')\Gamma_1, \omega, \Omega_{aa.a_\perp})$ in the parameter space $\Theta_c = \mathbf{R}^{s\times r} \times \mathbf{R}^{p\times r} \times \mathbf{R}^{s\times p} \times \mathbf{R}^{s\times(p-s)} \times \mathbf{D}(s)$.

The variables $\varepsilon_{a_\perp t}$ and $\varepsilon_{aa.a_\perp t}$ are independent and Gaussian with mean zero and variances given by $\Omega_{a_\perp a_\perp}$ and $\Omega_{aa.a_\perp} = \Omega_{aa} - \Omega_{aa_\perp}\Omega_{a_\perp a_\perp}^{-1}\Omega_{a_\perp a}$. We have used the notation $\Omega_{a_\perp a_\perp} = A_\perp'\Omega A_\perp$ and defined $\omega = \Omega_{aa_\perp}\Omega_{a_\perp a_\perp}^{-1}$.

The parameters ψ and β are easily found from the parameters in the conditional model, up to an normalization. The only thing left to prove is that the parameter space Θ is decomposed into a product space of Θ_m and Θ_c. This is seen by selecting arbitrary values for θ_m and θ_c satisfying the requirement that θ_{m2} and θ_{c5} are positive definite and then construct θ which satisfies the requirement that Ω is positive definite, such that $\theta \in \Theta$.

We construct θ in the following way. The parameters ψ and β are given directly from the partial model. The parameter Γ_1 is given by

$$\begin{aligned}
\Gamma_1 &= AA'\Gamma_1 + A_\perp A_\perp'\Gamma_1 \\
&= A[(A' - \omega A_\perp')\Gamma_1 + \omega A_\perp'\Gamma_1] + A_\perp A_\perp'\Gamma_1 \\
&= A[\theta_{c3} + \theta_{c4}\theta_{m1}] + A_\perp\theta_{m1}
\end{aligned}$$

and Ω is given by

$$\begin{aligned}
\Omega &= (\bar{A}, \bar{A}_\perp)(A, A_\perp)'\Omega(A, A_\perp)(\bar{A}, \bar{A}_\perp)' \\
&= (\bar{A}, \bar{A}_\perp)\begin{pmatrix} \Omega_{aa} & \Omega_{aa_\perp} \\ \Omega_{a_\perp a} & \Omega_{a_\perp a_\perp} \end{pmatrix}(\bar{A}, \bar{A}_\perp)' \\
&= (\bar{A}, \bar{A}_\perp)\begin{pmatrix} \theta_{c5} + \theta_{c4}\theta_{m2}\theta_{c4}' & \theta_{c4}\theta_{m2} \\ \theta_{m2}\theta_{c4}' & \theta_{m2} \end{pmatrix}(\bar{A}, \bar{A}_\perp)'.
\end{aligned}$$

That this value of Ω is positive definite is seen by checking that $x'\Omega x$ is positive for any vector $x \in \mathbf{R}^p$, $x \neq 0$:

$$\begin{aligned}
x'\Omega x &= x'(\bar{A}, \bar{A}_\perp)\begin{pmatrix} \theta_{c5} + \theta_{c4}\theta_{m2}\theta_{c4}' & \theta_{c4}\theta_{m2} \\ \theta_{m2}\theta_{c4}' & \theta_{m2} \end{pmatrix}(\bar{A}, \bar{A}_\perp)'x \\
&= y'\begin{pmatrix} \theta_{c5} + \theta_{c4}\theta_{m2}\theta_{c4}' & \theta_{c4}\theta_{m2} \\ \theta_{m2}\theta_{c4}' & \theta_{m2} \end{pmatrix}y \\
&= \begin{pmatrix} y_1 \\ y_2 \end{pmatrix}'\begin{pmatrix} \theta_{c5} + \theta_{c4}\theta_{m2}\theta_{c4}' & \theta_{c4}\theta_{m2} \\ \theta_{m2}\theta_{c4}' & \theta_{m2} \end{pmatrix}\begin{pmatrix} y_1 \\ y_2 \end{pmatrix} \\
&= y_1'\theta_{c5}y_1 + y_1'\theta_{c4}\theta_{m2}\theta_{c4}'y_1 + y_1'\theta_{c4}\theta_{m2}y_2 + y_2'\theta_{m2}\theta_{c4}'y_1 + y_2'\theta_{m2}y_2 \\
&= y_1'\theta_{c5}y_1 + (\theta_{c4}'y_1 + y_2)\theta_{m2}(\theta_{c4}'y_1 + y_2),
\end{aligned}$$

which is positive since θ_{c5} and θ_{m2} are positive definite.

The result for Ω is a consequence of the classic result of Barndorff-Nielsen (1978) that the parameters $\Omega_{a_\perp a_\perp}$, $\omega = \Omega_{aa_\perp}\Omega_{a_\perp a_\perp}^{-1}$ and $\Omega_{aa.a_\perp}$ are variation-free; see SJ, Theorem 8.1.

The hypothesis that $\alpha_\perp = (a_0, \varphi)$, where φ varies freely, is identical to the restriction that a_0 is orthogonal to α. Hence the hypothesis can be formulated as $\alpha = A\psi$ where $A = a_{0\perp}$ and hence $A_\perp = a_0$.

From the previous question we know that $a_0'X_t$ is weakly exogenous for (ψ, β). If we are interested in a specific equation, say the first, we choose a_0 to be the first unit vector $(1, 0, \ldots, 0)'$, and can thereby formulate the hypothesis that the first variable is weakly exogenous for (ψ, β).

5.5*

In the cointegration model

$$\Delta X_t = \alpha\beta' X_{t-1} + \varepsilon_t,$$

where $\varepsilon_1, \ldots, \varepsilon_T$ are independent Gaussian $N_p(0, \Omega)$, we split X_t into X_{1t} and X_{2t}, of dimensions p_1 and p_2 respectively, corresponding to two subsystems. We want to test if the cointegration in the full system can be expressed by requiring that the subsystems cointegrate. This is called separate cointegration. The precise definition is that there exist matrices β_1 $(p_1 \times r_1)$ and β_2 $(p_2 \times r_2)$ with $r_1 + r_2 = r$, such that the cointegrating relations $\beta' X_t$ are linear combinations of $\beta_1' X_{1t}$ and $\beta_2' X_{2t}$, that is, that there exist matrices A_1 $(r \times r_1)$ and A_2 $(r \times r_2)$, such that $\beta' X_t = A_1\beta_1' X_{1t} + A_2\beta_2' X_{2t}$.

1. Show that this hypothesis can be formulated as one of the hypotheses which is treated in Chapter 5 and discuss an algorithm for calculating the maximum likelihood estimator.

We call a system *strongly separated* if it is separated, if the equations for ΔX_{1t} contain only $\beta_1' X_{1t-1}$ and if the equations for ΔX_{2t} contain only $\beta_2' X_{2t-1}$.

2. Formulate this hypothesis as a hypothesis about α and show that even if the system is strongly separated it is not the case that X_{2t} is weakly exogenous for β_1; see Granger and Konishi (1993).

Solution to exercise 5.5

1. Since the cointegrating relations $\beta' X_t$ are linear combinations of $\beta_1' X_{1t}$ and $\beta_2' X_{2t}$, the parameter β has the structure

$$\beta' = (A_1, A_2)\begin{pmatrix} \beta_1 & 0 \\ 0 & \beta_2 \end{pmatrix}'$$

where the $r \times r$ matrix (A_1, A_2) has full rank r. By defining

$$\tilde{\beta} = \begin{pmatrix} \beta_1 & 0 \\ 0 & \beta_2 \end{pmatrix} \text{ and } \tilde{\alpha} = \alpha(A_1, A_2)$$

we can reparametrize the model by $\tilde{\alpha}$ and $\tilde{\beta}$ since

$$\alpha\beta' = \alpha(A_1, A_2) \begin{pmatrix} \beta_1 & 0 \\ 0 & \beta_2 \end{pmatrix}' = \tilde{\alpha}\tilde{\beta}',$$

which shows that the hypothesis can be formulated as

$$\tilde{\beta} = \left(\begin{pmatrix} I \\ 0 \end{pmatrix} \beta_1, \begin{pmatrix} 0 \\ I \end{pmatrix} \beta_2 \right),$$

since there are no restrictions on $\tilde{\alpha}$. The estimation problem is a multiple reduced rank regression problem which can be estimated as discussed in SJ, Chapter 7, p. 110.

2. If the system is strongly separated the Π matrix has the form

$$\Pi = \begin{pmatrix} \Pi_{11} & 0 \\ 0 & \Pi_{22} \end{pmatrix} = \begin{pmatrix} \alpha_1\beta_1' & 0 \\ 0 & \alpha_2\beta_2' \end{pmatrix} = \begin{pmatrix} \alpha_1 & 0 \\ 0 & \alpha_2 \end{pmatrix} \begin{pmatrix} \beta_1 & 0 \\ 0 & \beta_2 \end{pmatrix}',$$

which can be formulated as the joint hypothesis

$$\alpha = \left(\begin{pmatrix} I \\ 0 \end{pmatrix} \psi_1, \begin{pmatrix} 0 \\ I \end{pmatrix} \psi_2 \right) \text{ and } \beta = \left(\begin{pmatrix} I \\ 0 \end{pmatrix} \varphi_1, \begin{pmatrix} 0 \\ I \end{pmatrix} \varphi_2 \right).$$

The weak exogeneity is checked by splitting the model into a conditional model and a marginal model:

$$\begin{aligned} \Delta X_{1t} &= \Pi_{11} X_{1t} + \Omega_{12}\Omega_{22}^{-1}(\Delta X_{2,t-1} - \Pi_{22} X_{2,t-1}) + \varepsilon_{11.2t}, \\ \Delta X_{2t} &= \Pi_{22} X_{2t-1} + \varepsilon_{2t}. \end{aligned}$$

The parameters in the two models are

$$\begin{aligned} \theta_c &= (\theta_{c1}, \theta_{c2}, \theta_{c3}, \theta_{c4}) = (\Pi_{11}, \Omega_{12}\Omega_{22}^{-1}, \Omega_{12}\Omega_{22}^{-1}\Pi_{22}, \Omega_{11.2}) \\ \theta_m &= (\theta_{m1}, \theta_{m2}) = (\Pi_{22}, \Omega_{22}). \end{aligned}$$

We have the identity $\theta_{c2}\theta_{m1} = \theta_{c3}$, which defines a cross equation restriction on the two sets of parameters, such that we cannot maximize the partial likelihood and the marginal likelihood independently. If, however, $\Omega_{12} = 0$, that is, if ε_1 and ε_2 are independent, X_{2t} will be weakly exogenous for β_1.

It is not in general possible to estimate the cointegrating relations among the X_1 variables efficiently by considering a submodel which only contains the X_1 variables. As long as we have no reason to believe that $\Omega_{12} = 0$, we have to perform the estimation in the full model.

This exercise has an * because it illustrates how an intuitive idea of separate cointegration can be given a precise formulation which leads to the slightly surprising result that seemingly unrelated cointegrated systems should be analysed jointly because the errors can be correlated.

5.6

Consider the cointegration model

$$\Delta X_{1t} = \alpha_1 \beta' X_{t-1} + \varepsilon_{1t},$$
$$\Delta X_{2t} = \alpha_2 \beta' X_{t-1} + \varepsilon_{2t},$$

where $\varepsilon_1, \ldots, \varepsilon_T$ are independent Gaussian $N_p(0, \Omega)$.

1. Show how the hypothesis that X_2 is weakly exogenous for β can be formulated as a hypothesis on α.

We define the stochastic trends

$$\alpha'_\perp \sum_{i=1}^{t} \varepsilon_i.$$

2. Show that the hypothesis that the first component of $\sum_{i=1}^{t} \varepsilon_{1i}$ is a common stochastic trend can be formulated in the form

$$\alpha_\perp = (a_0, \psi)$$

and find a_0.

Assume that $X_t = (p^{au}, p^{us}, \text{exch}, i^{au}, i^{us})_t$, that is, prices and interest rates in Australia and the United States together with the exchange rate. We assume that the cointegrating rank is three, that is, that there are two common trends. We want to investigate if there is a stochastic trend that comes from the price variables (the goods sector) and another from the interest variables and the exchange rate (the financial sector).

3. Formulate this hypothesis as a hypothesis on $\alpha_\perp$.

Solution to exercise 5.6

1. The conditional model for ΔX_{1t} given ΔX_{2t} and X_{t-1} is

$$\Delta X_{1t} = \omega \Delta X_{2t} + (\alpha_1 - \omega \alpha_2)\beta' X_{t-1} + \varepsilon_{1t} - \omega \varepsilon_{2t}.$$

It is seen that β enters the marginal and the conditional model. Hence for X_{2t} to be weakly exogenous for β we must have $\alpha_2 = 0$.

Under this condition it is seen that X_{2t} is in fact weakly exogenous for β.

The restriction $\alpha_2 = 0$ can be formulated as $\alpha = A\psi$, where

$$A = \begin{pmatrix} I \\ 0 \end{pmatrix}.$$

2. The hypothesis that the first component of $\sum_{i=1}^{t} \varepsilon_{1i}$ $(= \sum_{i=1}^{t} \varepsilon_{11i})$ is a common stochastic trend, is equivalent to the first unit vector $e_1 = (1, 0, \ldots, 0)'$ being in the space spanned by $\alpha_\perp$. This can be formulated as

$$\alpha_\perp = (e_1, \psi).$$

Usually one would reformulate this hypothesis as a hypothesis on α, which in this case would be

$$\alpha = A\psi = (e_2, \ldots, e_p)\psi.$$

3. The hypothesis that one stochastic trend comes from the price variables and another from the interest rates and the exchange rate, is simply formulated as

$$\alpha_\perp = \left(\begin{pmatrix} 1\,0 \\ 0\,1 \\ 0\,0 \\ 0\,0 \\ 0\,0 \end{pmatrix} \begin{pmatrix} \psi_1 \\ \psi_2 \end{pmatrix}, \begin{pmatrix} 0\,0\,0 \\ 0\,0\,0 \\ 1\,0\,0 \\ 0\,1\,0 \\ 0\,0\,1 \end{pmatrix} \begin{pmatrix} \psi_3 \\ \psi_4 \\ \psi_5 \end{pmatrix} \right).$$

6

The Statistical Analysis of $I(1)$ Models

It is shown here that the derivation of test statistics and estimators from the Gaussian likelihood function leads to the technique of reduced rank regression and the analysis of eigenvalues and eigenvectors, as developed by Anderson (1951). Theorem 6.1 contains the main results on the calculation of estimators and likelihood ratio tests in terms of the eigenvectors in certain matrices. Briefly the technique is the following. The error correction model is a non-linear regression model and we first eliminate the linearly unrestricted parameters $(\Gamma_1, \ldots, \Gamma_{k-1}, \Phi)$ by regression. The residuals obtained from ΔX_t are R_{0t} and the residuals from X_{t-1} are R_{1t}. We form the product moments

$$S_{ij} = T^{-1} \sum_{t=1}^{T} R_{it} R'_{jt}, \qquad i, j = 0, 1, \tag{6.10}$$

and solve the eigenvalue problem

$$|\lambda S_{11} - S_{10} S_{00}^{-1} S_{01}| = 0,$$

for eigenvalues $1 > \hat{\lambda}_1 > \cdots > \hat{\lambda}_p > 0$, and eigenvectors $\hat{V} = (\hat{v}_1, \ldots, \hat{v}_p)$, normalized such that $\hat{V}' S_{11} \hat{V} = I$. The maximum likelihood estimator is

$$\hat{\beta} = (\hat{v}_1, \ldots, \hat{v}_r),$$
$$\hat{\alpha} = S_{01} \hat{\beta},$$
$$\hat{\Omega} = S_{00} - \hat{\alpha}\hat{\alpha}'.$$

The maximized likelihood function is found from

$$L_{\max}^{-\frac{2}{T}} = |S_{00}| \prod_{i=1}^{r} (1 - \hat{\lambda}_i).$$

The so-called trace test for the hypothesis $H(r)$ in $H(p)$ is given by

$$-2 \log Q(H(r)|H(p)) = -T \sum_{i=r+1}^{p} \log(1 - \hat{\lambda}_i). \tag{6.18}$$

We have also listed the asymptotic properties, which will be treated in more detail in the later chapters.

Theorem 6.2 contains the corresponding results for models defined by restricted deterministic terms. Note in particular the way the models with restricted constant term are estimated by extending X_{t-1} by 1; see (6.29). Exercise 6.2 discusses an identification, which is statistically interesting but not so useful for interpretation, and exercise 6.3 gives a possible formulation of a model with rational expectations in the vector autoregressive framework. Finally exercise 6.5 gives conditions on the parameters and develops tests in the case where a linear transformation of an autoregressive model is again autoregressive with the same lag length.

6.1

Consider the model

$$\Delta X_t = \alpha\beta' X_{t-1} + \mu_0 + \mu_1 t + \varepsilon_t.$$

We define the parameters

$$\mu_0 = \alpha\rho_0 + \alpha_\perp\gamma_0,$$

$$\mu_1 = \alpha\rho_1 + \alpha_\perp\gamma_1.$$

1. Show by Granger's representation theorem that X_t in general has a quadratic trend and show how this model can be estimated by reduced rank regression.

2. Show that if $\alpha'_\perp\mu_1 = 0$ then the quadratic trend disappears, but the process still has a linear trend given by

$$\tau_1 = \beta_\perp(\alpha'_\perp\beta_\perp)^{-1}\alpha'_\perp\alpha_\perp(\gamma_0 + (\alpha'_\perp\alpha_\perp)^{-1}\alpha'_\perp\beta(\beta'\beta)^{-1}\rho_1) - \beta(\beta'\beta)^{-1}\rho_1;$$

see SJ, formula (5.20).

3. Show how one can estimate the parameters of the model by reduced rank regression under the constraint $\alpha'_\perp\mu_1 = 0$.

4. What happens under the constraint $\alpha'_\perp\mu_0 = 0$ and μ_1 unrestricted?

5. Under the restriction $\alpha'_\perp\mu_1 = 0$, the hypothesis of trend stationarity of X_{1t}, say, can be formulated as the hypothesis that the unit vector $(1, 0, \ldots, 0)$ is one of the cointegrating vectors. Discuss how the parameters can be estimated by reduced rank regression in this case.

Solution to exercise 6.1

When one wants to investigate the properties of an $I(1)$ process with respect to deterministic trends, it is useful to consider the Granger representation.

1. In the case where X_t is $I(1)$ the representation is

$$X_t = C\sum_{i=1}^{t}(\varepsilon_i + \mu_0 + \mu_1 i) + C(L)(\varepsilon_t + \mu_0 + \mu_1 t) + A$$
$$= C\sum_{i=1}^{t}\varepsilon_i + \frac{1}{2}C\mu_1 t^2 + C\left(\mu_0 + \frac{1}{2}\mu_1\right)t + C(L)(\varepsilon_t + \mu_0 + \mu_1 t) + A.$$

So unless $C\mu_1 = 0$ or $\alpha'_\perp \mu_1 = 0$ we will have a quadratic trend with coefficient $\frac{1}{2}C\mu_1$. The parameters can be estimated by applying a reduced rank regression of R_{0t} on R_{1t}, where we define R_{0t} and R_{1t} as ΔX_t and X_{t-1} corrected for $Z_{2t} = (1, t)'$.

2. The assumption $\alpha'_\perp \mu_1 = 0$ implies that $C\mu_1 = 0$. Hence the process has only a linear trend $\tau_0 + \tau_1 t$. In order to see that the expression for τ_1 is as given we note that it is equivalent to the two statements

$$\alpha'_\perp \tau_1 = \alpha'_\perp \alpha_\perp \gamma_0,$$
$$\beta' \tau_1 = -\rho_1,$$

which we shall now show.

From the model equation we find

$$\alpha'_\perp \Delta X_t = \alpha'_\perp \mu_0 + \alpha'_\perp \varepsilon_t$$

such that

$$\alpha'_\perp \tau_1 = E(\alpha'_\perp \Delta X_t) = \alpha'_\perp \mu_0 = \alpha'_\perp \alpha_\perp \gamma_0.$$

We also find

$$\beta' \Delta X_t = \beta' \alpha \beta' X_{t-1} + \beta' \mu_0 + \beta' \alpha \rho_1 t + \beta' \varepsilon_t,$$

which for $E(\beta' X_t) = \beta' \tau_0 + \beta' \tau_1 t$ gives

$$\beta' \tau_1 = \beta' \alpha(\beta' \tau_0 + \beta' \tau_1 (t-1)) + \beta' \mu_0 + \beta' \alpha \rho_1 t.$$

The coefficients of t are the same and hence

$$\beta' \tau_1 = -\rho_1.$$

3. In case $\alpha'_\perp \mu_1 = 0$, we can reformulate the model as

$$\Delta X_t = \alpha(\beta', \rho_1)\begin{pmatrix} X_{t-1} \\ t \end{pmatrix} + \mu_0 + \varepsilon_t.$$

Expressed in the notation of SJ, Chapter 6, we get

$$Z_{0t} = \alpha\beta^{*\prime} Z_{1t} + \mu_0 Z_{2t} + \varepsilon_t,$$

where we define $Z_{0t} = \Delta X_t$, $Z_{1t} = (X_{t-1}', t)'$, $Z_{2t} = 1$ and $\beta^* = (\beta', \rho_1)'$. Hence the parameters can be estimated by a reduced rank regression of ΔX_t on (X_{t-1}', t) corrected for 1.

4. If $\alpha_\perp' \mu_0 = 0$ and μ_1 is unrestricted, we can write the process as

$$\Delta X_t = \alpha(\beta', \rho_0) \begin{pmatrix} X_{t-1} \\ 1 \end{pmatrix} + \mu_1 t + \varepsilon_t,$$

which can be estimated by a reduced rank regression of ΔX_t on $(X_{t-1}', 1)$ corrected for t.

Note that this model is characterized by a special relation between the deterministic quadratic trend and the deterministic linear trend $\tau_1 = \tau_2 + C(1)\mu_1$, which is hard to interpret.

5. The model is estimated as described in question 3 and the hypothesis is that the vector $(1, 0, \ldots, 0, a)$ is in the space $\text{sp}(\beta^*)$. In terms of H matrices the formulation is

$$\beta^* = \left(\begin{pmatrix} 1 & 0 \\ 0 & 0 \\ \vdots & \vdots \\ 0 & 0 \\ 0 & 1 \end{pmatrix} \varphi_1, \varphi_2 \right)$$

where φ_1 is a 2×1 matrix and φ_2 is a $(p+1) \times (r-1)$ matrix. The estimation is performed as in SJ, pp. 110–111.

6.2*

We now discuss a normalization or identification of the cointegrating vectors. Consider the model

$$\Delta X_t = \alpha\beta' X_{t-1} + \varepsilon_t.$$

The equation

$$|\lambda\Sigma_{\beta\beta} - \Sigma_{\beta 0}\Sigma_{00}^{-1}\Sigma_{0\beta}| = 0$$

has solutions $\lambda_1 > \cdots > \lambda_r$ and $V = (v_1, \ldots, v_r)$ normalized by $V'\Sigma_{\beta\beta}V = I$. Now define $\tilde{\beta} = \beta V$, that is, $\tilde{\beta}_i = \beta v_i$, and define $\tilde{\alpha} = \alpha V'^{-1}$, such that $\tilde{\alpha}\tilde{\beta}' = \alpha\beta'$.

1. Show that

$$\mathrm{Var}(\tilde{\beta}'X_t) = I,$$

$$\tilde{\alpha} = \Sigma_{0\tilde{\beta}} = \mathrm{Cov}(\Delta X_t, \tilde{\beta}'X_{t-1}),$$

$$\tilde{\alpha}'\Sigma_{00}^{-1}\tilde{\alpha} = \mathrm{diag}\left(\lambda_1, \ldots, \lambda_r\right).$$

2. Show that similar relations hold for the estimated values of α and β.

Solution to exercise 6.2

1. The relation $\tilde{\beta}'X_t = V'\beta'X_t$ implies

$$\Sigma_{\tilde{\beta}\tilde{\beta}} = \mathrm{Var}(\tilde{\beta}'X_t) = V'\mathrm{Var}(\beta'X_t)V = V'\Sigma_{\beta\beta}V = I.$$

Where the last identity holds by definition of the matrix of eigenvectors V.
Post-multiplying

$$\Delta X_t = \tilde{\alpha}\tilde{\beta}'X_{t-1} + \varepsilon_t$$

by $X_{t-1}'\tilde{\beta}$ and taking expectations gives us the second identity

$$\Sigma_{0\tilde{\beta}} = \tilde{\alpha}\Sigma_{\tilde{\beta}\tilde{\beta}} = \tilde{\alpha}.$$

The eigenvectors and eigenvalues satisfy the relations

$$\lambda_i\Sigma_{\beta\beta}v_i = \Sigma_{\beta 0}\Sigma_{00}^{-1}\Sigma_{0\beta}v_i,$$

$$v_i'\Sigma_{\beta\beta}v_j = \begin{cases} 1 & i = j \\ 0 & i \neq j. \end{cases}$$

In matrix notation this can be written as

$$\Sigma_{\beta\beta}V\Lambda = \Sigma_{\beta 0}\Sigma_{00}^{-1}\Sigma_{0\beta}V$$
$$V'\Sigma_{\beta\beta}V = I,$$

where $\Lambda = \mathrm{diag}(\lambda_1, \ldots, \lambda_r)$, which implies that

$$\Lambda = V'\Sigma_{\beta 0}\Sigma_{00}^{-1}\Sigma_{0\beta}V = \Sigma_{\tilde{\beta}0}\Sigma_{00}^{-1}\Sigma_{0\tilde{\beta}} = \tilde{\alpha}'\Sigma_{00}^{-1}\tilde{\alpha}.$$

2. For estimated values of α and β we have the same identities, though only in terms of the sample product moments. Thus

$$\hat{\beta}'S_{11}\hat{\beta} = \frac{1}{T}\sum_{t=1}^{T}\hat{\beta}'X_{t-1}X_{t-1}'\hat{\beta} = I$$

$$\hat{\alpha} = \hat{\alpha}(\hat{\beta}) = S_{01}\hat{\beta} = \frac{1}{T}\sum_{t=1}^{T} \Delta X_t X_{t-1}'\hat{\beta},$$

and

$$\hat{\alpha}' S_{00}^{-1} \hat{\alpha} = \hat{\beta}' S_{10} S_{00}^{-1} S_{01} \hat{\beta} = \hat{\Lambda}.$$

The $*$ for this exercise indicates that the convenient mathematical and numerical normalization (or identification) of the estimated cointegration vectors can be given an equivalent formulation in terms of identifying restrictions on the parameters.

6.3**

Consider the model-based or rational expectations that are formulated as

$$E_t(c_0' X_t + c_1' X_{t+1}) + c = 0, \tag{6.33}$$

for a process X_t which we assume is generated by the equation

$$\Delta X_t = \Pi X_{t-1} + \mu + \varepsilon_t, \qquad t = 1, \ldots, T. \tag{6.34}$$

Here X_t is p-dimensional and the matrix c is $q \times 1$ and c_0 and c_1 are $p \times q$ known matrices.

As an example consider the variables $(i_t^{\text{au}}, i_t^{\text{us}}, \text{exch}_t, p_t^{\text{us}}, p_t^{\text{au}})$. The hypothesis of uncovered interest parity is formulated as

$$i_t^{\text{us}} - i_t^{\text{au}} = E_t \Delta \text{exch}_{t+1}, \tag{6.35}$$

and the hypothesis of equal expected real interest rates is formulated as

$$i_t^{\text{us}} - E_t \Delta p_{t+1}^{\text{us}} = i_t^{\text{au}} - E_t \Delta p_{t+1}^{\text{au}}. \tag{6.36}$$

1. Show that (6.35) and (6.36) taken together are a special case of (6.33) and find the matrices c, c_0, and c_1.

2. Show that in order for (6.33) to be consistent with (6.34) we must have

$$c_1' \Pi = -(c_0 + c_1)' \text{ and } c_1' \mu + c = 0. \tag{6.37}$$

In the presence of cointegration these restrictions give more restrictions on the matrix Π and it is these restrictions that we want to test in the following. We define

$$a = c_1, \quad b = -(c_0 + c_1),$$

and assume that the matrix b has full rank.

3. Show that under the assumption that Π has reduced rank r $(0 < r < p)$ and the restrictions (6.37) hold, we have that a has full rank and that

$$(a, a_\perp)'\Pi(b, b_\perp) = \begin{pmatrix} b'b & 0 \\ \Theta & \xi\eta' \end{pmatrix},$$

for matrices ξ and η of dimension $(p-q) \times (r-q)$ and rank $(r-q)$ and a matrix Θ of dimension $(p-q) \times q$. Find Π as a function of Θ, ξ and η and show that this expression implies that Π has reduced rank and satisfies the restrictions (6.37).

4. Find the dimension of the parameter space spanned by Π and μ under the restrictions (6.37), and find an expression for the cointegration vectors β, in terms of η, and an expression for α.

5. Show by multiplying the equations for X_t by a and $a_\perp$ respectively that the estimators for η, ξ, Θ and μ can be determined by reduced rank regression.

6. Find an expression for the likelihood ratio test for the hypothesis (6.37). The asymptotic distribution is χ^2. Find the degrees of freedom.

Solution to exercise 6.3

1. The two equations can be rewritten as

$$\begin{aligned} -i_t^{\text{au}} + i_t^{\text{us}} + \text{exch}_t - E_t(\text{exch}_{t+1}) &= 0 \\ -i_t^{\text{au}} + i_t^{\text{us}} + p_t^{\text{us}} - p_t^{\text{au}} - E_t(p_{t+1}^{\text{us}}) + E_t(p_{t+1}^{\text{au}}) &= 0 \end{aligned}$$

which we formulate, in terms of the c matrices, as

$$c_0 = \begin{pmatrix} -1 & -1 \\ 1 & 1 \\ 1 & 0 \\ 0 & 1 \\ 0 & -1 \end{pmatrix}, \; c_1 = \begin{pmatrix} 0 & 0 \\ 0 & 0 \\ -1 & 0 \\ 0 & -1 \\ 0 & 1 \end{pmatrix}, \; c = \begin{pmatrix} 0 \\ 0 \end{pmatrix}.$$

2. Multiplying equation (6.34) by c_1' at time $t+1$, and taking expectations given the information available at time t, gives

$$E_t(c_1'\Delta X_{t+1}) = c_1'\Pi X_t + c_1'\mu,$$

which can be rewritten as

$$E_t(c_1' X_{t+1}) = c_1'(I + \Pi)X_t + c_1'\mu.$$

We can eliminate $E_t(c_1' X_{t+1})$ by applying equation (6.33), which gives the identity

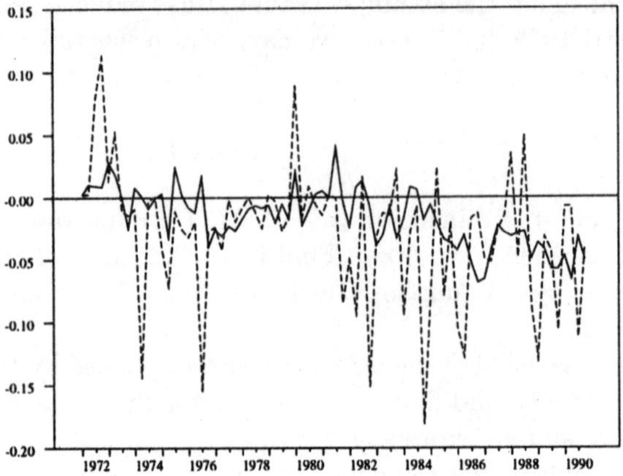

Fig. 6.1: PPP (solid line) and UIP (dotted line) (the Australian data set).

$$(c_1' + c_1'\Pi + c_0')X_t + (c + c_1'\mu) = 0. \tag{1}$$

Since the process X_t is not restricted from taking any values in $\mathbf{R}^p$, equation (1) is equivalent to the two identities

$$c_1'\Pi = -(c_0' + c_1'), \text{ and } c_1'\mu + c = 0.$$

By introducing the notation $a = c_1$ and $b = -(c_0 + c_1)$ the identities are expressed as

$$a'\Pi = b' \text{ and } a'\mu + c = 0.$$

3. From $b = \Pi' a$ it follows that

$$q = \text{rank}(b) \leq \text{rank}(\Pi) = r,$$

such that $r \geq q$. This restriction tells us that there have to be at least as many cointegrating relations, r, as there are restrictions derived from the hypothesis on rational expectations, q.

Similarly

$$q = \text{rank}(b) \leq \text{rank}(a) \leq q$$

such that a also has full rank q. The matrices $a_\perp$ and $b_\perp$ are therefore well defined, and are of dimension $p \times (p - q)$. Hence, the two $p \times p$ matrices $(a, a_\perp)$ and $(b, b_\perp)$ have full rank and

$$(a, a_\perp)'\Pi(b, b_\perp) = \begin{pmatrix} a'\Pi b & a'\Pi b_\perp \\ a_\perp'\Pi b & a_\perp'\Pi b_\perp \end{pmatrix} = \begin{pmatrix} b'b & b'b_\perp \\ a_\perp'\Pi b & a_\perp'\Pi b_\perp \end{pmatrix} = \begin{pmatrix} b'b & 0 \\ \Theta & \xi\eta' \end{pmatrix} \tag{2}$$

for some matrices ξ and η of dimension $(p - q) \times (r - q)$ with full rank $(r - q)$. That the matrix $a_\perp'\Pi b_\perp$ has reduced rank $r - q$, and can therefore be written as the product $\xi\eta'$, is seen from the identity

$$r = \text{rank}(\Pi) = \text{rank}(b'b) + \text{rank}(a'_\perp \Pi b_\perp) = q + (r - q).$$

By introducing $\bar{a} = a(a'a)^{-1}$ and $\bar{a}_\perp$, and similarly $\bar{b}$ and $\bar{b}_\perp$, we find the expression for Π,

$$\begin{aligned}
\Pi &= (a, a_\perp)'^{-1} \begin{pmatrix} b'b & 0 \\ \Theta & \xi\eta' \end{pmatrix} (b, b_\perp)^{-1} \\
&= (\bar{a}, \bar{a}_\perp) \begin{pmatrix} b'b & 0 \\ \Theta & \xi\eta' \end{pmatrix} (\bar{b}, \bar{b}_\perp)' \\
&= \bar{a}b'b\bar{b}' + \bar{a}_\perp\Theta\bar{b}' + \bar{a}_\perp\xi\eta'\bar{b}'_\perp \\
&= \left(\bar{a}b'b + \bar{a}_\perp\Theta,\, \bar{a}_\perp\xi\right) \begin{pmatrix} \bar{b}' \\ \eta'\bar{b}'_\perp \end{pmatrix} = \alpha\beta',
\end{aligned}$$

which represents Π as a function of the parameters Θ, ξ and η. The last expression shows that Π has reduced rank, since it is a product of two $p \times r$ matrices, and identifies the cointegrating vectors.

4. The identity (2) and the expression for Π show that there exists a bijective mapping

$$\Pi \leftrightarrow (\Theta, \xi\eta')$$

such that the dimension of the parameter space of Π can be found by calculating the dimension of the parameter space of Θ and $\xi\eta'$.

The parameter Θ varies freely in $\mathbf{R}^{(p-q)\times q}$ and the dimension of the parameter space of $\xi\eta'$ is, by applying Lemma 7.1, equal to

$$\begin{aligned}
[(p-q) + (p-q) - (r-q)](r-q) &= [2p - r - q](r - q) \\
&= 2p(r-q) - r^2 + q^2.
\end{aligned}$$

Hence, the number of free parameters in the Π matrix is

$$(p-q)q + 2p(r-q) - r^2 + q^2 = 2pr - pq - r^2.$$

The parameter μ has q restrictions, such that its parameter space has dimension $p - q$. The total number of parameters in the model is therefore

$$2pr - pq - r^2 + p - q.$$

Expressions for α and β were found in question 3:

$$\begin{aligned}
\alpha &= \left(\bar{a}b'b + \bar{a}_\perp\Theta,\, \bar{a}_\perp\xi\right) \\
\beta &= \left(\bar{b},\, \bar{b}_\perp\eta\right).
\end{aligned}$$

5. Applying the expression we found for Π leads to the equation

$$\Delta X_t = (\bar{a}b' + \bar{a}_\perp \Theta \bar{b}' + \bar{a}_\perp \xi \eta' \bar{b}'_\perp) X_{t-1} + \mu + \varepsilon_t.$$

Multiplying this by a' and $a'_\perp$ gives

$$\begin{aligned} a'\Delta X_t &= (b'X_{t-1} - c) + a'\varepsilon_t \\ a'_\perp \Delta X_t &= \Theta(\bar{b}'X_{t-1}) + \xi\eta'(\bar{b}'_\perp X_{t-1}) + a'_\perp \mu + a'_\perp \varepsilon_t. \end{aligned} \tag{3}$$

The introduction of the standard notation $\Omega_{aa} = a'\Omega a$ etc., and $\omega = \Omega_{a_\perp a}\Omega_{aa}^{-1}$, will enables us to decompose the likelihood function into a product of a marginal model (3) and a conditional model (4), where the residuals are independent.

In the marginal model we only have to estimate the variance, which is given by

$$\hat{\Omega}_{aa} = \frac{1}{T}\sum_{t=1}^{T}(a'\Delta X_t - b'X_{t-1} + c)(a'\Delta X_t - b'X_{t-1} + c)'.$$

The conditional model is

$$a'_\perp \Delta X_t = \xi\eta'\bar{b}'_\perp X_{t-1} + \omega a'\Delta X_t + (\Theta - \omega b'b)b'X_{t-1} + (\alpha'_\perp \mu + \omega c) + \varepsilon_{a_\perp . at}. \tag{4}$$

It is seen that the parameters ξ and η can be estimated by reduced rank regression of $a'_\perp \Delta X_t$ on $\bar{b}'_\perp X_{t-1}$ corrected for $a'\Delta X_t$, $b'X_{t-1}$, and 1. The estimate for the variance is denoted $\hat{\Omega}_{a_\perp a_\perp . a}$.

6. The method for deriving the likelihood ratio test is in principal the same as that for deriving tests for linear hypothesis on α, which is described in details in SJ, Chapter 8.

Under the hypothesis that $E_t(c_0'X_t + c_1'X_{t+1}) + c = 0$, the likelihood function is split into the product

$$L_{full} = L_{part}L_{marg}.$$

The maximized likelihood function from the marginal model is given by

$$\max L_{marg}^{-2/T} = |a'a||\hat{\Omega}_{aa}|,$$

and the maximized likelihood function from the conditional model is

$$\max L_{cond}^{-2/T} = |a'_\perp a_\perp||\hat{\Omega}_{a_\perp a_\perp . a}|.$$

In the unrestricted model we get

$$\max L_{full}^{-2/T} = |\hat{\Omega}|.$$

The likelihood ratio test is then given by

$$-2\log Q = T\log\frac{|a'a||a'_{\perp}a_{\perp}||\Omega_{aa}||\hat{\Omega}_{a_{\perp}a_{\perp}.a}|}{|\hat{\Omega}|}.$$

The degrees of freedom are equal to the decrease in dimension of the parameter space. The dimension of the parameter space for the unrestricted model is $(2p-r)r+p$, such that the degrees of freedom in the test are

$$(2p-r)r+p-(2pr-pq-r^2+p-q)=pq+q.$$

6.4

Discuss the estimation problem for the statistical models discussed in the exercises in Chapter 5.

Solution to exercise 6.4

The estimation problem for most of the hypotheses which appeared in the exercises in Chapter 5, can be solved by reduced rank regression. But some of the models have parameter restrictions which make it impossible to formulate them as reduced rank regressions, so other methods have to be applied. These methods are discussed in Chapters 7 and 8.

6.5*

Consider the model

$$\Delta X_t = \alpha\beta' X_{t-1} + \Gamma_1 \Delta X_{t-1} + \varepsilon_t. \tag{6.38}$$

Let H be a $p \times s$ matrix.

1. Show that the hypothesis

$$\Gamma_1 H_{\perp} = 0$$

can be formulated as $\Gamma_1 = \xi H'$ for some ξ $(p \times s)$ and derive the likelihood ratio test for this hypothesis. The asymptotic distribution of the test statistic is χ^2. Determine the degrees of freedom.

2. Show that if $\beta = H\varphi$ and $\Gamma_1 = \xi H'$ then $Y_t = H'X_t$ is an autoregressive process. Find the parameters and give the condition for the process Y_t to be an $I(1)$ process.

3. Consider now the following special case:

$$\Delta Y_t = \gamma \Delta Z_{t-1} + \varepsilon_{1t}, \tag{6.39}$$
$$\Delta Z_t = \alpha_2 (Y_{t-1} + \beta_2 Z_{t-1}) + \varepsilon_{2t}. \tag{6.40}$$

Find the characteristic polynomial and its roots and show that if

$$\begin{aligned} -1 &< \gamma\,\alpha_2 \\ \alpha_2(\gamma+\beta_2) &< 0 \\ \alpha_2(\gamma-\beta_2) &< 2 \end{aligned}$$

then the process $X_t = (Y_t, Z_t)'$ is an $I(1)$ process and $Y_t + \beta_2 Z_t$ is stationary.

4. For $H = (1, 0)'$ the hypothesis $\beta = H\varphi$ reduces to $\beta_2 = 0$. Find the autoregressive representation of Y_t given by (6.39) and (6.40) under the assumption that $\beta = H\varphi$ and $\Gamma_1 = \xi H'$ and determine the properties of the process depending on the parameters.

5. The problem is inspired by the following situation. In an investigation of money m_t, income y_t, prices p_t and interest rates i_{1t} and i_{2t}, both money and income are in nominal values. The variables m_t, y_t and p_t are in logarithms. An analysis of the data shows that a model with $r = 3$ and $k = 2$ describes the data. We now want to investigate if we could have analysed the variables in real terms, that is, the variables $(m_t - p_t,\ y_t - p_t,\ i_{1t},\ i_{2t})$.

Determine in this case the matrix H and determine explicitly the condition that Γ_1 has to satisfy in order that the real variables are described by an AR(2) model.

Solution to exercise 6.5

1. One can always decompose Γ_1 into the sum $\Gamma_1 = \xi H' + \tilde{\xi} H_\perp'$, for some matrices $\xi \in \mathbf{R}^{p\times s}$ and $\tilde{\xi} \in \mathbf{R}^{p\times(p-s)}$. This expression shows that the identities $\Gamma_1 H_\perp = 0$ and $\Gamma_1 = \xi H'$ imply the same restrictions on Γ_1.

The unrestricted model is analysed as in SJ, Chapter 6, pp. 90–92 (just define $Z_{2t} = \Delta X_{t-1}$), and the maximum value of the likelihood function is (up to a constant)

$$L_{\max}^{-2/T} = |S_{00}| \prod_{i=1}^{r} (1 - \hat{\lambda}_i),$$

where we have used the same notation as in SJ.

Under the hypothesis $\Gamma_1 = \xi H'$ we define the variable

$$\tilde{Z}_{2t} = H' \Delta X_{t-1},$$

and again have a reduced rank regression model in the usual form (see SJ, equation (6.2))

$$Z_{0t} = \alpha\beta' Z_{1t} + \xi \tilde{Z}_{2t} + \varepsilon_t.$$

Hence we get an expression for the maximum value of the likelihood function

$$\tilde{L}_{\max}^{-2/T} = |\tilde{S}_{00}| \prod_{i=1}^{r} (1 - \tilde{\lambda}_i).$$

The likelihood ratio test is given by

$$-2 \log Q = T \log \frac{|\tilde{S}_{00}| \prod_{i=1}^{r} (1 - \tilde{\lambda}_i)}{|S_{00}| \prod_{i=1}^{r} (1 - \hat{\lambda}_i)}$$
$$= T \log \frac{|\tilde{S}_{00}|}{|S_{00}|} + \sum_{i=1}^{r} [\log(1 - \tilde{\lambda}_i) - \log(1 - \hat{\lambda}_i)].$$

The degrees of freedom are equal to the decrease in dimension of the parameter space.

In the unrestricted model the dimension of the parameter space for Γ_1 is p^2, while under the hypothesis it is ps. The other parameters have the same parameter spaces, and hence the degrees of freedom of the test are $p^2 - ps = p(p - s)$.

2. In the case where $\beta = H\varphi$ and $\Gamma_1 = \xi H'$ we can multiply the model equation by H' and find

$$\Delta H' X_t = H' \alpha \varphi' H' X_{t-1} + H' \xi H' \Delta' X_{t-1} + H' \varepsilon_t,$$

which shows that $Y_t = H' X_t$ satisfies the autoregression equation

$$\Delta Y_t = (H' \alpha) \varphi' Y_{t-1} + (H' \xi) \Delta Y_{t-1} + \tilde{\varepsilon}_t,$$

which has parameters $(H'\alpha, \varphi, H'\xi)$ and $\tilde{\Omega} = H' \Omega H$.

The conditions for the process to be an $I(1)$ process are the three conditions given by Granger's representation theorem.

We simplify the notation by writing

$$(a, b, G_1) = (H'\alpha, \varphi, H'\xi),$$

so that the model becomes

$$\Delta Y_t = ab' Y_{t-1} + G_1 \Delta Y_{t-1} + \tilde{\varepsilon}_t.$$

The conditions are that the matrix ab' has reduced rank, the matrix $a_\perp'(I - G_1)b_\perp$ has full rank and the roots in the characteristic polynomial are either outside the unit disc or equal to one.

3. The equations (6.39) and (6.40) can be written as

$$\Delta \begin{pmatrix} Y_t \\ Z_t \end{pmatrix} = \begin{pmatrix} 0 \\ \alpha_2 \end{pmatrix} (1, \beta_2) \begin{pmatrix} Y_{t-1} \\ Z_{t-1} \end{pmatrix} + \begin{pmatrix} 0 & \gamma \\ 0 & 0 \end{pmatrix} \begin{pmatrix} \Delta Y_{t-1} \\ \Delta Z_{t-1} \end{pmatrix} + \varepsilon_t.$$

The characteristic polynomial of the process is given by

$$\begin{aligned} A(z) &= I(1-z) - \begin{pmatrix} 0 \\ \alpha_2 \end{pmatrix} (1, \beta_2) z - \begin{pmatrix} 0 & \gamma \\ 0 & 0 \end{pmatrix} (1-z) z \\ &= \begin{pmatrix} (1-z) & -\gamma(1-z)z \\ -\alpha_2 z & (1-z) - \alpha_2\beta_2 z \end{pmatrix} \end{aligned}$$

and has determinant

$$\begin{aligned} |A(z)| &= (1-z)\left((1-z) - \alpha_2\beta_2 z\right) - \alpha_2 z\gamma(1-z)z \\ &= (1-z)\left((1-z) - \alpha_2\beta_2 z - \alpha_2\gamma z^2\right) \\ &= (1-z)\left(1 - (1+\alpha_2\beta_2)z - \alpha_2\gamma z^2\right). \end{aligned}$$

The roots of the polynomial

$$1 - (1+\alpha_2\beta_2)z - \alpha_2\gamma z^2 = 0$$

correspond to stationary solutions if the following inequalities are satisfied:

$$\begin{aligned} &\alpha_2\gamma > -1, \\ &\alpha_2\gamma < 1 - (1+\alpha_2\beta_2), \\ &\alpha_2\gamma < 1 + (1+\alpha_2\beta_2); \end{aligned}$$

see Box and Jenkins (1976). Hence under these restrictions we can conclude that the process is $I(1)$ and that the cointegrating relation $Y_t + \beta_2 Z_t$ has a stationary representation.

4. For $H = (1,0)'$, the condition $\Gamma_1 = \xi H'$ implies that $\gamma = 0$. Hence the autoregressive representation of Y_t is

$$Y_t = Y_{t-1} + \varepsilon_{1t},$$

that is, Y_t is a random walk. The equation for Z_t, when $\beta_2 = 0$, is

$$\Delta Z_t = \alpha_2 Y_{t-1} + \varepsilon_{2t},$$

such that Z_t is $I(2)$ when $\alpha_2 \neq 0$, since its difference is $I(1)$. In the case where $\alpha_2 = 0$, the variable Z_t is $I(1)$, and the process $(Y_t, Z_t)'$ does not cointegrate.

5. In the case where $X_t = (m, y, p, i_1, i_2)'_t$ the H matrix is given by

$$H = \begin{pmatrix} 1 & 0 & 0 & 0 \\ 0 & 1 & 0 & 0 \\ -1 & -1 & 0 & 0 \\ 0 & 0 & 1 & 0 \\ 0 & 0 & 0 & 1 \end{pmatrix}.$$

The condition on Γ_1 is that $\Gamma_1 H_\perp = 0$, where $H_\perp = (1, 1, 1, 0, 0)'$, or equivalently, that the first three elements in Γ_1 sum to zero:

$$\sum_{j=1}^{3} \gamma_{ij} = 0, \qquad i = 1, \ldots, 5,$$

where γ_{ij} are the elements in the matrix Γ_1.

In many situations it is tempting to transform the data before analysing them. This exercise shows how one can instead ask what restrictions one should impose on the original data to find that the transformation suggested is the natural one. Once this has been achieved one can derive a test for the restrictions.

7

Hypothesis Testing for the Long-Run Coefficients β

Chapter 7 gives a number of hypotheses on the long-run coefficients and discusses how they can be estimated. A general point of view is that we want to find all the models that can be treated by the same reduced rank regression algorithm based on eigenvalues, so we try as far as possible to reduce the estimation problem to a question of a reduced rank regression. Lemma 7.1 contains a useful result about the number of free parameters in these models which is needed for calculating the degrees of freedom for the various tests. The hypotheses are basically linear restrictions on the cointegrating space and it turns out that these are surprisingly often exactly those that are interesting in the applications. More general linear restrictions are also formulated and estimation and identification are discussed. We also include here an analysis of the data, where the rank is determined and then various tests are performed to investigate economic hypotheses.

Only two exercises are given. The first illustrates how careful one has to be when formulating restrictions on the parameters, and the second discusses a situation where the estimation involves two reduced rank matrices.

7.1*

Consider the model

$$\Delta X_{1t} = \tfrac{1}{2}\left(X_{1t-1} - \beta_1 X_{2t-1}\right) + \varepsilon_{1t},$$

$$\Delta X_{2t} = \tfrac{1}{2}\left(X_{1t-1} - \beta_2 X_{2t-1}\right) + \varepsilon_{2t},$$

where ε_t, $t = 1, \ldots, T$, are i.i.d. $N_2(0, \Omega)$. Find the maximum likelihood estimator of β_1 and β_2 and derive the likelihood ratio test of the hypothesis $\beta_1 = \beta_2$. Discuss the properties of the process X_t when $\beta_1 = \beta_2$, and when $\beta_1 \neq \beta_2$.

Solution to exercise 7.1

The equations of the model can be written as

$$\Delta X_{1t} - \frac{1}{2}X_{1t-1} = -\frac{1}{2}\beta_1 X_{2t-1} + \varepsilon_{1t},$$
$$\Delta X_{2t} - \frac{1}{2}X_{1t-1} = -\frac{1}{2}\beta_2 X_{2t-1} + \varepsilon_{2t}.$$

Since the two equations have the same regressors the model can be estimated by single equation regression; we find residuals $\hat{\varepsilon}_{1t}$ and $\hat{\varepsilon}_{2t}$, estimate the variance matrix by $\hat{\Omega} = T^{-1}\sum_t \hat{\varepsilon}_t\hat{\varepsilon}_t'$, and find $L_{\max}^{-\frac{2}{T}} = \left|\hat{\Omega}\right|$.

Under the hypothesis that $\beta_1 = \beta_2 (= \beta)$ we have a cross equation restriction and we decompose the model into a marginal and a conditional model by multiplying by $\alpha_\perp' = (1, -1)$ and $\bar{\alpha}' = (2, 2)$:

$$\alpha_\perp' \Delta X_t = \alpha_\perp' \varepsilon_t \quad (1)$$
$$\bar{\alpha}' \Delta X_t = (1, -\beta)X_{t-1} + \omega(\alpha_\perp' \Delta X_t) + (\bar{\alpha}' - \omega\alpha_\perp')\varepsilon_t. \quad (2)$$

The residuals in the two equations are Gaussian and independent, so the parameter estimates for β and ω are found by regressing $(\bar{\alpha}'\Delta X_t - X_{1,t-1})$ on $(-X_{2,t-1}, \alpha_\perp'\Delta X_t)'$. If we let $\hat{\varepsilon}_{ct}$ be the estimated residuals, we have that the estimated variance in the condition model (2) is

$$\hat{\Omega}_c = \frac{1}{T}\sum_{t=1}^{T} \hat{\varepsilon}_{ct}\hat{\varepsilon}_{ct}',$$

and the variance in the marginal model (1) is

$$\hat{\Omega}_m = \frac{1}{T}\sum_{t=1}^{T} \alpha_\perp' \Delta X_t \Delta X_t' \alpha_\perp.$$

The value of the likelihood function is the product of the contributions from the marginal and condition model, hence the likelihood ratio test is

$$Q^{-2/T} = \frac{|\hat{\Omega}_c|\,|\hat{\Omega}_m|}{|\hat{\Omega}|\,|\alpha_\perp'\alpha_\perp|\,|\alpha'\alpha|}.$$

We will now investigate the properties of the process. The roots of the characteristic polynomial are given as the solutions to

$$\left|\begin{pmatrix} 1 - z - \frac{1}{2}z & \frac{\beta_1}{2}z \\ -\frac{1}{2}z & 1 - z + \frac{\beta_2}{2}z \end{pmatrix}\right| = 0$$

which is equivalent to

$$1-\frac{10-2\beta_2}{4}z-\frac{3\beta_2-\beta_1-6}{4}z^2=0.$$

This problem is identical to the problem we solved in question 3 of exercise 6.5, and the solutions will all be larger than one in absolute value if β_1 and β_2 fulfil the restrictions

$$\begin{aligned}\frac{3\beta_2-\beta_1-6}{4}&>-1\\ \frac{3\beta_2-\beta_1-6}{4}&<1-\frac{10-2\beta_2}{4}\\ \frac{3\beta_2-\beta_1-6}{4}&<1+\frac{10-2\beta_2}{4}.\end{aligned}$$

The restrictions can be rewritten as

$$\begin{aligned}\beta_1&<3\beta_2-2\\ \beta_1&>\beta_2\\ \beta_1&>5\beta_2-20,\end{aligned}$$

which defines an open triangle, with corners $(1,1)$, $(5,5)$ and $(25,9)$. Hence if the parameters (β_1,β_2) lie inside the triangle, the process is stationary.

The polynomial $1-\rho_1 z-\rho_2 z^2$ has a unit root if

$$\begin{aligned}1=\rho_1+\rho_2&=\frac{10-2\beta_2}{4}+\frac{3\beta_2-\beta_1-6}{4}\\ &=\frac{4+\beta_2-\beta_1}{4}=1+\frac{\beta_2-\beta_1}{4},\end{aligned}$$

that is, if $\beta_1=\beta_2$. Hence if $\beta_1\neq\beta_2$ the characteristic polynomial has no unit roots, and the process is therefore not $I(1)$.

In the case where $\beta_1=\beta_2=\beta$, the process has a unit root. So if the other root is larger than one in absolute value, the process is $I(1)$; if it is equal to one, the process is $I(2)$; otherwise it is explosive (or seasonal cointegrated). The second root of the characteristic polynomial is

$$z=\frac{2}{3-\beta}$$

which is larger the one in absolute value if and only if $\beta\in]1,5[$.

The condition for $I(2)$-ness is

$$\alpha'_\perp\beta_\perp=(1,-1)\begin{pmatrix}\beta\\1\end{pmatrix}=\beta-1=0,$$

which shows that $\beta=1$ gives an $I(2)$ process.

In general, we have that the model ($a \neq 0$)

$$\Delta X_t = a \begin{pmatrix} 1 \\ 1 \end{pmatrix} (1, -\beta) X_{t-1} + \varepsilon_t$$

is $I(2)$ if $\beta = 1$; $I(1)$ if $\beta \in]1; \frac{a+2}{a}[$; and explosive otherwise (seasonal cointegrated for $\beta = \frac{a+2}{a}$).

This simple model illustrates an important point. A seemingly innocent hypothesis on the coefficients β_1 and β_2 is in fact a question about cointegration. Moreover, if the common value is one, suddenly the process is $I(2)$. Thus the condition on the roots of the characteristic polynomial should be carefully checked, even under the various null hypotheses that we investigate.

7.2*

A special type of regression problem which occurs in various hypotheses on the cointegrating relations is

$$Z_{0t} = \Pi^1 Z_{1t}^1 + \Pi^2 Z_{1t}^2 + \varepsilon_t,$$

where the parameters Π^1 and Π^2 both have reduced rank, such that, as usual, we can write the reduced rank parameters as a product of two full rank matrices. We then get the equation

$$\begin{aligned} Z_{0t} &= \alpha_1 \beta_1' Z_{1t}^1 + \alpha_2 \beta_2' Z_{1t}^2 + \varepsilon_t \\ &= [\alpha_1, \alpha_2] \begin{pmatrix} \beta_1 & 0 \\ 0 & \beta_2 \end{pmatrix}' \begin{pmatrix} Z_{1t}^1 \\ Z_{1t}^2 \end{pmatrix} + \varepsilon_t \\ &= \tilde{\alpha} \tilde{\beta}' \tilde{Z}_{1t} + \varepsilon_t. \end{aligned} \tag{1}$$

This type of regression, which may have more than two reduced rank conditions, is called multiple reduced rank regression, and is typically solved by applying a switching algorithm, see SJ, pp. 110–111.

1. Consider the model

$$\Delta X_t = \alpha \beta' X_{t-1} + \Gamma_1 \Delta X_{t-1} + \varepsilon_t.$$

Show that the hypothesis

$$\beta = (H_1 \varphi_1, \ldots, H_r \varphi_r),$$

leads to a multiple reduced rank regression.

Now consider the model

$$\Delta X_t = \alpha_t \beta_t' X_{t-1} + \Gamma_1 \Delta X_{t-1} + \varepsilon_t,$$

where we allow for a structural break at time τ, such that the parameters have the form

$$\alpha_t = \begin{cases} \alpha_1, & t = 1, \ldots, \tau - 1 \\ \alpha_2, & t = \tau, \ldots, T, \end{cases} \quad \text{and } \beta_t = \begin{cases} \beta_1, & t = 1, \ldots, \tau - 1 \\ \beta_2, & t = \tau, \ldots, T. \end{cases}$$

2. Show that this hypothesis leads to a multiple reduced rank regression. Note that this general formulation allows for not only a change in the values of the parameters but also a change in the number of cointegrating relations. For example, we could have r_1 cointegrating relations before time τ and $r_2 > r_1$ cointegrating relations after time τ. Assume that this is the case, and that we would like to test if the r_1 cointegrating relations are the same throughout the sample, and that at time τ there are added $r_2 - r_1$ to the system, or equivalently that $\text{sp}(\beta_1) \subset \text{sp}(\beta_2)$.

3. Show that this hypothesis can be formulated as a multiple reduced rank regression, and find the degrees of freedom for the test against the alternative where the r_1 cointegrating relations are not necessarily the same before and after time τ.

4. Show that the hypothesis on a structural break in the cointegrating relation β_t with α constant throughout the sample can be formulated as a reduced rank regression; see equation (6.9).

5. Show that the hypothesis on a break in α_t, with β constant throughout the sample, is not covered by the multiple reduced rank regression formulation.

Solution to 7.2

1. We regress ΔX_t and X_{t-1} on lagged differences and get residuals R_{0t} and R_{1t}. The concentrated model for these residuals is

$$\begin{aligned} R_{0t} &= \alpha\beta' R_{1t} + \tilde{\varepsilon}_t \\ &= \alpha(H_1\varphi_1, \ldots, H_r\varphi_r)' R_{1t} + \tilde{\varepsilon}_t \\ &= \alpha_1\varphi_1' H_1' R_{1t} + \cdots + \alpha_r\varphi_r' H_r' R_{1t} + \tilde{\varepsilon}_t \\ &= \alpha_1\varphi_1' R_{11t} + \cdots + \alpha_r\varphi_r' R_{1rt} + \tilde{\varepsilon}_t, \end{aligned}$$

where $R_{1it} = H_i' R_{1t}$, $i = 1, \ldots, r$.

2. By defining the variables

$$\begin{aligned} X_t^1 &= X_t I_{\{t<\tau\}} \\ X_t^2 &= X_t I_{\{t\geq\tau\}}, \end{aligned}$$

where $I_{\{.\}}$ is an indicator function, the model can be written as

$$\Delta X_t = \alpha_1\beta_1' X_{t-1}^1 + \alpha_2\beta_2' X_{t-1}^2 + \Gamma_1 \Delta X_{t-1} + \varepsilon_t,$$

which is concentrated to the multiple reduced rank regression model

$$R_{0t} = \alpha_1\beta_1' R_{11t} + \alpha_2\beta_2' R_{12t} + \tilde{\varepsilon}_t,$$

where R_{0t} are the residuals for regressing ΔX_t on ΔX_{t-1} and (R_{11t}', R_{12t}') are the residuals from regressing $(X_t^{1\prime}, X_t^{2\prime})$ on ΔX_{t-1}.

3. For this hypothesis we let α_1, β_1 be $p \times r_1$ and α_2, β_2 be $p \times (r_2 - r_1)$ and have the concentrated model

$$R_{0t} = \alpha_1\beta_1' R_{11t} + \alpha_2\beta_2' R_{12t} + \tilde{\varepsilon}_t,$$

where R_{0t} is defined as previously and $(R_{11t}', R_{12t}')'$ are the residuals from regressing $(X_t', X_t^{2\prime})'$ on ΔX_{t-1}.

The degrees of freedom are found by applying Lemma 7.1. Under the general hypothesis we find the number of parameters in (α_t, β_t) to be

$$(2p - r_1)r_1 + (2p - r_2)r_2.$$

Under the hypothesis with r_1 constant cointegrating relations the degrees of freedom are calculated as follows. In the second period some of the cointegrating relations are identical to the cointegrating relations in the first period β_1. Thus $\beta_2 = (\beta_1, \phi)$. The relations ϕ, however, can be chosen orthogonal to β_1, such that for $\alpha_2 = (\alpha_{21}, \alpha_{22})$ we get the equation

$$\alpha_1\beta_1' X_{t-1}^1 + \alpha_{21}\beta_1' X_{t-1}^2 + \alpha_{22}\xi'\beta_{\perp 1}' X_{t-1}^2,$$

where α_{22} is $p \times (r_2 - r_1)$ and ξ is $(p - r_1) \times (r_2 - r_1)$. We can then determine the parameters as pr_1 for α_1, $(p - r_1)r_1$ for β_1 normalized as $\beta_1 = (I, \beta_*)'$, where β_* is $(p - r_1) \times r_1$. Next we have pr_1 parameters from α_{21}. Finally we get from SJ, Lemma 7.1, that $\alpha_{22}\xi'$ contains $p(r_2 - r_1) + (r_2 - r_1)(p - r_2)$. Adding the contributions, we find

$$\begin{aligned} &pr_1 + (p - r_1)r_1 + pr_1 + p(r_2 - r_1) + (r_2 - r_1)(p - r_2) \\ &= 2pr_1 - r_1^2 + 2pr_2 - r_2^2 - r_1(p - r_2), \end{aligned}$$

giving $r_1(p - r_2)$ degrees of freedom for the test.

4. The model, under the hypothesis that there is only a break in β_t, while α_t is constant, is

$$\begin{aligned} \Delta X_t &= \alpha\beta_1' R_{11t} + \alpha\beta_2' R_{12t} + \tilde{\varepsilon}_t \\ &= \alpha\,(\beta_1', \beta_2') \begin{pmatrix} R_{11t} \\ R_{12t} \end{pmatrix} + \tilde{\varepsilon}_t, \end{aligned}$$

which is a simple reduced rank regression with no restrictions on the reduced rank parameters.

5. The hypothesis on a shift in α_t and while β_t is constant leads to the model

$$\begin{aligned}\Delta X_t &= \alpha_1\beta' R_{11t} + \alpha_1\beta' R_{12t} + \tilde{\varepsilon}_t \\ &= (\alpha_1, \alpha_2)\begin{pmatrix}\beta & 0\\ 0 & \beta\end{pmatrix}'\begin{pmatrix}R_{11t}\\ R_{12t}\end{pmatrix} + \tilde{\varepsilon}_t.\end{aligned}$$

This structure in the parameters is not covered by the multiple reduced rank regression formulation because there are cross restrictions on the $\tilde{\beta}$ parameter; see equation (1). The parameters can therefore not be estimated by applying the algorithm described in SJ, pp. 110–111. One has to apply a more general optimization algorithm.

The formulation given here is a general framework for a number of different and often occurring problems. We still need to find a general algorithm that converges for this type of problem.

8

Hypothesis Testing for α

In Chapter 8 a partial system is defined and a result is proved which gives conditions for the conditioning variable to be weakly exogenous for the parameter of interest β, such that inference can be conducted in the partial system; see Theorem 8.1. The situation is the following. We decompose the process into X_{1t} and X_{2t}. The equations are then given by

$$\Delta X_{1t} = \alpha_1 \beta' X_{t-1} + \sum_{i=1}^{k-1} \Gamma_{1i} \Delta X_{t-i} + \Phi_1 D_t + \varepsilon_{1t}, \tag{8.1}$$

$$\Delta X_{2t} = \alpha_2 \beta' X_{t-1} + \sum_{i=1}^{k-1} \Gamma_{2i} \Delta X_{t-i} + \Phi_2 D_t + \varepsilon_{2t}. \tag{8.2}$$

The conditional model for ΔX_{1t} given ΔX_{2t} and the past is given by

$$\Delta X_{1t} = (\alpha_1 - \omega \alpha_2) \beta' X_{t-1} + \sum_{i=1}^{k-1} \tilde{\Gamma}_{1i} \Delta X_{t-i} + \tilde{\Phi}_1 D_t + \tilde{\varepsilon}_{1t},$$

and it is seen that if $\alpha_2 = 0$, then the parameter β can be estimated efficiently from this partial model as long as no further restrictions are imposed on the parameters. The test for weak exogeneity, $\alpha_2 = 0$, is thus a linear restriction on the adjustment coefficients

$$\alpha = A\psi.$$

It is shown in Theorem 8.2 that a suitable reduced rank regression again provides the maximum likelihood estimator such that the test statistic can be calculated. Theorem 8.4 gives the results for hypotheses where some α are known.

The chapter concludes by showing how $\alpha_\perp$ can be determined by an eigenvalue problem, where R_{0t} and R_{1t} are interchanged.

The first exercise illustrates that the problem that we exemplified in exercise 7.1 can also occur in a test on the adjustment coefficients; the second exercise discusses the concept of co-feature vectors, and various questions are asked relating to estimation.

8.1

Consider the model

$$\Delta X_{1t} = \alpha_1 (X_{1t-1} - X_{2t-1}) + \varepsilon_{1t},$$

$$\Delta X_{2t} = \alpha_2 (X_{1t-1} - X_{2t-1}) + \varepsilon_{2t},$$

where ε_t, $t = 1, \ldots, T$, are i.i.d. $N_2(0, \Omega)$. Find the maximum likelihood estimator of α_1 and α_2 and derive the likelihood ratio test of the hypothesis $\alpha_1 = \alpha_2$. Discuss the properties of the process X_t when $\alpha_1 = \alpha_2$, and when $\alpha_1 \neq \alpha_2$.

Solution to exercise 8.1

The maximum likelihood estimator is determined by regressing ΔX_t on $X_{1t-1} - X_{2t-1}$; we find the usual result that

$$L_{\max}^{-2/T} = \left|\hat{\Omega}\right|,$$

and the estimator of α is given by $\hat{\alpha} = S_{0b} S_{bb}^{-1}$, where $S_{b0} = \frac{1}{T}\sum_{t=1}^{T}(X_{1t-1} - X_{2t-1})\Delta X_t'$ and $S_{bb} = \frac{1}{T}\sum_{t=1}^{T}(X_{1t-1} - X_{2t-1})^2$.

Under the hypothesis that $\alpha_1 = \alpha_2 (= \psi)$ we have a cross equation restriction and we can decompose the model into a marginal and a conditional model by defining $A = (1, 1)'$ and $A_\perp = (1, -1)'$. We find

$$\begin{aligned} A_\perp' \Delta X_t &= A_\perp' \varepsilon_t \\ A' \Delta X_t &= A' A \psi (X_{1t-1} - X_{2t-1}) + \omega A_\perp' \Delta X_t + (A' - \omega A_\perp')\varepsilon_t, \end{aligned}$$

and by defining the variable

$$Z_t = \begin{pmatrix} X_{1,t-1} - X_{2,t-1} \\ A_\perp' \Delta X_t \end{pmatrix}$$

we have

$$\begin{aligned} \hat{\Omega}_m &= A_\perp' S_{00} A_\perp \\ \hat{\Omega}_c &= A' S_{00} A - A' S_{0z} S_{zz}^{-1} S_{z0} A \end{aligned}$$

and hence

$$L_{\max}^{-2/T}(\alpha_1 = \alpha_2) = \frac{|A_\perp' S_{00} A_\perp|}{|A_\perp' A_\perp|} \frac{|A'(S_{00} - S_{0z} S_{zz}^{-1} S_{z0}) A|}{|A'A|}.$$

The likelihood ratio test is then given by

$$Q^{-2/T} = \frac{|A'_\perp S_{00} A_\perp| \, |A'(S_{00} - S_{0z} S_{zz}^{-1} S_{z0}) A|}{|A'A| \, |A'_\perp A_\perp| \, |S_{00} - S_{0b} S_{bb}^{-1} S_{b0}|}.$$

The process will be $I(1)$ when $\alpha_1 \neq \alpha_2$, since $\alpha'_\perp \beta_\perp = \alpha_2 - \alpha_1 \neq 0$, and $I(2)$ when $\alpha_1 = \alpha_2$, provided that the roots of the characteristic polynomial satisfies Assumption 1; see SJ, p. 14.

8.2*

Let the p-dimensional process be given by the equation

$$\Delta X_t = \alpha\beta' X_{t-1} + \Gamma_1 \Delta X_{t-1} + \varepsilon_t, \qquad t = 1, \ldots, T, \tag{1}$$

where α and β are $p \times r$ matrices of rank r, Γ_1 is a $p \times p$ matrix and $\varepsilon_1, \ldots, \varepsilon_T$ are i.i.d. Gaussian variables $N_p(0, \Omega)$.

The process X_t is said to have common features if a vector, ζ, eliminates all short-run dynamics, that is, if $\zeta' X_t$ is a random walk. The vector ζ is then called a co-feature vector.

To illustrate the idea, we consider the case where $p = 2$ and $\zeta = (1, -1)'$. In general ΔX_{1t} and ΔX_{2t} will be complicated stationary processes, but they have the same complicated structure (the same features) if $\Delta X_{1t} - \Delta X_{2t}$ is a simple white noise process, such that $X_{1t} - X_{2t}$ is a random walk.

1. Give the conditions for ζ to be a co-feature vector of the process X_t given by equation (1) and show that there exists a co-feature vector if and only if the matrix (α, Γ_1) has reduced rank m, where $r \leq m \leq p$. Determine in this case the number of linearly independent co-feature vectors, and show that a co-feature vector can be written as $\zeta = \alpha_\perp \theta$ for a suitable θ.

2. Apply the result found in question 1 to discuss co-feature vectors and cointegration vectors of the process given by

$$\Delta X_t = \Phi \Psi' \begin{pmatrix} \beta' X_{t-1} \\ \Delta X_{t-1} \end{pmatrix} + \varepsilon_t, \qquad t = 1, \ldots, T, \tag{2}$$

where Φ is a $p \times m$ matrix, Ψ is a $(p + r) \times m$ matrix and β is a $p \times r$ matrix.

3. Discuss the maximum likelihood estimation of the parameters in model (2) in the case where β is known and Φ, Ψ, Ω vary freely, and in the case where Φ is known and the other parameters vary freely. Use the result to suggest an algorithm to derive the estimators in the model, and the likelihood ratio test of model (2) against model (1).

4. Determine the number of parameters in models (1) and (2). The difference is the degrees of freedom in the asymptotic χ^2 test.

If in model (1) we want linear combinations of the process $\eta' X_t$ (and not $\eta' \Delta X_t$) to be white noise, we get a more complicated problem.

5. Show that if $\eta' X_t$ is white noise then η is a linear combination of the cointegrating relations $\eta = \beta v$ for a suitable v, and that the following relations hold:

$$v'(I + \beta'\alpha) = 0,$$
$$v'\beta'\Gamma_1 = 0.$$

Show that if one wants, for fixed β, to investigate the presence of cointegrating relations which are white noise, one could work within the model

$$\beta' X_t = \delta\tau' \begin{pmatrix} \beta' X_{t-1} \\ \Delta X_{t-1} \end{pmatrix} + \beta'\varepsilon_t, \qquad t = 1, \ldots, T,$$

$$\beta'_\perp \Delta X_t = \kappa \begin{pmatrix} \beta' X_{t-1} \\ \Delta X_{t-1} \end{pmatrix} + \beta'_\perp\varepsilon_t, \qquad t = 1, \ldots, T.$$

6. Determine α and Γ_1 as functions of δ, τ, κ and β, and determine the number of parameters when δ, τ and κ vary freely, where δ is an $r \times m$ matrix, τ is a $(p+r) \times m$ matrix and κ is a $(p-r) \times (p+r)$ matrix.

7. Discuss estimation of δ, τ and κ, when β is known.

Solution to exercise 8.2

1. The model is rewritten as

$$\Delta X_t = (\alpha, \Gamma_1) \begin{pmatrix} \beta' X_{t-1} \\ \Delta X_{t-1} \end{pmatrix} + \varepsilon_t,$$

such that multiplication by ζ' gives

$$\zeta'\Delta X_t = \zeta'(\alpha, \Gamma_1) \begin{pmatrix} \beta' X_{t-1} \\ \Delta X_{t-1} \end{pmatrix} + \zeta'\varepsilon_t.$$

For $\zeta'\Delta X_t$ to be a white noise process the relation $\zeta'(\alpha, \Gamma_1) = 0$ must hold, hence (α, Γ_1) has to have reduced rank m, for some $m < p$. Since α is assumed to have rank r, we have the relation $r \leq m < p$. The number of co-feature vectors is then $p - m$. Furthermore, since $\zeta'\alpha = 0$, we have $\zeta = \alpha_\perp\theta$ for some θ.

2. The model is reparametrized as

$$\Delta X_t = \Phi\Psi' \begin{pmatrix} \beta' X_{t-1} \\ \Delta X_{t-1} \end{pmatrix} + \varepsilon_t. \tag{2}$$

If $\zeta'\Phi = 0$ then $\zeta'\Delta X_t$ is a white noise process, and the common feature vectors are the $p - m$ columns in $\Phi_\perp$, if the rank of Φ is m. Since the hypothesis on common features is a hypothesis on the short-term dynamics

(α, Γ_1) the cointegration vectors are still given by β provided that the conditions of Granger's representation theorem holds.

3. Estimating the parameters in model (2) when β is known is simply a reduced rank regression of ΔX_t on $\begin{pmatrix} \beta' X_{t-1} \\ \Delta X_{t-1} \end{pmatrix}$. Estimation when Φ is known is similar to estimation of the parameters in the standard error correcting model, under linear restrictions on α; see SJ, Chapter 8. So we multiply by $\bar{\Phi}'$ and $\Phi'_\perp$ and get, for $\Psi' = (\Psi'_1, \Psi'_2)$,

$$\begin{aligned} \bar{\Phi}' \Delta X_t &= \Psi'_1 \beta' X_{t-1} + \Psi'_2 \Delta X_{t-1} + \bar{\Phi}' \varepsilon_t \\ \Phi'_\perp \Delta X_t &= \Phi'_\perp \varepsilon_t, \end{aligned} \tag{3}$$

such that

$$\bar{\Phi}' \Delta X_t = \Psi'_1 \beta' X_{t-1} + \Psi'_2 \Delta X_{t-1} + \omega \Phi'_\perp \Delta X_t + \bar{\Phi}' \varepsilon_t - \omega \Phi'_\perp \varepsilon_t, \tag{4}$$

where

$$\omega = \mathrm{Cov}(\bar{\Phi}' \varepsilon_t, \Phi'_\perp \varepsilon_t) \mathrm{Var}(\Phi'_\perp \varepsilon_t)^{-1}.$$

The parameters in (3) and (4) are variation-independent, and the errors are independent, such that the equations can be analysed independently. Equation (3) is easy to estimate by regression, and (4) is estimated by reduced rank regression of $\bar{\Phi}' \Delta X_t$ on X_{t-1} corrected for ΔX_{t-1} and $\Phi'_\perp \Delta X_t$.

If all parameters are unknown, one can apply an algorithm, which in step one estimates $(\alpha, \beta, \Gamma_1)$ unrestricted, in step two estimates Φ and Ψ by a reduced rank regression keeping β fixed, and then in step three estimates β and Ψ keeping Φ fixed, switching between steps two and three until convergence. There is no proof of convergence, but it will probably occur in practice, since each step maximizes the likelihood function for fixed values of the other parameters.

Finally the hypothesis on common features can be tested by comparing the derived maxima. Note that the hypothesis is on the short-run parameters (α, Γ_1) such that the test is an asymptotic χ^2 test.

4. The number of parameters can be determined as follows. For fixed β one can apply Lemma 7.1. For fixed Φ one can rewrite the model as above and then apply Lemma 7.1. But we have to determine the number of parameters when all parameters (Φ, Ψ, β) vary freely.

We note that

$$\Phi \Psi' \begin{pmatrix} \beta' & 0 \\ 0 & I \end{pmatrix} = \Phi \xi \xi^{-1} \Psi' \begin{pmatrix} \beta' & 0 \\ 0 & I \end{pmatrix}$$

for any $m \times m$ matrix ξ of full rank. So by defining

$$\begin{pmatrix} \Phi_1 \\ \Phi_2 \end{pmatrix} = \Phi$$

and choosing $\xi = \Phi_1^{-1}$, we see that there is no loss of generality in assuming $\Phi_1 = I$. Similarly

$$\Phi\Psi' \begin{pmatrix} \beta' & 0 \\ 0 & I \end{pmatrix} = \Phi\Psi' \begin{pmatrix} \rho & 0 \\ 0 & I \end{pmatrix} \begin{pmatrix} \rho^{-1} & 0 \\ 0 & I \end{pmatrix} \begin{pmatrix} \beta' & 0 \\ 0 & I \end{pmatrix}$$

for any $r \times r$ matrix ρ of full rank, such that we can identify

$$\beta = \begin{pmatrix} \beta_1 \\ \beta_2 \end{pmatrix}$$

by choosing $\rho = \beta_1^{-1}$, and assume, again without loss of generality, that $\beta_1 = I$. Hence the number of parameters in the model is equal to the number of parameters in the matrix

$$\begin{pmatrix} I \\ \Phi_2 \end{pmatrix} \Psi' \begin{pmatrix} I & \beta_2' & 0 \\ 0 & 0 & I \end{pmatrix}$$

which is equal to $(p-m)m + m(r+p) + r(p-r)$. The variance matrix Ω has $\frac{1}{2}p(p+1)$ parameters since it is symmetric.

5. From

$$\Delta X_t = \alpha\beta' X_{t-1} + \Gamma_1 \Delta X_{t-1} + \varepsilon_t,$$

we get

$$\beta' X_t = (I + \beta'\alpha, \beta'\Gamma_1) \begin{pmatrix} \beta' X_{t-1} \\ \Delta X_{t-1} \end{pmatrix} + \beta'\varepsilon_t$$

and

$$\beta_\perp' \Delta X_t = \beta_\perp'(\alpha, \Gamma_1) \begin{pmatrix} \beta' X_{t-1} \\ \Delta X_{t-1} \end{pmatrix} + \beta_\perp'\varepsilon_t.$$

If $\eta' X_t$ is white noise, it is stationary. Therefore η has to be a linear combination of the vectors in β, hence $\eta = \beta v$ for some v. From

$$\eta' X_t = v'\beta' X_t = v'(I + \beta'\alpha, \beta'\Gamma_1) \begin{pmatrix} \beta' X_{t-1} \\ \Delta X_{t-1} \end{pmatrix} + v'\beta'\varepsilon_t$$

we see that $\eta' X_t$ is white noise if and only if $v'(I + \beta'\alpha, \beta'\Gamma_1) = 0$. Hence $(I + \beta'\alpha, \beta'\Gamma_1)$ has to have reduced rank, such that it can be written as a product

$$(I + \beta'\alpha, \beta'\Gamma_1) = \delta\tau'.$$

By defining

$$\kappa = \beta_\perp'(\alpha, \Gamma_1)$$

we find the model given in the question.

6. We split the matrices into two parts, $\kappa = (\kappa_1, \kappa_2)$ and $\tau' = (\tau_1', \tau_2')$, and get the equations to determine α and Γ_1,

$$\beta_\perp' \Gamma_1 = \kappa_2, \quad \beta' \Gamma_1 = \delta \tau_2',$$

$$\beta_\perp' \alpha = \kappa_1, \quad I + \beta' \alpha = \delta \tau_1',$$

such that

$$\Gamma_1 = \bar{\beta}_\perp \kappa_2 + \bar{\beta} \delta \tau_2',$$
$$\alpha = \bar{\beta}_\perp \kappa_1 + \bar{\beta}(\delta \tau_1' - I).$$

The number of parameters is found by applying Lemma 7.1 to the matrix $\delta\tau'$, and is $r(r+p) - (r-m)(r+p-m)$ if the matrix $\delta\tau'$ has rank $m < r$. The matrix κ has $(p-r)(p+r)$ parameters.

7. The two equations have correlated errors, since $\text{Cov}(\beta'\varepsilon_t, \beta_\perp'\varepsilon_t) = \beta'\Omega\beta_\perp' \neq 0$. We can apply the usual trick by considering one of the equations given the other. The only question is which equation we want to condition on. We choose the first, and consider the first equation, and the second equation conditioned on the first, and get

$$\beta_\perp' \Delta X_t = (\kappa - \omega\delta\tau') \begin{pmatrix} \beta' X_{t-1} \\ \Delta X_t \end{pmatrix} + \omega \beta' X_t + \beta_\perp' \varepsilon_t - \omega \beta' \varepsilon_t,$$

where the errors are now independent since $\omega = \beta_\perp' \Omega \beta (\beta' \Omega \beta)^{-1}$. Furthermore, the parameters $(\delta, \tau, \Omega_{\beta\beta})$ are variation-independent of the parameters $(\kappa - \omega\delta\tau', \omega, \Omega_{\beta_\perp\beta_\perp.\beta})$. The estimation is performed by applying a reduced rank regression of $\beta' X_t$ on $\begin{pmatrix} \beta' X_{t-1} \\ \Delta X_t \end{pmatrix}$, to determine δ, τ and $\Omega_{\beta\beta}$, and a regression of $\beta_\perp' \Delta X_t$ on $\begin{pmatrix} \beta' X_{t-1} \\ \Delta X_t \end{pmatrix}$ and $\beta' X_t$ to determine κ, ω and $\Omega_{\beta_\perp\beta_\perp.\beta}$. For more information on this model, see Engle and Kozicki (1993).

9

The $I(2)$ Model and a Test for $I(2)$

Chapter 9 is a brief introduction to the analysis of the $I(2)$ model. The chapter contains the definition of the I(2) model as a submodel of the error correction model. We reformulate the error correction model as

$$\Delta^2 X_t = \alpha\beta' X_{t-1} - \Gamma X_{t-1} + \sum_{i=1}^{k-2} \Psi_i \Delta^2 X_{t-i} + \Phi D_t + \varepsilon_t, \qquad (9.2)$$

where $\Psi_i = -\sum_{j=i+1}^{k-1} \Gamma_j$. The $I(2)$ model is then defined by the further reduced rank restriction,

$$\alpha'_\perp \Gamma \beta_\perp = \xi\eta',$$

where ξ and η are $(p-r) \times s$; see Definition 9.1. By deriving a marginal model for $\alpha'_\perp \Delta^2 X_t$ and a conditional model for $\alpha' \Delta^2 X_t$ given $\alpha'_\perp \Delta^2 X_t$ and the past, we can construct a test statistic for the hypothesis that the process is $I(2)$ against the hypothesis that it is $I(1)$. We give two exercises. The first suggests a different parametrization of the $I(2)$ model, which leads to an iterative algorithm for estimating the model by maximum likelihood. The second shows that the concept of multi-cointegration is only possible in an $I(2)$ model. Other problems involving $I(2)$ variables can be found in exercises 3.2, 3.3, 3.4, 4.4, 4.13, 4.14, 7.1, 10.2 and 10.3.

9.1**

The $I(2)$ model is defined as a submodel of the vector autoregressive model with two reduced rank restrictions; see SJ, Definition 9.1. We give here a different parametrization, which has the advantage that the parameters are allowed to vary freely in their domain of definition, thereby making inference via the likelihood function easier. We focus on the model with two lags.

The new parametrization of the $I(2)$ model is

$$\Delta^2 X_t = \alpha(\rho'\tau' X_{t-1} + \psi' \Delta X_{t-1}) + \Omega\alpha_\perp(\alpha'_\perp \Omega \alpha_\perp)^{-1} \kappa' \tau' \Delta X_{t-1} + \varepsilon_t.$$

The parameters, which vary freely, are as follows:

$$\alpha_{p\times r},\ \rho_{(r+s)\times r},\ \tau_{p\times(r+s)},\ \psi_{p\times r},\ \kappa_{(r+s)\times(p-r)},\ \Omega_{p\times p}.$$

1. Find the matrices Π and Γ from the representation (9.2), and show that Π has reduced rank. If α, ρ and τ have full rank, show that the rank of α and $\beta = \tau\rho$ is r and that $\alpha_\perp'\Gamma\beta_\perp$ has reduced rank s, and find expressions for the matrices ξ and η; see (9.4). Show that the coefficient τ reduces the order of the process from 2 to 1, and that $\rho'\tau' X_{t-1} + \psi'\Delta X_{t-1}$ is stationary under the assumption (4.27).

2. In the $I(1)$ model the parameters α and β are not identified, and $\alpha\xi$ and $\beta\xi^{-1\prime}$ give the same probability measure. Show, for the $I(2)$ model, that the parameter transformations

$$(\alpha, \rho, \tau, \psi, \kappa, \alpha_\perp) \mapsto (\alpha\xi, \theta\rho\xi^{-1\prime}, \tau\theta^{-1}, \psi\xi^{-1\prime}, \theta\kappa\nu, \alpha_\perp\nu^{-1})$$

all give the same probability measure, where the matrices $\xi_{r\times r}$, $\theta_{(r+s)\times(r+s)}$ and $\nu_{(p-r)\times(p-r)}$ are square full rank matrices. Note that this yields a number of identification problems when the parameters are estimated.

3. Show that the equations for $\alpha_\perp'\Delta^2 X_t$ and the equation for $\bar{\alpha}'\Delta X_t$ given $\alpha_\perp'\Delta^2 X_t$, X_{t-1} and X_{t-2}, are the following:

$$\alpha_\perp'\Delta^2 X_t = \kappa'\tau'\Delta X_{t-1} + \alpha_\perp'\varepsilon_t, \tag{9.12}$$

$$\bar{\alpha}'\Delta X_t = \omega\alpha_\perp'\Delta^2 X_t + \rho'\tau' X_{t-1} + \psi'\Delta X_{t-1} + \bar{\alpha}'\varepsilon_t - \omega\alpha_\perp'\varepsilon_t, \tag{9.13}$$

where $\omega = \bar{\alpha}'\Omega\alpha_\perp(\alpha_\perp'\Omega\alpha_\perp)^{-1}$.

4. Apply the result in question 3 to show that for fixed α and τ the estimation of ρ, ψ, κ and Ω is a simple regression, and that the maximized likelihood function is given by

$$L_{\max}^{-2/T}(\alpha, \tau) = \frac{|\bar{\alpha}' SS(\Delta^2 X_t | \alpha_\perp'\Delta^2 X_t, \tau' X_{t-1}, \Delta X_{t-1})\bar{\alpha}|}{|\bar{\alpha}'\bar{\alpha}|} \times \frac{|\alpha_\perp' SS(\Delta^2 X_t | \tau'\Delta X_{t-1})\alpha_\perp|}{|\alpha_\perp'\alpha_\perp|},$$

where $SS(\Delta^2 X_t | \tau'\Delta X_{t-1})$ is the normalized product moment of $\Delta^2 X_t$ corrected for $\tau'\Delta X_{t-1}$ and $SS(\Delta^2 X_t | \alpha_\perp'\Delta^2 X_t, \tau' X_{t-1}, \Delta X_{t-1})$ is the normalized product moment of $\Delta^2 X_t$ corrected for $\alpha_\perp'\Delta^2 X_t, \tau' X_{t-1}, \Delta X_{t-1}$.

5. Apply the result to show that for fixed τ the parameter α can be found as a solution to an eigenvalue problem. Finally, for fixed values of $(\alpha, \rho, \Omega, \psi, \kappa)$, the estimator of τ can be found by generalized least squares, and by switching between these steps we can calculate the maximum likelihood estimator. See Johansen (1997) for further details.

Solution to 9.1

1. By comparing coefficients we find

$$\Pi = \alpha\rho'\tau' \text{ and } \Gamma = -\alpha\psi' - \Omega\alpha_\perp(\alpha_\perp'\Omega\alpha_\perp)^{-1}\kappa'\tau'.$$

Since $\beta = \tau\rho$ has dimension $p \times r$ the matrix Π has reduced rank.

If α, ρ and τ have full rank, then β has rank r and $\alpha_\perp$ and $\beta_\perp$ have rank $p - r$. We calculate the matrix

$$\begin{aligned}\alpha'_\perp \Gamma \beta_\perp &= -\kappa' \tau' \beta_\perp = -\kappa'(\bar{\rho}\rho' + \bar{\rho}_\perp \rho'_\perp)\tau'\beta_\perp \\ &= -\kappa'\bar{\rho}\rho'\tau'\beta_\perp - \kappa'\bar{\rho}_\perp\rho'_\perp\tau'\beta_\perp = -\kappa'\bar{\rho}_\perp\rho'_\perp\tau'\beta_\perp,\end{aligned}$$

since $\rho'\tau'\beta_\perp = \beta'\beta_\perp = 0$. Defining $\xi_{(p-r)\times s} = -\kappa'\bar{\rho}_\perp$ and $\eta_{(p-r)\times s} = \beta'_\perp \tau \rho_\perp$, we see that $\alpha'_\perp \Gamma \beta_\perp = \xi\eta'$ has reduced rank s.

Thus we find $\beta_1 = \bar{\beta}_\perp \eta = \bar{\beta}_\perp \beta'_\perp \tau \rho_\perp$ and $\beta = \tau\rho$, such that

$$\mathrm{sp}(\beta, \beta_1) = \mathrm{sp}(\tau\rho, \tau\rho_\perp) = \mathrm{sp}(\tau).$$

Hence $\tau'\Delta X_t$ is stationary and $\beta_2 = \tau_\perp$. Finally we have the stationary polynomial cointegrating relations as given by

$$\begin{aligned}\beta' X_t - \bar{\alpha}'\Gamma\bar{\tau}_\perp\tau'_\perp\Delta X_t &= \rho'\tau' X_t + (\psi' + \bar{\alpha}'\Omega\alpha_\perp(\alpha'_\perp\Omega\alpha_\perp)^{-1}\kappa'\tau')\bar{\tau}_\perp\tau'_\perp\Delta X_t \\ &= \rho'\tau' X_t + \psi'\bar{\tau}_\perp\tau'_\perp\Delta X_t.\end{aligned}$$

Since $\tau'\Delta X_t$ is stationary we also get that $\rho'\tau' X_{t-1} + \psi'\Delta X_{t-1}$ is stationary.

2. The parameters enter the model through the three products

$$\alpha\rho'\tau', \alpha\psi', \Omega\alpha_\perp(\alpha'_\perp\Omega\alpha_\perp)^{-1}\kappa'\tau',$$

which are seen to be invariant under the parameter transformations, thus leaving the density the same.

3. This follows easily by multiplication by $\bar{\alpha}'$ and $\alpha'_\perp$. Notice that the model looks a lot simpler in this formulation, which is the reason for choosing it.

4. The errors in equation (9.12) and equation (9.13) are independent and the parameters ω, ρ, ψ and $\Omega_{\alpha\alpha.\alpha_\perp}$ enter only in (9.13), whereas the parameters κ and $\Omega_{\alpha_\perp\alpha_\perp}$ enter only in (9.12). The estimates of the variances are

$$\begin{aligned}\hat{\Omega}_{\alpha\alpha.\alpha_\perp} &= \bar{\alpha}' SS(\Delta^2 X_t | \alpha'_\perp \Delta^2 X_t, \tau' X_{t-1}, \Delta X_{t-1})\bar{\alpha}, \\ \hat{\Omega}_{\alpha_\perp\alpha_\perp} &= \alpha'_\perp SS(\Delta^2 X_t | \tau'\Delta X_{t-1})\alpha_\perp.\end{aligned}$$

This gives the desired expression for the maximized likelihood function, remembering the Jacobian $(|\bar{\alpha}'\bar{\alpha}||\alpha'_\perp\alpha_\perp|)^{-1}$.

5. From SJ, p. 130, we have the identity

$$\begin{aligned}&|\alpha'_\perp SS(\Delta^2 X_t | \tau' X_{t-1}, \Delta X_{t-1})\alpha_\perp| \\ &\times |\bar{\alpha}' SS(\Delta^2 X_t | \alpha'_\perp\Delta^2 X_t, \tau' X_{t-1}, \Delta X_{t-1})\bar{\alpha}| \\ &= |\bar{\alpha}'\bar{\alpha}||\alpha'_\perp\alpha_\perp| \, |SS(\Delta^2 X_t | \tau' X_{t-1}, \Delta X_{t-1})|,\end{aligned}$$

which shows that

$$\begin{aligned} &L_{\max}^{-2/T}(\alpha,\tau) \\ &= \left|SS(\Delta^2 X_t|\tau' X_{t-1}, \Delta X_{t-1})\right| \frac{|\alpha_\perp' SS(\Delta^2 X_t|\tau'\Delta X_{t-1})\alpha_\perp|}{|\alpha_\perp' SS(\Delta^2 X_t|\tau' X_{t-1}, \Delta X_{t-1})\alpha_\perp|}. \end{aligned}$$

Minimizing this expression is possible by solving the eigenvalue problem

$$\left|\lambda SS(\Delta^2 X_t|\tau' X_{t-1}, \Delta X_{t-1}) - SS(\Delta^2 X_t|\tau'\Delta X_{t-1})\right| = 0,$$

for eigenvalues $\hat{\lambda}_1 > \cdots > \hat{\lambda}_p$ and eigenvectors $V = (v_1, \ldots, v_p)$. The solution is then given by the eigenvectors $\hat{\alpha}_\perp = (v_{r+1}, \ldots, v_p)$.

9.2

Let X_t be an $I(1)$ process satisfying the usual model

$$\Delta X_t = \alpha\beta' X_{t-1} + \sum_{i=1}^{k-1} \Gamma_i \Delta X_{t-i} + \varepsilon_t,$$

such that $\alpha_\perp' \Gamma \beta_\perp$ has full rank. Granger's representation theorem shows that

$$X_t = C\sum_{i=1}^{t} \varepsilon_i + Y_t + A,$$

where A depends on initial conditions, such that $\beta' A = 0$ and Y_t is stationary.

1. Show that $Z_t = \sum_{i=1}^t \beta' X_i$ is an $I(1)$ process and find the coefficient matrix for the random walk in its Granger representation.

2. Show that there are no coefficients γ and $\delta \neq 0$ such that

$$\gamma' X_t + \delta' \sum_{i=1}^{t} \beta' X_i$$

is stationary. This shows that we cannot have cointegration between the cumulated disequilibrium errors and the process itself as long as the process is generated by the autoregressive model.

3. Finally assume that the process no longer satisfies the autoregressive model for $I(1)$ variables but that $W_t = \sum_{i=1}^t X_i$ is generated by the autoregressive model for $I(2)$ variables. Show that in this case we can have cointegration between the cumulated disequilibrium errors $\sum_{i=1}^t \beta' X_{i-1}$ and the process X_t.

Solution to 9.2

1. Let the functions $C(L)$ and $C^*(L)$ be given by

$$Y_t = C(L)\varepsilon_t = C(1)\varepsilon_t + C^*(L)\Delta\varepsilon_t.$$

It follows that

$$Z_t = \sum_{i=1}^{t} \beta' X_i = \sum_{i=1}^{t} \beta' Y_i = \beta' C(1) \sum_{i=1}^{t} \varepsilon_t + C^*(L)(\varepsilon_t - \varepsilon_0).$$

We want to find the matrix $\beta' C(1)$ and show that it is non-zero, such that Z_t is $I(1)$. We therefore insert the expression for $\beta' Y_t = \beta' X_t$ and ΔX_t in the equation for X_t:

$$\begin{aligned} \Delta X_t &= (C + C(1)\Delta + C^*(L)\Delta^2)\varepsilon_t \\ &= \alpha(\beta' C(1) L + \beta' C^*(L) L \Delta)\varepsilon_t \\ &\quad + \sum_{i=1}^{k-1} \Gamma_i (C L^i + C(1) L^i \Delta + C^*(L) L^i \Delta^2)\varepsilon_t + \varepsilon_t. \end{aligned}$$

The coefficients on the levels of ε_t have to match, so we get

$$C = \alpha\beta' C(1) + \sum_{i=1}^{k-1} \Gamma_i C + I$$

or

$$\Gamma C - I = \alpha\beta' C(1),$$

which shows that

$$\beta' C(1) = \bar{\alpha}'(\Gamma C - I) \neq 0.$$

This shows that the process Z_t is $I(1)$.

2. Next assume that there exist coefficients δ and γ such that

$$\gamma' X_t + \delta' \beta' \sum_{i=1}^{t} X_i$$

is stationary. Inserting the random walk part of the processes which we have just found, we get that the following identity should hold:

$$\gamma' C + \delta' \bar{\alpha}'(\Gamma C - I) = 0.$$

Multiplying from the right by α, and using that $C\alpha = 0$, we get that $\delta = 0$.

3. Let W_t satisfy the $I(2)$ model with two lags; see exercise 9.1,

$$\Delta^2 W_t = \alpha(\rho'\tau' W_{t-1} + \psi'\Delta W_{t-1}) + \Omega\alpha_\perp(\alpha_\perp'\Omega\alpha_\perp)^{-1}\kappa'\tau'\Delta W_{t-1} + \varepsilon_t.$$

We find the equation for the process $X_t = \Delta W_t$ and let $\beta = \tau\rho$:

$$\Delta X_t = \alpha\left(\sum_{i=1}^{t-1}\beta' X_i + \psi' X_{t-1}\right) + \Omega\alpha_\perp(\alpha_\perp'\Omega\alpha_\perp)^{-1}\kappa'\tau' X_{t-1} + \varepsilon_t.$$

In this model we have not only the error correction term $\kappa'\tau' X_{t-1}$ but also an integral correction term $\alpha\sum_{i=1}^{t-1}\beta' X_i$. Since, under the I(2) assumption, we have that

$$\rho'\tau' W_{t-1} + \psi'\Delta W_{t-1} = \sum_{i=1}^{t-1}\beta' X_i + \psi' X_{t-1}$$

is stationary, it follows that in this model for X_t the phenomenon of multicointegration can occur; see Granger and Lee (1989) and Engsted and Johansen (1997).

10

Probability Properties of $I(1)$ Processes

In Chapter 10 we discuss properties of $I(1)$ processes given by the autoregressive equations allowing for a constant term. The basic limit results we need are discussed in Appendix B:

$$T^{-\frac{1}{2}}\sum_{t=1}^{[Tu]}\varepsilon_t \xrightarrow{w} W(u), \tag{B.12}$$

$$T^{-2}\sum_{t=1}^{[Tu]}\left(\sum_{i=1}^{t}\varepsilon_i\right)\left(\sum_{i=1}^{t}\varepsilon_i\right)' \xrightarrow{w} \int_0^1 W(u)W(u)'du, \tag{B.13}$$

$$T^{-1}\sum_{t=1}^{[Tu]}\left(\sum_{i=1}^{t-1}\varepsilon_i\right)\varepsilon_t{}' \xrightarrow{w} \int_0^1 W(dW)', \tag{B.14}$$

where $W(u)$ is a Brownian motion and $\xrightarrow{w}$ denotes weak convergence of the processes. The process X_t is given by Granger's representation theorem as the sum of a trend, a random walk and a stationary process:

$$X_t = C\sum_{i=1}^{t}\varepsilon_i + C\mu t + C(L)(\varepsilon_t + \mu) + A,$$

where $C = \beta_\perp(\alpha'_\perp\Gamma\beta_\perp)^{-1}\alpha'_\perp$, and where A depends on initial conditions and $\beta' A = 0$. We give in Lemma 10.1 some finite sample results on the variances and covariances of the stationary processes ΔX_t and $\beta' X_t$; see also exercises 4.10, 4.11 and 4.12.

The asymptotic properties of X_t are derived in Lemma 10.2 from the Granger representation. The process is dominated by a linear trend $\tau t = C\mu t$, and we see that

$$T^{-1}\bar{\tau}' X_{[Tu]} \xrightarrow{w} u,$$

where $\bar{\tau} = \tau(\tau'\tau)^{-1}$. If we choose the directions β the process $\beta' X_t$ is stationary without a trend, since $\beta' C\mu = 0$. Finally we choose directions γ, such that γ is orthogonal to both τ and β, and find, since the trend is eliminated,

$$T^{-\frac{1}{2}}\bar{\gamma}'X_{[Tu]} \overset{w}{\to} \bar{\gamma}'CW(u).$$

We then derive in Lemma 10.3 the asymptotic properties of the moment matrices S_{11}, S_{10} and S_{00}, applying the limit results in Appendix B. The asymptotic properties of S_{00} follow from the law of large numbers for stationary processes and the properties of S_{11} from the continuous mapping theorem for weak convergence of stochastic processes; see (B.13). Finally the properties of S_{01} involve weak convergence to a stochastic integral, as discussed in Appendix B; see (B.14).

The results obtained in Chapter 10 are applied in Chapters 11 and 13 to study the large sample properties of estimators and tests. The exercises are meant to illustrate the techniques when non-stationary processes are involved. It is a good idea to start with exercise 10.3, which deals with the simple regression estimator.

10.1*

Consider the model

$$\Delta X_t = \Pi X_{t-1} + \Gamma_1 \Delta X_{t-1} + \varepsilon_t, \qquad t = 1, \ldots, T.$$

In Chapter 2 it is mentioned that the likelihood ratio test for $\Gamma_1 = 0$ in the unrestricted vector autoregressive model is asymptotically distributed as χ^2 with p^2 degrees of freedom.

With the notation

$$Z_{0t} = \Delta X_t,\ Z_{1t} = X_{t-1},\ Z_{2t} = \Delta X_{t-1},$$

we define

$$M_{ij} = T^{-1}\sum_{t=1}^{T} Z_{it}Z_{jt}', \qquad i, j = 0,\ 1,\ 2.$$

1. Show that the estimator of Ω is given by

$$\hat{\Omega} = M_{00.12} = M_{00} - \begin{pmatrix} M_{10} \\ M_{20} \end{pmatrix}' \begin{pmatrix} M_{11}\ M_{12} \\ M_{21}\ M_{22} \end{pmatrix}^{-1} \begin{pmatrix} M_{10} \\ M_{20} \end{pmatrix},$$

whereas the estimator under the null hypothesis that $\Gamma_1 = 0$ is given by

$$\hat{\Omega}_0 = M_{00.1} = M_{00} - M_{01}M_{11}^{-1}M_{10}.$$

2. Find an expression for the likelihood ratio test statistic for the null hypothesis that $\Gamma_1 = 0$, in terms of $\hat{\Omega}$ and $\hat{\Omega}_0$.

3. Show that if also $\Pi = 0$ such that the process X_t is a random walk, then $T(\hat{\Omega}_0 - \hat{\Omega})$ has the same limit distribution as $TM_{02}M_{22}^{-1}M_{20}$, which implies that $-2\log Q(\Gamma_1 = 0) \overset{w}{\to} \chi^2(p^2)$. Hence the asymptotic distribution does not depend on the presence of $I(1)$ variables in this case.

Solution to exercise 10.1

1. In the unrestricted model

$$\Delta X_t = \Pi X_{t-1} + \Gamma_1 \Delta X_{t-1} + \varepsilon_t,$$

the parameters can be estimated by regressing ΔX_t on X_{t-1} and ΔX_{t-1}. So we apply formulae (2.10) and (2.11), which give

$$\begin{aligned}(\hat{\Pi}, \hat{\Gamma}_1) &= \left(T^{-1}\sum_{i=1}^{T} \Delta X_t (X'_{t-1}, \Delta X'_{t-1})\right) \\ &\quad \times \left(T^{-1}\sum_{i=1}^{T} \begin{pmatrix} X_{t-1} \\ \Delta X_{t-1}\end{pmatrix} (X'_{t-1}, \Delta X'_{t-1})\right)^{-1} \\ &= (M_{01}, M_{02}) \begin{pmatrix} M_{11} & M_{12} \\ M_{21} & M_{22}\end{pmatrix}^{-1}\end{aligned}$$

and

$$\hat{\Omega} = M_{00.12} = M_{00} - (M_{01}, M_{02}) \begin{pmatrix} M_{11} & M_{12} \\ M_{21} & M_{22}\end{pmatrix}^{-1} \begin{pmatrix} M_{10} \\ M_{20}\end{pmatrix}.$$

Applying the same formula in the case where $\Gamma_1 = 0$, we find

$$\begin{aligned}\hat{\Pi}_0 &= M_{01} M_{11}^{-1} \\ \hat{\Omega}_0 &= M_{00.1} = M_{00} - M_{01} M_{11}^{-1} M_{10}.\end{aligned}$$

2. The likelihood ratio test is given by

$$-2\log Q = -2\log \frac{L_{\max}(\Pi, \Omega)}{L_{\max}(\Pi, \Gamma_1, \Omega)} = -2\log \frac{|\hat{\Omega}_0|^{-T/2}}{|\hat{\Omega}|^{-T/2}} = T \log \frac{|\hat{\Omega}_0|}{|\hat{\Omega}|}.$$

3. The moment matrix $M_{00.12}$ can be rewritten as

$$M_{00.12} = M_{00.1} - M_{02.1} M_{22.1}^{-1} M_{20.1},$$

where

$$M_{ij.k} = M_{ij} - M_{ik} M_{kk}^{-1} M_{kj},$$

such that

$$\hat{\Omega}_0 - \hat{\Omega} = M_{02.1} M_{22.1}^{-1} M_{20.1}.$$

We now investigate the moment matrices when $\Pi = 0$, that is, when X_t is a random walk. We find

$$M_{01} = T^{-1} \sum_{t=1}^{T} \varepsilon_t \sum_{i=1}^{t-1} \varepsilon'_i \in O_P(1),$$

$$M_{11} = T^{-1}\sum_{t=1}^{T}\sum_{i=1}^{t-1}\varepsilon_i\sum_{i=1}^{t-1}\varepsilon_i' \in O_P(T),$$

$$M_{12} = T^{-1}\sum_{t=1}^{T}\sum_{i=1}^{t-1}\varepsilon_i\varepsilon_{t-1}' \in O_P(1),$$

and similarly M_{00}, M_{01}, M_{02}, $M_{22} \in O_p(1)$.

Thus

$$\begin{aligned}
M_{00.1} - M_{00} &= -M_{01}M_{11}^{-1}M_{10} \in O_p(T^{-1}),\\
M_{02.1} - M_{02} &= -M_{01}M_{11}^{-1}M_{12} \in O_p(T^{-1}),\\
M_{22.1} - M_{22} &= -M_{21}M_{11}^{-1}M_{12} \in O_p(T^{-1}).
\end{aligned}$$

Since

$$\hat{\Omega}_0 - \hat{\Omega} = M_{02.1}M_{22.1}^{-1}M_{20.1} = M_{02}M_{22}^{-1}M_{20} + O_P(T^{-1}),$$

we find that $T^{\frac{1}{2}}(\hat{\Omega}_0 - \hat{\Omega})$ has the same limit distribution as $T^{\frac{1}{2}}M_{02}M_{22}^{-1}M_{20}$.

In order to find the asymptotic distribution of $-2\log Q$, we apply the expansion in Lemma A.8 in the form

$$\log(|I+h|) = tr(h) + O(|h|^2),$$

and find

$$\begin{aligned}
\log\frac{|\hat{\Omega}_0|}{|\hat{\Omega}|} &= \log|I + \hat{\Omega}^{-1}(\hat{\Omega}_0 - \hat{\Omega})|\\
&= tr\{\hat{\Omega}^{-1}(\hat{\Omega}_0 - \hat{\Omega})\} + O_P(|\hat{\Omega}^{-1}(\hat{\Omega}_0 - \hat{\Omega})|^2)\\
&= tr\{\hat{\Omega}^{-1}(\hat{\Omega}_0 - \hat{\Omega})\} + O_P(T^{-1}),
\end{aligned}$$

which shows that $-2\log Q$ has the same limit as $Ttr\{\hat{\Omega}^{-1}(\hat{\Omega}_0 - \hat{\Omega})\}$. The law of large numbers implies that $\hat{\Omega} \xrightarrow{P} \Omega$ and that $M_{22} \xrightarrow{P} \Omega$, and the central limit theorem shows that $T^{\frac{1}{2}}M_{02} \xrightarrow{w} N(0, \Omega\otimes\Omega)$, thus

$$\begin{aligned}
-2\log Q &\simeq tr\{\hat{\Omega}^{-1}(T^{\frac{1}{2}}M_{02})M_{22}^{-1}(T^{\frac{1}{2}}M_{20})\}\\
&\xrightarrow{w} tr\{\Omega^{-1}N(0,\Omega\otimes\Omega)\Omega^{-1}N(0,\Omega\otimes\Omega)\}\\
&= tr\{N(0, I\otimes I)N(0, I\otimes I)\}\\
&= \chi^2(p^2).
\end{aligned}$$

Thus even though the process X_t is non-stationary, the usual inference applies for testing hypotheses on the coefficients of ΔX_{t-1}; see Stock and Watson (1988).

10.2

Let the $I(2)$ process X_t be given as a cumulated random walk

$$X_t = \sum_{i=1}^{t} \sum_{j=1}^{i} \varepsilon_j,$$

where, as usual, the ε are i.i.d. with mean zero and finite variance. Consider the mapping from $C[0,1]$ to $C[0,1]$ given by associating to every continuous function f its integral $F(\cdot) = \int_0^{\cdot} f(u)du$.

1. Prove by the continuous mapping theorem applied to this functional that

$$T^{-\frac{3}{2}} X_{[Tu]} \xrightarrow{w} \int_0^u W(s)ds.$$

2. Use the result in question 1 to show that

$$T^{-4} \sum_{t=1}^{T} X_t X_t' \xrightarrow{w} \int_0^1 \left(\int_0^u W(s)ds \right) \left(\int_0^u W(s)'ds \right) du.$$

Solution to exercise 10.2

1. We first show that the mapping from $C(0,1)$ to $C(0,1)$ defined by F is continuous in the uniform topology. Thus for any two continuous functions x_1 and x_2 we evaluate

$$\begin{aligned} |F(x_1) - F(x_2)| &= \sup_u \left| \int_0^u (x_1(s) - x_2(s))ds \right| \\ &\leq \sup_s |x_1(s) - x_2(s)| = |x_1 - x_2|. \end{aligned}$$

This shows that if $x_n \to x$ uniformly, then also $F(x_n) \to F(x)$ uniformly and hence that F is continuous. In the rest of the exercise we work on $D(0,1)$ because some of the calculations are easier on this space.

We define the processes $Y_T(\cdot)$ and $W(\cdot)$ by

$$Y_T(s) = T^{-\frac{1}{2}} \sum_{j=1}^{[Ts]} \varepsilon_j \xrightarrow{w} W(s),$$

where $\xrightarrow{w}$ indicates weak convergence of the processes, not just weak convergence for a particular value of s. Then for $\frac{i}{T} \leq u < \frac{i+1}{T}$ we have $[Tu] = i$ and

$$\int_0^u Y_T(s)ds = T^{-\frac{3}{2}} \sum_{j=1}^{i} \sum_{k=1}^{j} \varepsilon_k - T^{-\frac{1}{2}} \left(\frac{i+1}{T} - u \right) \sum_{k=1}^{i} \varepsilon_k$$
$$= T^{-\frac{3}{2}} X_{[Tu]} - T^{-\frac{1}{2}} \left(\frac{i+1}{T} - u \right) \sum_{k=1}^{i} \varepsilon_k.$$

By the weak convergence of $Y_T(\cdot)$ and the continuous mapping theorem applied to F, we have

$$\int_0^u Y_T(s)ds \xrightarrow{w} \int_0^u W(s)ds,$$

as processes. Hence weak convergence of $T^{-\frac{3}{2}} X_{[Tu]}$ follows if we can show that the remainder term tends uniformly in u to zero in probability:

$$\left| T^{-\frac{1}{2}} \left(\frac{i+1}{T} - u \right) \sum_{k=1}^{i} \varepsilon_k \right| \leq \frac{1}{T} \sup_{t \leq T} \left| T^{-\frac{1}{2}} \sum_{k=1}^{t} \varepsilon_k \right| = T^{-1} \sup_s |Y_T(s)|.$$

The weak convergence of the process $Y_T(\cdot)$ and the continuity of the mapping $x \to \sup_u |x(u)| = |x|$ show that $\sup_s |Y_T(s)| \xrightarrow{w} \sup_s |W(s)|$ and hence that

$$\frac{1}{T} \sup_s |Y_T(s)| \in O_P(T^{-1}).$$

Combining these results, we find that $T^{-\frac{3}{2}} X_{[Tu]}$ has the same limit as $\int_0^u Y_T(s)ds$, which was to be shown.

2. Let us first show that the mapping defined on $C(0,1)^n$ by $L : x \mapsto \int_0^1 x(u)x'(u)du$ is continuous in the uniform topology. We find, for any two continuous functions x_1 and x_2, that

$$|L(x_1) - L(x_2)| = \left| \int_0^1 x_1 x_1' du - \int_0^1 x_2 x_2' du \right|$$
$$\leq \left| \int_0^1 x_2(x_1 - x_2)' + (x_1 - x_2)x_2' + (x_1 - x_2)(x_1 - x_2)' du \right|$$
$$\leq |x_2|\,|x_1 - x_2| + |x_1 - x_2||x_2| + |x_1 - x_2|^2.$$

This again proves continuity of the mapping L.

Next we define the process

$$U_T(s) = T^{-\frac{3}{2}} X_{[Ts]} = T^{-\frac{3}{2}} \sum_{j=1}^{[Ts]} \sum_{k=1}^{j} \varepsilon_k \xrightarrow{w} \int_0^s W(u)du,$$

and investigate the integral

$$\int_0^1 U_T(s)U_T(s)'ds = \sum_{i=0}^{T-1} \int_{\frac{i}{T}}^{\frac{i+1}{T}} U_T(s)U_T(s)'ds$$
$$= \sum_{i=0}^{T-1} T^{-1}T^{-\frac{3}{2}}X_iT^{-\frac{3}{2}}X_i'$$
$$= T^{-4}\sum_{i=0}^{T-1} X_iX_i'.$$

Finally we apply the continuous mapping theorem to the mapping L and the process $U_T(\cdot)$ and get the result.

10.3

Consider the regression

$$Y_t = \beta' X_t + \varepsilon_t,$$

where $\{\varepsilon_t\}$ is as before, and X_t is a random walk with finite variance which is independent of the ε.

1. Find the limit distribution of the regression estimator for β,

$$\hat{\beta}_{\text{ols}} = \left(\sum_{t=1}^{T} X_tX_t'\right)^{-1}\left(\sum_{t=1}^{T} X_tY_t'\right).$$

2. Solve the same problem if X_t is an $I(2)$ process given as a cumulated random walk, but still independent of the ε.

Solution to exercise 10.3

1. The regression estimator satisfies

$$T(\hat{\beta}_{\text{ols}} - \beta) = \left(T^{-2}\sum_{t=1}^{T} X_tX_t'\right)^{-1} T^{-1}\sum_{t=1}^{T} X_t\varepsilon_t'.$$

Let the random walk X_t be given by the equations

$$\Delta X_t = \delta_t,$$

where δ_t is i.i.d. with mean zero and finite variance. Let us define the processes W_ε and W_δ as the limits

$$T^{-\frac{1}{2}}\sum_{j=1}^{[Tu]} \varepsilon_j \xrightarrow{w} W_\varepsilon(u),$$

$$T^{-\frac{1}{2}}X_{[Tu]} = T^{-\frac{1}{2}}\sum_{j=1}^{[Tu]}\delta_j \xrightarrow{w} W_\delta(u).$$

The continuous mapping theorem, applied to $L : x \mapsto \int_0^1 xx'du$ and the process $T^{-\frac{1}{2}}X_{[Tu]}$, shows that

$$T^{-2}\sum_{t=1}^{T} X_t X_t' \xrightarrow{w} \int_0^1 W_\delta(u)W_\delta(u)'du = \int_0^1 W_\delta W_\delta{}'du.$$

In order to find the limit of the $T^{-1}\sum_{t=1}^{T} X_t\varepsilon_t'$ we have to apply the results on convergence to stochastic integrals. We write the product moment as

$$\begin{aligned} T^{-1}\sum_{t=1}^{T} X_t\varepsilon_t' &= \sum_{t=1}^{T} T^{-\frac{1}{2}}X_t T^{-\frac{1}{2}}\left(\sum_{i=1}^{t}\varepsilon_i - \sum_{i=1}^{t-1}\varepsilon_i\right)' \\ &\xrightarrow{w} \int_0^1 W_\delta(dW_\varepsilon)'; \end{aligned}$$

see Theorem B.13. We write it this way to indicate that the process $T^{-\frac{1}{2}}X_t$ converges and $T^{-\frac{1}{2}}\left(\sum_{i=1}^{t}\varepsilon_i - \sum_{i=1}^{t-1}\varepsilon_i\right)$ is the increment of the process $T^{-\frac{1}{2}}\sum_{i=1}^{t}\varepsilon_i$. Hence

$$T(\hat\beta_{\text{ols}} - \beta) \xrightarrow{w} \left(\int_0^1 W_\delta W_\delta{}'du\right)^{-1}\int_0^1 W_\delta(dW_\varepsilon)',$$

which is mixed Gaussian since we assumed that ε and δ are independent.

2. If X_t is an $I(2)$ process we normalize as follows:

$$T^2(\hat\beta_{\text{ols}} - \beta) = \left(T^{-4}\sum_{t=1}^{T} X_t X_t'\right)^{-1} T^{-2}\sum_{t=1}^{T} X_t\varepsilon_t'.$$

Let X_t be given by the equations

$$\Delta^2 X_t = \delta_t,$$

such that

$$T^{-\frac{3}{2}}X_{[Tu]} \xrightarrow{w} \int_0^u W_\delta(s)ds.$$

The continuous mapping theorem, applied to the mapping $L : x \mapsto \int_0^1 xx'du$ and the process $T^{-\frac{3}{2}}X_{[Tu]}$, implies that

$$T^{-4}\sum_{t=1}^{T} X_t X_t' \xrightarrow{w} \int_0^1 \left(\int_0^s W_\delta(u)du\right)\left(\int_0^s W_\delta(u)'du\right)ds.$$

The other product moment involves a limiting stochastic integral and we apply the results in Theorem B.13 to find

$$T^{-2}\sum_{t=1}^{T} X_t\varepsilon_t' = \sum_{t=1}^{T} T^{-\frac{3}{2}} X_t T^{-\frac{1}{2}}\left(\sum_{i=1}^{t}\varepsilon_i - \sum_{i=1}^{t-1}\varepsilon_i\right)'$$
$$\overset{w}{\to} \int_0^1\left(\int_0^s W_\delta(u)du\right)(dW_\varepsilon)'.$$

Combining these two results, we get the asymptotic distribution of the regression estimator for an $I(2)$ regression as a mixed Gaussian distribution.

Note that in this last case the limit could be found without the limit results for stochastic integrals. This is seen by the partial summation

$$T^{-2}\sum_{t=1}^{T} X_t\varepsilon_t' = \left(T^{-\frac{3}{2}}X_T\right)\left(T^{-\frac{1}{2}}\sum_{t=1}^{T}\varepsilon_t'\right) - T^{-2}\sum_{t=2}^{T}(X_t - X_{t-1})\sum_{i=1}^{t-1}\varepsilon_i'$$
$$= \left(T^{-\frac{3}{2}}X_T\right)\left(T^{-\frac{1}{2}}\sum_{i=1}^{T}\varepsilon_i'\right) - T^{-2}\sum_{t=2}^{T}\left(\sum_{i=1}^{t}\delta_i\right)\left(\sum_{i=1}^{t-1}\varepsilon_i'\right).$$

Now the continuous mapping theorem will imply that

$$T^{-2}\sum_{t=1}^{T} X_t\varepsilon_t' \overset{w}{\to} \int_0^1 W_\delta du W_\varepsilon(1)' - \int_0^1 W_\delta W_\varepsilon' du,$$

which by a partial integration equals the expression we found above.

11

The Asymptotic Distribution of the Test for Cointegrating Rank

The main result here is Theorem 11.1 which gives various forms for the limit distribution for the likelihood ratio test for cointegrating rank. The simplest result is that the test statistic of $H_2(r)$ in $H_2(p)$,

$$-2\log Q(H_2(r)|H_2(p)) = -T\sum_{i=r+1}^{p}\log(1-\hat{\lambda}_i),$$

has a limit distribution of the form

$$-2\log Q(H_2(r)|H_2(p)) \xrightarrow{w} tr\left\{\int_0^1 (dB)B'\left(\int_0^1 BB'du\right)^{-1}\int_0^1 B(dB)'\right\}, \tag{11.9}$$

where B is a standard Brownian motion in $p-r$ dimensions.

Theorem 11.1 contains the various modifications of this result for the models $H_1(r)$ and $H(r)$. The asymptotic tests are not similar since the limit distribution depends on the presence or absence of the trend in the process. Theorem 11.2, however, gives the result for the models $H_1^*(r)$ and $H^*(r)$ where the deterministic term is restricted. It turns that the tests here are asymptotically similar, such that inference is much easier in this case. Finally there is a result concerning the test of restrictions on the deterministic term, which has a standard asymptotic χ^2 distribution, and a discussion of the test for $I(2)$, which can be used as a multivariate test for misspecification of the $I(1)$ model.

The exercises exemplify the techniques in the proofs by asking how they should be modified in some special cases not considered in the book.

11.1**

Consider the model

$$\Delta X_t = \alpha\beta' X_{t-1} + \mu + \varepsilon_t,$$

and the test statistic of the hypothesis $H_1(r)$ in $H_1(p)$; see Chapter 5. In Chapters 10 and 11 the asymptotic properties of X_t, S_{ij} and the test statistic $-2\log Q(H_1(r)|H_1(p))$ were discussed under the assumption that $\text{rank}(\alpha) = \text{rank}(\beta) = r$ and that $\alpha'_\perp \mu \neq 0$. In the following assume that $\alpha'_\perp \mu = 0$.

1. Show that

$$T^{-\frac{1}{2}} \beta'_\perp X_{[Tu]} \xrightarrow{w} \beta'_\perp C W(u).$$

2. Show that

$$T^{-1}\beta'_\perp S_{11}\beta_\perp \xrightarrow{w} \beta'_\perp C \textstyle\int_0^1 (W(u) - \bar{W})(W(u) - \bar{W})' du C'\beta_\perp,$$

$$\beta'_\perp S_{10}\alpha_\perp \xrightarrow{w} \beta'_\perp C \textstyle\int_0^1 (W - \bar{W})(dW)'\alpha_\perp.$$

3. Finally show that

$$-2\log Q(H_1(r)|H_1(p)) \xrightarrow{w} tr\left\{\int_0^1 (dB)F' \left(\int_0^1 FF'du\right)^{-1} \int_0^1 F(dB)'\right\},$$

where $F = B - \bar{B}$.

Solution to exercise 11.1

1. Granger's representation theorem shows that the process has the form

$$X_t = C\sum_{i=1}^{t}(\varepsilon_i + \mu) + C(L)(\varepsilon_t + \mu) + A,$$

where $\beta' A = 0$, $C = \beta_\perp(\alpha'_\perp\beta_\perp)^{-1}\alpha'_\perp$ and A depends on initial conditions. The assumption $\alpha'_\perp\mu = 0$ implies that the trend is absent in the process, such that the stationary process ΔX_t has expectation zero. Multiplication by $T^{-\frac{1}{2}}\beta'_\perp$ gives

$$T^{-\frac{1}{2}}\beta'_\perp X_{[Tu]} = T^{-\frac{1}{2}}\beta'_\perp C\sum_{i=1}^{[Tu]}\varepsilon_i + T^{-\frac{1}{2}}\beta'_\perp C(L)(\varepsilon_{[Tu]} + \mu) + T^{-\frac{1}{2}}\beta'_\perp A.$$

The first term converges to a Brownian motion

$$T^{-\frac{1}{2}}\beta'_\perp C\sum_{i=1}^{[Tu]}\varepsilon_i \xrightarrow{w} \beta'_\perp CW(u).$$

The second term tends to zero in probability, uniformly in u since the process $C(L)\varepsilon_t$ is a linear process (see (B.17)). Finally the third term tends to zero. Thus we have proved the first result.

2. We recall the definitions

$$\bar{X} = T^{-1}\sum_{t=1}^{T} X_{t-1},$$

$$S_{11} = T^{-1}\sum_{t=1}^{T}(X_{t-1} - \bar{X})(X_{t-1} - \bar{X})'.$$

We apply the continuous mapping theorem to the mappings $x \mapsto \int_0^1 x du$ and $x \mapsto \int_0^1 xx' du$ and the process $T^{-\frac{1}{2}}\beta_\perp' X_{[Tu]}$ and find

$$T^{-\frac{1}{2}}\beta_\perp'\bar{X} \overset{w}{\to} \beta_\perp' C \int_0^1 W du = \beta_\perp' C\bar{W}$$

(see (B.18)) and

$$T^{-1}\beta_\perp' S_{11}\beta_\perp \overset{w}{\to} \beta_\perp' C \int_0^1 (W - \bar{W})(W - \bar{W})' du C'\beta_\perp$$

(see (B.19)).

Finally the limit of $\beta_\perp' S_{10}\alpha_\perp$ is given by a stochastic integral,

$$\begin{aligned} \beta_\perp' S_{10}\alpha_\perp &= \sum_{t=1}^{T} T^{-\frac{1}{2}}(X_{t-1} - \bar{X})T^{-\frac{1}{2}}\left(\sum_{i=1}^{t}\varepsilon_i - \sum_{i=1}^{t-1}\varepsilon_i\right)'\alpha_\perp \\ &\overset{w}{\to} \beta_\perp' C \int_0^1 (W - \bar{W})(dW)'\alpha_\perp \end{aligned}$$

(see (B.20)).

3. In order to find the limit distribution of the likelihood ratio test, in the case where there is no trend, we have to mimic the proof in SJ, pp. 158–160. The test is based upon the solutions to the equation

$$|\lambda S_{11} - S_{10}S_{00}^{-1}S_{01}| = 0, \tag{1}$$

and we define the normalization matrix as $A_T = (\beta, T^{-\frac{1}{2}}\beta_\perp)$ since in this case there is no trend to take into account.

We multiply (1) by A_T' and A_T and go to the limit and find (11.16) and (11.20) with

$$G = \beta_\perp' C(W - \bar{W}),$$

instead of the process defined by (10.12).

We define the standard Brownian motion

$$B = (\beta_\perp' C\Omega C'\beta_\perp)^{-\frac{1}{2}}\beta_\perp' CW,$$

and find from equation (11.20) that the limit of the log likelihood ratio test is given as the sum of the $p-r$ roots in the equation

$$\left|\rho\int_0^1 (B-\bar{B})(B-\bar{B})'du - \int_0^1 (B-\bar{B})(dB)'\int_0^1 (dB)(B-\bar{B})'\right| = 0,$$

hence

$$-2\log Q(H_1(r)|H_1(p)) \xrightarrow{w} tr\left\{\int_0^1 (dB)F'\left(\int_0^1 FF'du\right)^{-1}\int_0^1 F(dB)'\right\},$$

where $F = B - \bar{B}$.

This is therefore the limit distribution of the test statistic that allows an unrestricted constant in the model equations when in fact the trend is absent. The result shows that we get two limit distributions under the null hypothesis. One is given in (11.12) if in fact the trend is present, that is $\alpha_\perp' \neq 0$, and the other is found above. The limit distribution has the usual form, only F is changed and reflects the properties of the process $X_t - \bar{X}$. Simulations show that the tails of this distribution are thicker than the distribution derived when the trend is present.

The next exercise deals with the situation where we assume from the outset that the model equations do not allow a trend. This restriction clearly changes the test statistic, and in exercise 11.2 we want to find the limit distribution of this different statistic.

11.2**

Consider the model

$$\Delta X_t = \alpha\beta' X_{t-1} + \alpha\rho + \varepsilon_t,$$

and the test statistic of the hypothesis $H_1^*(r)$ in $H_1^*(p)$; see Chapter 5.

Assume again that $\text{rank}(\alpha) = \text{rank}(\beta) = r$.

1. Show that

$$T^{-\frac{1}{2}}\beta_\perp' X_{[Tu]} \xrightarrow{w} \beta_\perp' CW(u).$$

2. Show that if $\bar{X} = T^{-1}\sum_{t=1}^T X_{t-1}$ and $\bar{\Delta X} = T^{-1}\sum_{t=1}^T \Delta X_t$, then

$$S_{11}^* = \begin{pmatrix} S_{xx} & \bar{X} \\ \bar{X}' & 1 \end{pmatrix} \text{ and } S_{10}^* = \begin{pmatrix} S_{x0} \\ \bar{\Delta X}' \end{pmatrix}.$$

Hence

$$T^{-1}\begin{pmatrix}\beta_\perp & 0\\ 0 & T^{\frac{1}{2}}\end{pmatrix}' S_{11}^{*}\begin{pmatrix}\beta_\perp & 0\\ 0 & T^{\frac{1}{2}}\end{pmatrix}$$

$$\xrightarrow{w}\begin{pmatrix}\beta_\perp' C\int_0^1 WW'duC'\beta_\perp & \beta_\perp' C\int_0^1 W(u)du\\ \int_0^1 W(u)'duC'\beta_\perp & 1\end{pmatrix},$$

and

$$\begin{pmatrix}\beta_\perp & 0\\ 0 & T^{\frac{1}{2}}\end{pmatrix}' S_{10}^{*}\alpha_\perp \xrightarrow{w}\begin{pmatrix}\beta_\perp' C\int_0^1 W(dW)'\alpha_\perp\\ \int_0^1 (dW)'\alpha_\perp\end{pmatrix}.$$

3. Finally show that

$$-2\log Q\left(H_1^*(r)|H_1^*(p)\right)\xrightarrow{w} tr\left\{\int_0^1 (dB)F'\left(\int_0^1 FF'du\right)^{-1}\int_0^1 F(dB)'\right\},$$

where $F' = (B', 1)$.

Solution to exercise 11.2

1. Granger's representation theorem shows that the process has the form

$$\begin{aligned} X_t &= C\sum_{i=1}^{t}(\varepsilon_i+\alpha\rho)+C(L)(\varepsilon_t+\alpha\rho)+A\\ &= C\sum_{i=1}^{t}\varepsilon_i+C(L)(\varepsilon_t+\alpha\rho)+A, \end{aligned}$$

where $\beta' A = 0$, $C = \beta_\perp(\alpha_\perp'\beta_\perp)^{-1}\alpha_\perp'$ and A depends on initial conditions. Again the assumption $\mu = \alpha\rho$ implies that the trend is absent in the process, such that ΔX_t has expectation zero. This time the assumption changes the test statistic which involves a reduced rank regression of ΔX_t on $X_t^* = (X_{t-1}', 1)'$ corrected for the remaining regressors. Multiplication by $T^{-\frac{1}{2}}\beta_\perp'$ gives

$$T^{-\frac{1}{2}}\beta_\perp' X_{[Tu]} = T^{-\frac{1}{2}}\beta_\perp' C\sum_{i=1}^{[Tu]}\varepsilon_i + T^{-\frac{1}{2}}\beta_\perp' C(L)(\varepsilon_{[Tu]}+\alpha\rho)+T^{-\frac{1}{2}}\beta_\perp' A.$$

This converges towards the Brownian motion $\beta_\perp' CW(u)$, just as in the solution to exercise 11.1.

2. In section 6.2 the moment matrices are found to be

$$S_{11}^* = T^{-1}\sum_{t=1}^{T}\begin{pmatrix} X_{t-1} \\ 1 \end{pmatrix}\begin{pmatrix} X_{t-1} \\ 1 \end{pmatrix}'$$
$$= \begin{pmatrix} T^{-1}\sum_{t=1}^{T} X_{t-1}X_{t-1}' & T^{-1}\sum_{t=1}^{T} X_{t-1} \\ T^{-1}\sum_{t=1}^{T} X_{t-1}' & T^{-1}\sum_{t=1}^{T} 1 \end{pmatrix} = \begin{pmatrix} S_{xx} & \bar{X} \\ \bar{X}' & 1 \end{pmatrix}.$$

$$S_{10}^* = T^{-1}\sum_{t=1}^{T}\begin{pmatrix} X_{t-1} \\ 1 \end{pmatrix}\Delta X_t' = \begin{pmatrix} T^{-1}\sum_{t=1}^{T} X_{t-1}\Delta X_t' \\ T^{-1}\sum_{t=1}^{T} \Delta X_t' \end{pmatrix} = \begin{pmatrix} S_{x0} \\ \bar{\Delta X}' \end{pmatrix}.$$

The continuous mapping theorem gives the weak convergence of the product moments expressed as

$$T^{-1}\begin{pmatrix} \beta_\perp & 0 \\ 0 & T^{\frac{1}{2}} \end{pmatrix}' S_{11}^* \begin{pmatrix} \beta_\perp & 0 \\ 0 & T^{\frac{1}{2}} \end{pmatrix} \overset{w}{\to} \begin{pmatrix} \beta_\perp' C\int_0^1 WW'duC'\beta_\perp & \beta_\perp' C\int_0^1 Wdu \\ \int_0^1 W'duC'\beta_\perp & 1 \end{pmatrix},$$

which can also be expressed as

$$T^{-1}\begin{pmatrix} \beta_\perp & 0 \\ 0 & T^{\frac{1}{2}} \end{pmatrix}' S_{11}^* \begin{pmatrix} \beta_\perp & 0 \\ 0 & T^{\frac{1}{2}} \end{pmatrix} \overset{w}{\to} \int_0^1 GG'du,$$

with

$$G(u) = \begin{pmatrix} \beta_\perp' CW(u) \\ 1 \end{pmatrix}.$$

The other limit involves a stochastic integral:

$$\begin{pmatrix} \beta_\perp & 0 \\ 0 & T^{\frac{1}{2}} \end{pmatrix}' S_{10}^*\alpha_\perp = \begin{pmatrix} T^{-1}\sum_{t=1}^{T}\beta_\perp' X_{t-1}\Delta X_t'\alpha_\perp \\ T^{-\frac{1}{2}}\sum_{t=1}^{T}\Delta X_t'\alpha_\perp \end{pmatrix}$$
$$= \begin{pmatrix} T^{-1}\sum_{t=1}^{T} T^{-\frac{1}{2}}\beta_\perp' X_{t-1}T^{-\frac{1}{2}}(\sum_{i=1}^{t}\varepsilon_i - \sum_{i=1}^{t-1}\varepsilon_i)'\alpha_\perp \\ T^{-\frac{1}{2}}\sum_{t=1}^{T}\varepsilon_t'\alpha_\perp \end{pmatrix}$$
$$\overset{w}{\to} \begin{pmatrix} \beta_\perp' C\int_0^1 W(dW)'\alpha_\perp \\ W(1)'\alpha_\perp \end{pmatrix}$$
$$= \begin{pmatrix} \beta_\perp' C\int_0^1 W(dW)'\alpha_\perp \\ \int_0^1 (dW)'\alpha_\perp \end{pmatrix} = \int_0^1 G(dW)'\alpha_\perp.$$

3. The test statistic $Q(H_1^*(r)|H_1^*(p))$ is derived from the solutions to the equation

$$|\lambda S_{11}^* - S_{10}^* S_{00}^{*-1} S_{01}^*| = 0.$$

The proof of the result on the asymptotic distribution follows the same idea as that given in SJ, and applied in the solution to exercise 11.1. We introduce the normalization matrix

$$A_T = \begin{pmatrix} \beta\, T^{-\frac{1}{2}}\beta_\perp\, 0 \\ 0 \quad 0 \quad 1 \end{pmatrix},$$

and find again that equations (11.16) and (11.20) hold, but this time with the definition of the function G given above. The limit distribution of the test statistic is then given by the sum of the $p - r + 1$ roots of equation (11.20). Note that the smallest is zero. We introduce the normalized Brownian motion as before by

$$B = (\beta_\perp' C \Omega C' \beta_\perp)^{-\frac{1}{2}} \beta_\perp' C W$$

and the process $F' = (B', 1)$. Then the result follows. Note again how F reflects the asymptotic properties of X_t^*.

11.3*

Consider the model

$$\Delta X_t = \alpha\beta' X_{t-1} + \varepsilon_t,$$

and the test statistic of the hypothesis $H_2(r)$ in $H_2(p)$; see Chapter 5.

In Chapters 10 and 11 the asymptotic properties of the test statistic $-2\log Q(H_1(r)|H_1(p))$, X_t and S_{ij} were discussed under the assumption that $\mathrm{rank}(\alpha) = \mathrm{rank}(\beta) = r$. In the following assume that $\mathrm{rank}(\alpha) = \mathrm{rank}(\beta) = 0$.

1. Show that

$$T^{-\frac{1}{2}} X_{[Tu]} \overset{w}{\to} W(u).$$

2. Show that

$$T^{-1} S_{11} \overset{w}{\to} \int_0^1 W(u)W(u)'du,$$

$$S_{10} \overset{w}{\to} \int_0^1 W(dW)'.$$

3. Finally show that

$$-2\log Q(H_2(r)|H_2(p)) \overset{w}{\to} tr_{p-r}\left\{\int_0^1 (dB)B' \left(\int_0^1 BB'du\right)^{-1} \int_0^1 B(dB)'\right\},$$

that is, the sum of the $p - r$ smallest solutions of the equation

$$\left|\lambda \int_0^1 BB'du - \int_0^1 B(dB)' \int_0^1 (dB)B'\right| = 0,$$

where B is p-dimensional Brownian motion.

Solution to exercise 11.3

1. When $\text{rank}(\alpha) = \text{rank}(\beta) = r = 0$, we have that $\beta_\perp = C = I$, such that

$$X_t = \sum_{i=1}^{t} \varepsilon_i + X_0$$

and therefore

$$T^{-\frac{1}{2}} X_{[Tu]} \overset{w}{\to} W(u).$$

2. The continuous mapping theorem implies that

$$T^{-1} S_{11} \overset{w}{\to} \int_0^1 WW' du,$$

and from (B.14) we find

$$S_{10} = \sum_{t=1}^{T} (T^{-\frac{1}{2}} X_{t-1}) T^{\frac{1}{2}} \Delta X_t \overset{w}{\to} \int_0^1 W(dW)'.$$

3. Applying the results found in question 2, and substituting W by $\Omega^{\frac{1}{2}} B$, we have

$$\Omega^{-\frac{1}{2}} \left(T^{-1} S_{11} - S_{10} S_{00}^{-1} S_{01} \right) \Omega^{-\frac{1}{2}} \overset{w}{\to} \int_0^1 BB' du \; - \int_0^1 B(dB)' \int_0^1 (dB)B',$$

from which it immediately follows that the p eigenvalues, normalized by T, of

$$|\rho T^{-1} S_{11} - S_{10} S_{00}^{-1} S_{01}| = 0$$

converge to the p eigenvalues of

$$\left| \rho \int_0^1 BB' du \; - \int_0^1 B(dB)' \int_0^1 (dB)B' \right| = 0.$$

Hence the test statistic has the limit required.

11.4

Consider next the model

$$\Delta X_t = \alpha\beta' X_{t-1} + \mu + \Phi D_t + \varepsilon_t,$$

where D_t are three quarterly dummies, which have been orthogonalized to the constant term, that is, they sum to zero over a year. Consider again the test statistic of the hypothesis $H_1(r)$ in $H_1(p)$ (see Chapter 5), and assume that α and β have full rank r, and that $\alpha'_\perp\mu \neq 0$. Granger's theorem shows that

$$X_t = C\sum_{i=1}^{t}(\varepsilon_i + \mu + \Phi D_i) + C_0(L)(\varepsilon_t + \mu + \Phi D_t) + A,$$

for $C = \beta_\perp(\alpha'_\perp\beta_\perp)^{-1}\alpha'_\perp$. Let $\tau = C\mu \neq 0$ and define the coordinate system $(\beta,\ \gamma,\ \tau)$ which spans $\mathbf{R}^p$. The purpose of this exercise is to show that the seasonal dummies do not matter for the asymptotics, once they have been orthogonalized to the constant.

1. Show that (10.10) and (10.11) hold.
2. Use this to show that Lemma 10.3 holds.
3. Finally show that

$$-2\log Q(H_1(r)|H_1(p)) \xrightarrow{w} tr\left\{\int_0^1(dB)F'\left(\int_0^1 FF'du\right)^{-1}\int_0^1 F(dB)'\right\},$$

where F is given by (11.12), so that the conclusions of Theorem 11.1 hold.

Solution to exercise 11.4

1. Since the seasonal dummies sum to zero over a year the partial sums $\sum_{i=1}^t D_i$ are bounded, such that

$$T^{-\frac{1}{2}}\bar{\gamma}'C\Phi\sum_{i=1}^{t}D_i \text{ and } T^{-1}\bar{\tau}'C\Phi\sum_{i=1}^{t}D_i$$

both tend to zero. This shows that (10.10) and (10.11) hold in this case.

2. From the representation of X_t we find that

$$\Delta X_t = C(\varepsilon_t + \mu + \Phi D_t) + C_0(L)(1-L)(\varepsilon_t + \mu + \Phi D_t),$$

which shows that ΔX_t has a periodic mean. This shows that correcting ΔX_t for the constant and the centred seasonal dummies will give residuals with mean zero. Hence we find that $S_{00} \xrightarrow{P} \Sigma_{00}$, $S_{01}\beta \xrightarrow{P} \Sigma_{0\beta}$, and $\beta' S_{11}\beta \xrightarrow{P} \Sigma_{\beta\beta}$, and the remaining results from Lemma 10.3 follow similarly using the result from question 1.

3. From the fact that Lemma 10.3 holds we can go through the proof in SJ, pp. 158–160, and see that the presence of centred seasonal dummies do not change the limit results.

11.5*

Consider the model $H_2(r)$, where $\Phi D_t = 0$. Show that the asymptotic distribution of the test statistic λ_{max} (see (6.19)), is given as the largest eigenvalue of the matrix

$$\int_0^1 (dB)B' \left(\int_0^1 BB'du \right)^{-1} \int_0^1 B(dB)',$$

where B is a $(p-r)$-dimensional standard Brownian motion.

Solution to exercise 11.5

The test statistic of $H_2(r)$ in $H_2(r+1)$ is given by

$$-2\log Q(H_2(r)|H_2(r+1)) = -T\log(1-\hat{\lambda}_{r+1})$$

(see (6.19)), where the $\hat{\lambda}$ are the solutions to the equation

$$|\lambda S_{11} - S_{10}S_{00}^{-1}S_{01}| = 0.$$

When the true model is $H_2(r)$ and the rank is r, the $p-r$ smallest solutions, that is $(\hat{\lambda}_{r+1}, \dots, \hat{\lambda}_p)$, normalized by T converge to those of the equation

$$\left|\rho \int_0^1 BB'du - \int_0^1 B(dB)' \int_0^1 (dB)B'\right| = 0$$

(see (11.21) with $F = B$), since in this case there is no constant term in the equations.

By (A.14) and (A.15) the solutions are the same as those of the equation

$$\left|\rho I - \int_0^1 (dB)B' \left(\int_0^1 BB'du \right)^{-1} \int_0^1 B(dB)'\right| = 0.$$

Hence the limit distribution of $-T\log(1-\hat{\lambda}_{r+1})$, when $H_2(r)$ holds and the rank is r, is the largest eigenvalue of the matrix as indicated in the question.

12

Determination of Cointegrating Rank

The determination of the cointegrating rank is based upon the trace statistic, and it is shown in Chapter 12 how a procedure adopted from Pantula (1989) serves to produce an estimator of the rank with desirable properties. As an example of the results obtained, consider the model without a constant term $H_2(r)$. Let

$$Q_r = -T \sum_{i=r+1}^{p} \log(1 - \hat{\lambda}_i)$$

be the trace statistic for testing $H_2(r)$ in $H_2(p)$, and let c_{p-r} be the $1 - \delta$ quantile in the limit distribution of Q_r, as given by (11.9),

$$tr\left\{\int_0^1 (dB)F' \left(\int_0^1 FF'du\right)^{-1} \int_0^1 F(dB)'\right\},$$

where $F = B$ is a $(p - r)$-dimensional Brownian motion; see (11.14).

In Theorem 12.2 the size and asymptotic power of the trace test is given. The test that rejects $H_2(r)$ on the set

$$\{Q_0 > c_p, \ldots, Q_r > c_{p-r}\},$$

has asymptotic size δ and asymptotic power 1.

In Theorem 12.3 the tests are used to construct an estimator of the rank $\hat{r}$ by the definition

$$\{\hat{r} = r\} = \{Q_0 > c_p, \ldots, Q_{r-1} > c_{p-r+1}, Q_r \leq c_{p-r}\}.$$

This estimator has the property that it converges to the true value with probability $1 - \delta$. The results are also given for the model $H_1(r)$ with a linear term in Theorems 12.5 and 12.7, if δ is kept fixed. Models with a linear term are briefly discussed in section 12.3 and it is pointed out that rank determination is easier in the models $H_1^*(r)$ and $H^*(r)$, where the deterministic term is restricted.

The exercises show that the same result cannot be obtained for the $\lambda_{\max}$ test (see (6.19)), and that the trace test in the models $H_1^*(r)$ and $H^*(r)$ has a nice invariance property.

12.1*

In (6.19) the test of $H(r)$ in $H(r+1)$ is given. This test statistic is sometimes called the $\lambda_{\max}$ statistic. Discuss its properties with respect to size and power as a procedure for selecting the cointegrating rank.

Solution to exercise 12.1

We discuss the model without deterministic terms. The $\lambda_{\max}$ test is derived as the likelihood ratio test of $H_2(r)$ in $H_2(r+1)$ and the size will be evaluated under the assumption that there are exactly r cointegrating relations.

The limit distribution of

$$Q_r = -2\log Q(H_2(r)|H_2(r+1)) = -T\log(1-\hat{\lambda}_{r+1})$$

is given by the largest eigenvalue of the $(p-r)\times(p-r)$ stochastic matrix

$$\int_0^1 (dB)B' \left(\int_0^1 BB'du\right)^{-1} \int_0^1 B(dB)'; \tag{1}$$

see exercise 11.5.

The distribution of this largest eigenvalue determines the critical values used in the test and makes sure that the asymptotic size of the test is correct.

In order to investigate the power we take a parameter point in $H(r+1)$ which is not in $H(r)$, that is, we assume that there are $r+1$ cointegrating relations. In this case $\lambda_{r+1} > 0$ and hence $-T\log(1-\hat{\lambda}_{r+1}) \to \infty$, which shows that the power of the test tends to 1.

If we want to use the $\lambda_{\max}$ test for an estimation of the unknown r we first check $Q_{p-1} = -T\log(1-\hat{\lambda}_p)$, that is, use the smallest eigenvalue as a test statistic.

We then take $\hat{r} = p$ if Q_{p-1} is rejected, that is, if $Q_{p-1} > c_{p-1}$, where c_{p-r} is defined for some level δ such that

$$P_r(Q_r \geq c_{p-r}) \to \delta.$$

Here P_r is the probability measure when the rank of Π is exactly r. If Q_{p-1} is accepted we investigate Q_{p-2} and choose $\hat{r} = p-1$ if Q_{p-2} is rejected, etc.

Thus

$$\{\hat{r} = k\} = \{Q_{p-1} \leq c_{p-1}, \ldots, Q_k \leq c_k, Q_{k-1} > c_{k-1}\}.$$

If r is the true cointegrating rank one can now calculate the probability of finding the correct value to be

$$P_r\{\hat{r}=r\} = P_r\{Q_{p-1} \leq c_{p-1},\ldots,Q_r \leq c_r, Q_{r-1} > c_{r-1}\}$$

$$\to P_r\{Q_{p-1} \leq c_{p-1},\ldots,Q_r \leq c_r\}$$

since $Q_{r-1} \to \infty$ under P_r. The limit probability is a complicated expression involving all the roots of (1). Thus the rank determination using the $\lambda_{\max}$ test is not as neat at the procedure we get from the trace test, since we cannot control the probability of finding the correct value. We can of course always solve this problem by letting the level $\delta = \delta_T \to 0$, as $T \to \infty$.

12.2

1. Show that the distribution of the likelihood ratio test statistic

$$Q_r^* = -2\log Q(H_1^*(r)|H_1^*(p))$$

does not depend on the parameter ρ_0; see (5.15).

2. Show that the distribution of the likelihood ratio test statistic

$$Q_r^* = -2\log Q(H^*(r)|H^*(p))$$

does not depend on the parameters μ_0 and ρ_1; see (5.13).

Solution to exercise 12.2

1. The test statistic is a function of the solutions to

$$|\lambda S_{11}^* - S_{10}^* S_{00}^{-1} S_{01}^*| = 0,$$

which are identical to the solutions to

$$|A(\lambda S_{11}^* - S_{10}^* S_{00}^{-1} S_{01}^*)A'| = |\lambda A S_{11}^* A' - A S_{10}^* S_{00}^{-1} S_{01}^* A'| = 0$$

for any full rank $(p+1) \times (p+1)$ matrix A. In the model the process has no trend but the parameter ρ_0 appears in the level which is $\tau_0 = C(1)\rho_0$. By choosing

$$A = \begin{pmatrix} I_p & -\tau_0 \\ 0 & 1 \end{pmatrix},$$

we see that we can always remove the mean from X_t by the linear transformation A, since

$$AX_t^* = \begin{pmatrix} X_t - \tau_0 \\ 1 \end{pmatrix}.$$

This shows that the distribution of the test statistic does not involve the value of ρ_0.

2. The process X_t has the form

$$X_t = C \sum_{i=1}^{t} \varepsilon_i + \tau_0 + \tau_1 t + Z_t + A,$$

where μ_0 and ρ_1 enter through the parameters τ_0 and τ_1. By choosing

$$A = \begin{pmatrix} I_p & -\tau_1 \\ 0 & 1 \end{pmatrix}$$

we eliminate the trend from the process by the transformation

$$AX_t^* = \begin{pmatrix} I_p & -\tau_1 \\ 0 & 1 \end{pmatrix} \begin{pmatrix} X_{t-1} \\ t \end{pmatrix} = \begin{pmatrix} X_{t-1} - \tau_1(t-1) - \tau_1 \\ t \end{pmatrix}.$$

Since the calculations involve subtracting the mean of the process, the roots, and hence the test statistic, do not depend on either τ_0 or τ_1.

13

Asymptotic Properties of the Estimators

This chapter starts with a brief discussion of the mixed Gaussian distribution, and a discussion of the normalization of the estimator β. If we write $\beta = (\beta_1', \beta_2')'$ and assume that β_1 has full rank then we can normalize β in the form $\beta' = (I, B)$. We work with a different normalization and normalize the estimated eigenvectors using first the true value $\bar{\beta} = \beta(\beta'\beta)^{-1}$. Thus $\tilde{\beta} = \hat{\beta}(\bar{\beta}'\hat{\beta})^{-1}$. We also work with the normalization on a matrix c with the property that $c'\beta$ full rank. The most important result is given in Lemma 13.2 for $\tilde{\beta}$ and in Theorem 13.3 for $\hat{\beta} = \hat{\beta}_c = \hat{\beta}(c'\hat{\beta})^{-1}$. The asymptotic behaviour is different in different directions given by the matrices β, γ and τ; see the introduction to Chapter 10.

The result is expressed as follows:

$$T(\hat{\beta} - \beta) \xrightarrow{w} (I - \beta c')\bar{\gamma} \left(\int_0^1 G_{1.2} G_{1.2}' \right)^{-1} \int_0^1 G_{1.2} (dV_a)',$$

where

$$G(u) = \begin{pmatrix} \bar{\gamma}' C(W(u) - \bar{W}) \\ u - \frac{1}{2} \end{pmatrix},$$

$$V_\alpha(u) = (\alpha'\Omega^{-1}\alpha)^{-1}\alpha'\Omega^{-1}W(u)$$

and

$$G_{1.2}(u) = G_1(u) - \int_0^1 G_1 G_2' du \left(\int_0^1 G_2 G_2' du \right)^{-1} G_2(u).$$

Since V_α is independent of G, the limit distribution conditional on $G_{1.2}$ is Gaussian with mean zero, that is, the asymptotic distribution of $\hat{\beta}$ is mixed Gaussian. We also give a result on the asymptotic distribution of $\hat{\beta}$ under identifying restrictions, and the steps of the proof are given in exercise 13.7. We give the asymptotic distributions of the other parameters in Theorems 13.5 and 13.6. In particular in Theorem 13.5 we show that the asymptotic distribution of the estimators of the parameters $(\alpha, \Gamma_1, \ldots, \Gamma_{k-1})$ is Gaussian. In Theorem 13.6 we give the asymptotic distribution of the estimator of the constant μ. This distribution is the focus of exercise 13.5. It is a good idea to start with exercises 13.4 and 13.3, where there is not so much notation.

We conclude the chapter with some results on the asymptotic distribution of tests on the cointegrating coefficients. These are all χ^2 distributions.

13.1*

Consider the cointegration model

$$\Delta X_t = a\tau b' X_{t-1} + \varepsilon_t,$$

where a and b are known $p \times r$ matrices of order $r < p$, Ω is a known variance matrix, whereas τ is the unknown parameter, which varies freely in the space of $r \times r$ matrices.

1. Find the maximum likelihood estimator of τ.
2. Find the likelihood ratio test for the hypothesis $\tau = 0$.

Under the null hypothesis X_t is a random walk and we define the Brownian motion W by

$$T^{-\frac{1}{2}} X_{[Tu]} = T^{-\frac{1}{2}} \sum_{t=1}^{[Tu]} \varepsilon_t \xrightarrow{w} W(u).$$

3. Show that under the null hypothesis, $T\hat{\tau}$ will converge weakly towards a stochastic variable Z, and determine Z in terms of W. Find the distribution of Z given $b'W$.

4. Find also the distribution of the likelihood ratio test for the hypothesis $\tau = 0$. Show that when $a'b = 0$, the likelihood ratio test is asymptotically χ^2 distributed with r^2 degrees of freedom, and when $b = \Omega^{-1}a$, the likelihood ratio test is asymptotically distributed as

$$tr \left\{ \int_0^1 (dB) B' \left(\int_0^1 BB' du \right)^{-1} \int_0^1 B (dB)' \right\},$$

where B is an r-dimensional standard Brownian motion.

Solution to exercise 13.1

1. Since a and b are known we can transform the model into the equations

$$\bar{a}'\Delta X_t = \tau b' X_{t-1} + \bar{a}'\varepsilon_t$$
$$a_\perp' \Delta X_t = a_\perp' \varepsilon_t.$$

We replace the first by the conditional model given the second and get

$$\bar{a}'\Delta X_t = \tau(b'X_{t-1}) + \omega(a_\perp' \Delta X_t) + \varepsilon_{aa.a_\perp,t}.$$

Since the parameters in the marginal and conditional model are variation-independent, the estimator of τ and the test for $\tau = 0$ are found from the conditional model, which we concentrate to

$$R_{0t} = \tau R_{1t} + \tilde{\varepsilon}_t,$$

where

$$\begin{aligned} R_{0t} &= \bar{a}'\Delta X_t - M_{aa_\perp} M_{a_\perp a_\perp}^{-1} a_\perp' \Delta X_t, \\ R_{1t} &= b' X_{t-1} - M_{ba_\perp} M_{a_\perp a_\perp}^{-1} a_\perp' \Delta X_t. \end{aligned}$$

The estimator of τ is given by

$$\begin{aligned} \hat{\tau} &= S_{01} S_{11}^{-1} \\ &= (M_{ab} - M_{aa_\perp} M_{a_\perp a_\perp}^{-1} M_{a_\perp b})(M_{bb} - M_{ba_\perp} M_{a_\perp a_\perp}^{-1} M_{a_\perp b})^{-1} \\ &= M_{ab.a_\perp} M_{bb.a_\perp}^{-1}, \end{aligned}$$

where the indices a, b and $a_\perp$ correspond to $\bar{a}'\Delta X_t$, $b'X_{t-1}$ and $a_\perp'\Delta X_t$ respectively.

2. The variance estimator in the conditional model when $\tau = 0$ is given by

$$\hat{\Omega}_{aa.a_\perp} = M_{aa.a_\perp},$$

whereas the variance estimator, if the regressor $b'X_{t-1}$ is also present, is

$$\hat{\Omega}_{aa.a_\perp b} = M_{aa.a_\perp b} = M_{aa.a_\perp} - M_{ab.a_\perp} M_{bb.a_\perp}^{-1} M_{ba.a_\perp},$$

and the likelihood ratio test is therefore given by

$$Q^{-2/T} = \frac{|\hat{\Omega}_{aa.a_\perp}|}{|\hat{\Omega}_{aa.a_\perp b}|}.$$

3. Under the null hypothesis X_t is a random walk which implies

$$\begin{aligned} T^{-1} M_{bb} &\xrightarrow{w} b'(\int_0^1 WW'du)b \\ T^{-1} M_{ba_\perp} M_{a_\perp a_\perp}^{-1} M_{a_\perp b} &\xrightarrow{P} 0 \\ T^{-1} M_{bb.a_\perp} &\xrightarrow{w} b'(\int_0^1 WW'du)b \\ M_{ab} &\xrightarrow{w} \bar{a}'(\int_0^1 (dW)W')b \\ M_{aa_\perp} &\xrightarrow{P} \bar{a}'\Omega a_\perp \end{aligned}$$

$$
\begin{aligned}
M_{a_\perp a_\perp} &\xrightarrow{P} a_\perp' \Omega a_\perp \\
M_{a_\perp b} &\xrightarrow{w} a_\perp' (\int_0^1 (dW)W')b \\
M_{ab.a_\perp} &\xrightarrow{w} \bar{a}' \int_0^1 (dW)W'b - \bar{a}'\Omega a_\perp \left(a_\perp'\Omega a_\perp\right)^{-1} a_\perp' \int_0^1 (dW)W'b \\
&= \left(a'\Omega^{-1}a\right)^{-1} a'\Omega^{-1} \int_0^1 (dW)W'b,
\end{aligned}
$$

where we have used the identity

$$I = \Omega a_\perp \left(a_\perp'\Omega a_\perp\right)^{-1} a_\perp' + a\left(a'\Omega^{-1}a\right)^{-1} a'\Omega^{-1}.$$

Hence we find the limit distribution

$$
\begin{aligned}
T\hat{\tau} &= M_{ab.a_\perp}(T^{-1}M_{bb.a_\perp})^{-1} \\
&\xrightarrow{w} \left(a'\Omega^{-1}a\right)^{-1} a'\Omega^{-1} \int_0^1 (dW)W'b \left(\int_0^1 b'WW'bdu\right)^{-1}.
\end{aligned}
$$

It follows that the distribution of Z depends on the two Brownian motions

$$
\begin{aligned}
W_1 &= a'\Omega^{-1}W, \\
W_2 &= b'W,
\end{aligned}
$$

such that

$$Z = \text{Var}(W_1)^{-1} \int_0^1 (dW_1)W_2' \left(\int_0^1 W_2 W_2' du\right)^{-1}.$$

In general W_1 and W_2 are correlated with

$$\text{Cov}(W_1, W_2) = a'\Omega^{-1}\Omega b = a'b.$$

Thus they are independent if $a'b = 0$, in which case Z is mixed Gaussian. If $b = \Omega^{-1}a$ the two processes are identical and Z has a multivariate unit root distribution.

In general W_1 and W_2 are not independent or identical so we decompose the process W_1 using the identity

$$W_1 = E(W_1|W_2) + (W_1 - E(W_1|W_2))$$

or

$$\begin{aligned}
a'\Omega^{-1}W &= a'b(b'\Omega b)^{-1}b'W + (a'\Omega^{-1}W - a'b(b'\Omega b)^{-1}b'W) \\
&= a'b(b'\Omega b)^{-1}b'W + a'\Omega^{-1}(I - \Omega b(b'\Omega b)^{-1}b')W) \\
&= a'b(b'\Omega b)^{-1}b'W + a'\Omega^{-1}b_\perp(b_\perp'\Omega^{-1}b_\perp)^{-1}b_\perp'\Omega^{-1}W \\
&= a'b(b'\Omega b)^{-1}W_2 + W_{1.2},
\end{aligned}$$

where $W_{1.2}$ and W_2 are independent. The stochastic process Z is decomposed similarly and we find

$$\begin{aligned}
Z = \mathrm{Var}(W_1)^{-1}a'b(b'\Omega b)^{-1} & \int_0^1 (dW_2)W_2' \left(\int_0^1 W_2W_2'du\right)^{-1} \\
+\mathrm{Var}(W_1)^{-1} & \int_0^1 (dW_{1.2})W_2' \left(\int_0^1 W_2W_2'du\right)^{-1}.
\end{aligned}$$

The first term is a unit root distribution and the last one is a mixed Gaussian distribution. Thus, given the process $W_2 = b'W$, the distribution of Z is Gaussian with the first term as its mean, and variance given by

$$\mathrm{Var}(W_1)^{-1}\mathrm{Var}(W_{1.2})\mathrm{Var}(W_1)^{-1} \otimes \left(\int_0^1 W_2W_2'du\right)^{-1}.$$

If $b'a = 0$ the first term is zero and Z is mixed Gaussian, and if $b = \Omega^{-1}a$ we have $W_1 = W_2$ and the distribution of Z is the multivariate unit root distribution.

4. The asymptotic distribution of the likelihood ratio test is found as follows:

$$Q^{-2/T} = \frac{|\hat\Omega_{aa.a_\perp}|}{|\hat\Omega_{aa.a_\perp b}|} = \frac{|M_{aa.a_\perp}|}{|M_{aa.a_\perp} - M_{ab.a_\perp}M_{bb.a_\perp}^{-1}M_{ba.a_\perp}|},$$

which implies that

$$\begin{aligned}
-2\log Q &= -T\log\left|I - M_{aa.a_\perp}^{-1}M_{ab.a_\perp}M_{bb.a_\perp}^{-1}M_{ba.a_\perp}\right| \\
&= tr\{M_{aa.a_\perp}^{-1}M_{ab.a_\perp}(T^{-1}M_{bb.a_\perp})^{-1}M_{ba.a_\perp}\} + o_P(1) \\
&\xrightarrow{w} tr\left\{\mathrm{Var}(W_1)^{-1}\int_0^1 (dW_1)W_2'\left(\int_0^1 W_2W_2'du\right)^{-1}\int_0^1 W_2(dW_1)'\right\}
\end{aligned}$$

We have used the identities

$$\begin{aligned}
M_{aa.a_\perp} \xrightarrow{w} \Omega_{aa.a_\perp} &= \bar a'\Omega\bar a - \bar a'\Omega a_\perp\left(a_\perp'\Omega a_\perp\right)^{-1}a_\perp'\Omega\bar a \\
&= \bar a'\Omega(I - a_\perp\left(a_\perp'\Omega a_\perp\right)^{-1}a_\perp'\Omega)\bar a \\
&= \bar a'\Omega(\Omega^{-1}a(a'\Omega^{-1}a)^{-1}a')\bar a \\
&= (a'\Omega^{-1}a)^{-1} = \mathrm{Var}(W_1)^{-1}.
\end{aligned}$$

It follows from the expression for the limit distribution that we can replace W_1 and W_2 by the standard Brownian motions

$$B_1 = (a'\Omega^{-1}a)^{-\frac{1}{2}}a'\Omega^{-1}W,$$
$$B_2 = (b'\Omega b)^{-\frac{1}{2}}b'W,$$

without changing the distribution. The covariance between these is

$$\mathrm{Cov}(B_1, B_2) = (a'\Omega^{-1}a)^{-\frac{1}{2}}a'b(b'\Omega b)^{-\frac{1}{2}}.$$

In the special case where $b'a = 0$, we find that B_1 and B_2 are independent and the distribution is given by

$$tr\left\{\int_0^1 (dB_1)B_2' \left(\int_0^1 B_2B_2'du\right)^{-1} \int_0^1 B_2(dB_1)'\right\},$$

which is $\chi^2(r^2)$. In the special case where $b = \Omega^{-1}a$, we have $B_1 = B_2$ such that the distribution is given by the expression

$$tr\left\{\int_0^1 (dB)B' \left(\int_0^1 BB'du\right)^{-1} \int_0^1 B(dB)'\right\},$$

where B is an r-dimensional Brownian motion.

13.2

Let, as before,

$$\Delta X_t = \alpha\beta' X_{t-1} + \varepsilon_t.$$

Let $X_t = (X_{1t}', X_{2t}')'$, where the dimension of X_{1t} is m and that of X_{2t} is $p - m$. Let α and Ω be decomposed similarly.

1. Find the distribution $f_{\alpha,\beta,\Omega}(\Delta X_{1t}|\Delta X_{2t}, X_{t-1})$ and find the partial likelihood function

$$L_{part}(\alpha, \beta, \Omega_{11.2}) = \prod_{t=1}^{T} f_{\alpha,\beta,\Omega}(\Delta X_{1t}|\Delta X_{2t}, X_{t-1}). \tag{13.19}$$

2. Show that the partial maximum likelihood estimator of β based on (13.19) is given by reduced rank regression if $r \leq m$, and find those functions of α and Ω that can be estimated. Show that if $\alpha_2 = 0$ one can estimate α_1 and β and then the estimator of β is the maximum likelihood estimator.

3. In the model with $\operatorname{rank}(\Pi) = \operatorname{rank}(\alpha\beta') \leq p$ find the likelihood ratio test for the hypothesis $\Pi = 0$ based upon the partial likelihood function and sketch the proof that the asymptotic distribution of the likelihood ratio test is given by

$$tr\left\{\int_0^1 (dB_1)\, B' \left(\int_0^1 BB'du\right)^{-1} \int_0^1 B\,(dB_1')\right\},$$

where B is a p-dimensional Brownian motion decomposed as $B = (B_1',\ B_2')'$ of dimension m and $p - m$ respectively.

In the above situation inference about β is difficult, and the next questions are attempts to find conditions for inference to be easier.

4. Assume again that α and Ω are known. Show that β can be estimated by regression and find the expression for the estimator of β based upon the partial likelihood function.

5. Show that the asymptotic distribution of $T(\hat{\beta}-\beta)$ is mixed Gaussian, but that the Brownian motions entering the asymptotic expression for the limit distribution are not independent.

6. Show that they are independent if $\alpha_2 = 0$.

Solution to exercise 13.2

1. The conditional distribution is found from the partial model

$$\begin{aligned}\Delta X_{1t} &= \alpha_1\beta' X_{t-1} + \Omega_{12}\Omega_{22}^{-1}(\Delta X_{2t} - \alpha_2\beta' X_{t-1} - \varepsilon_{2t}) + \varepsilon_{1t} \\ &= (\alpha_1 - \omega\alpha_2)\beta' X_{t-1} + \omega\Delta X_{2t} + \varepsilon_{1.2t},\end{aligned} \tag{1}$$

where $\omega = \Omega_{12}\Omega_{22}^{-1}$, such that $f_{\alpha,\beta,\Omega}(\Delta X_{1t}|\Delta X_{2t}, X_{t-1})$ is Gaussian with mean

$$(\alpha_1 - \omega\alpha_2)\beta' X_{t-1} + \omega\Delta X_{2t}$$

and variance

$$\Omega_{11.2} = \Omega_{11} - \Omega_{12}\Omega_{22}^{-1}\Omega_{21}.$$

The partial likelihood function is given by

$$L_{part}(\alpha, \beta, \Omega_{11.2}) = \prod_{t=1}^{T} (2\pi)^{-\frac{m}{2}} |\Omega_{11.2}|^{-\frac{1}{2}} \exp\left\{-\frac{1}{2}\varepsilon_{1.2,t}'\Omega_{11.2}^{-1}\varepsilon_{1.2t}\right\}$$

where $\varepsilon_{1.2t}$ is given by (1).

2. Equation (1) shows that the estimation problem is a reduced rank regression where $(\alpha_1 - \omega\alpha_2)$ is $m \times r$, β is $p \times r$ and ω varies freely in $\mathbf{R}^{m\times(p-m)}$.

The parameters which can be estimated from the partial model are $\alpha_1 - \omega\alpha_2$, β, ω and $\Omega_{11.2}$. Hence functions of these can be estimated. When

$\alpha_2 = 0$ the conditional parameters are $(\alpha_1, \beta, \omega, \Omega_{11.2})$, showing that α_1 and β can be estimated. The only parameter in the marginal model in this case is the variance, Ω_{22}. The parameters in the marginal and conditional model are variation-independent and β and α_1 can be recovered from the conditional parameters. Hence X_{2t} is weakly exogenous for β and α_1 and maximization of the full likelihood function with respect to β is the same as maximization of the partial likelihood function with respect to β. Thus the estimator derived from the full likelihood is the same as the estimator derived from the partial likelihood.

3. The eigenvalue problem to be solved is

$$|\lambda S_{11} - S_{10} S_{00}^{-1} S_{01}| = 0,$$

where

$$S_{ij} = T^{-1} \sum_{t=1}^{T} R_{it} R_{jt}, \qquad i, j = 0, 1,$$

and R_{0t} and R_{1t} are ΔX_{1t} and X_{t-1} corrected for ΔX_{2t}.

Under the null hypothesis X_t is a random walk such that

$$T^{-\frac{1}{2}} X_{[Tu]} \xrightarrow{w} W(u) = \begin{pmatrix} W_1(u) \\ W_2(u) \end{pmatrix}.$$

We define $W_{1.2} = W_1(u) - \Omega_{12}\Omega_{22}^{-1} W_2(u)$, which is independent of $W_2(u)$ and has variance $\Omega_{11.2}$. Note that $W_{1.2}$ is generated by the errors in the conditional model. It then follows that

$$\begin{aligned} S_{00} &\xrightarrow{P} \Omega_{11.2}, \\ S_{10} &\xrightarrow{w} \int_0^1 W (dW_1)', \\ T^{-1} S_{11} &\xrightarrow{w} \int_0^1 W W' du, \end{aligned}$$

and hence

$$-2 \log Q \xrightarrow{w} tr \left\{ \left(\int_0^1 W W' du \right)^{-1} \int_0^1 W (dW_{1.2})' \Omega_{11.2}^{-1} \int_0^1 (dW_{1.2}) W' \right\},$$

which, by the substitutions $B_1 = \Omega_{11.2}^{-\frac{1}{2}} W_{11.2}$, $B_2 = \Omega_{22}^{-\frac{1}{2}} W_2$ and $B = (B_1', B_2')'$ equals

$$tr \left\{ \int_0^1 (dB_1) B' \left(\int_0^1 B B' du \right)^{-1} \int_0^1 B (dB_1)' \right\}.$$

Note how B is the limit of all the common trends in the process X_t, whereas B_1 is the limit of those common trends that are generated by the errors in the conditional model. Thus the limit distribution depends on two indices; see Harbo et al. (1998) for details.

4. The partial model (1) is clearly linear in β. Estimation, however, involves the known variance matrix $\Omega_{11.2}$. Let $\tilde{\alpha} = \alpha_1 - \omega\alpha_2$. The first-order condition is found to be

$$tr\left\{\tilde{\alpha}'\Omega_{11.2}^{-1}\sum_{t=1}^{T}(\Delta X_{1t} - \omega\Delta X_{2t} - \tilde{\alpha}\beta' X_{t-1})X_{t-1}'h\right\} = 0,$$

for all h. This implies that

$$\tilde{\alpha}'\Omega_{11.2}^{-1}\tilde{\alpha}\beta' S_{xx} = \tilde{\alpha}'\Omega_{11.2}^{-1}(I, -\omega)S_{\Delta x}$$

or

$$\hat{\beta} = S_{xx}^{-1}S_{x\Delta}(I, -\omega)'\Omega_{11.2}^{-1}\tilde{\alpha}\left(\tilde{\alpha}'\Omega_{11.2}^{-1}\tilde{\alpha}\right)^{-1},$$

such that

$$\begin{aligned}\hat{\beta} - \beta &= S_{xx}^{-1}S_{x\varepsilon}(I, -\omega)'\Omega_{11.2}^{-1}\tilde{\alpha}\left(\tilde{\alpha}'\Omega_{11.2}^{-1}\tilde{\alpha}\right)^{-1}\\ &= S_{xx}^{-1}S_{x\varepsilon_{1.2}}\Omega_{11.2}^{-1}\tilde{\alpha}\left(\tilde{\alpha}'\Omega_{11.2}^{-1}\tilde{\alpha}\right)^{-1}.\end{aligned}$$

5. We find

$$\begin{aligned}T\bar{\beta}_\perp'(\hat{\beta} - \beta) &= \bar{\beta}_\perp'(T^{\frac{1}{2}}\beta, \beta_\perp)\begin{pmatrix}\beta' S_{xx}\beta & T^{-\frac{1}{2}}\beta' S_{xx}\beta_\perp\\ T^{-\frac{1}{2}}\beta_\perp' S_{xx}\beta & T^{-1}\beta_\perp' S_{xx}\beta_\perp\end{pmatrix}^{-1}\\ &\quad\times\begin{pmatrix}T^{\frac{1}{2}}\beta' S_{x\varepsilon_{1.2}}\\ \beta_\perp' S_{x\varepsilon_{1.2}}\end{pmatrix}\Omega_{11.2}^{-1}\tilde{\alpha}\left(\tilde{\alpha}'\Omega_{11.2}^{-1}\tilde{\alpha}\right)^{-1}\\ &\overset{w}{\rightarrow}(0, I)\begin{pmatrix}\Sigma_{\beta\beta} & 0\\ 0 & \beta_\perp' C\int_0^1 WW'duC'\beta_\perp\end{pmatrix}^{-1}\\ &\quad\times\begin{pmatrix}N(0, \Sigma_{\beta\beta}\otimes\Omega_{11.2})\\ \beta_\perp' C\int_0^1 W(dW_{1.2})'\end{pmatrix}\Omega_{11.2}^{-1}\tilde{\alpha}\left(\tilde{\alpha}'\Omega_{11.2}^{-1}\tilde{\alpha}\right)^{-1}.\end{aligned}$$

This shows that

$$\begin{aligned}T\bar{\beta}_\perp'(\hat{\beta} - \beta) \overset{w}{\rightarrow} &\left(\beta_\perp' C\int_0^1 WW'duC'\beta_\perp\right)^{-1}\\ &\times\beta_\perp' C\int_0^1 W(dW_{1.2})'\Omega_{11.2}^{-1}\tilde{\alpha}\left(\tilde{\alpha}'\Omega_{11.2}^{-1}\tilde{\alpha}\right)^{-1}.\end{aligned}$$

We next introduce the standard Brownian motions

$$F = (\alpha_\perp'\Omega\alpha_\perp)^{-\frac{1}{2}}\alpha_\perp' W$$

$$G = (\tilde{\alpha}'\Omega_{11.2}^{-1}\tilde{\alpha})^{-\frac{1}{2}}\,\tilde{\alpha}'\Omega_{11.2}^{-1}W_{1.2}$$

which have covariance

$$\mathrm{Cov}(F, G) = (\alpha_\perp'\Omega\alpha_\perp)^{-\frac{1}{2}}\alpha_\perp'\Omega(I, -\omega)'\Omega_{11.2}^{-1}\tilde{\alpha}\,(\tilde{\alpha}'\Omega_{11.2}^{-1}\tilde{\alpha})^{-\frac{1}{2}}.$$

By noting that

$$\begin{aligned}\Omega(I, -\omega)'\Omega_{11.2}^{-1} &= \begin{pmatrix}\Omega_{11} & \Omega_{12}\\ \Omega_{21} & \Omega_{22}\end{pmatrix}\begin{pmatrix} I \\ -\Omega_{22}^{-1}\Omega_{21}\end{pmatrix}\Omega_{11.2}^{-1}\\ &= \begin{pmatrix}\Omega_{11.2}\\ 0\end{pmatrix}\Omega_{11.2}^{-1} = \begin{pmatrix} I \\ 0\end{pmatrix},\end{aligned}$$

the covariance simplifies to

$$\mathrm{Cov}(F, G) = (\alpha_\perp'\Omega\alpha_\perp)^{-\frac{1}{2}}\alpha_\perp'\begin{pmatrix}\tilde{\alpha}\\ 0\end{pmatrix}(\tilde{\alpha}'\Omega_{11.2}^{-1}\tilde{\alpha})^{-\frac{1}{2}}.$$

6. If we now assume that $\alpha_2 = 0$, then we see that $\tilde{\alpha} = \alpha_1$ and that

$$\alpha_\perp = \begin{pmatrix}\alpha_{1\perp} & 0\\ 0 & I\end{pmatrix},$$

such that

$$\alpha_\perp'\begin{pmatrix}\tilde{\alpha}\\ 0\end{pmatrix} = \begin{pmatrix}\alpha_{1\perp} & 0\\ 0 & I\end{pmatrix}'\begin{pmatrix}\alpha_1\\ 0\end{pmatrix} = 0,$$

thus the two Brownian motions are independent in this case.

13.3

Consider the usual model

$$\Delta X_t = \alpha\beta' X_{t-1} + \varepsilon_t.$$

1. Find the estimator of α for fixed β and Ω, and find the asymptotic distribution of

$$T^{\frac{1}{2}}(\hat{\alpha}(\beta) - \alpha).$$

2. Find the estimator of β for fixed α and Ω, and find the asymptotic distribution of

$$T\beta_\perp'(\hat{\beta}(\alpha) - \beta).$$

Solution to exercise 13.3

1. For fixed β the maximum likelihood estimator is the usual regression estimator given by

$$\hat{\alpha} = \sum_{t=1}^{T} \Delta X_t X_{t-1}' \beta \left(\beta' \sum_{t=1}^{T} X_{t-1} X_{t-1}' \beta \right)^{-1}$$

which satisfies the equality

$$T^{\frac{1}{2}}(\hat{\alpha} - \alpha) = T^{-\frac{1}{2}} \sum_{t=1}^{T} \varepsilon_t X_{t-1}' \beta \left(T^{-1} \beta' \sum_{t=1}^{T} X_{t-1} X_{t-1}' \beta \right)^{-1}.$$

The process $\beta' X_t$ is stationary such that

$$T^{-1} \beta' \sum_{t=1}^{T} X_{t-1} X_{t-1}' \beta \xrightarrow{P} E(\beta' X_{t-1} X_{t-1}' \beta) = \mathrm{Var}(\beta' X_t) = \Sigma_{\beta\beta}, \qquad (1)$$

which has been found in exercise 4.12.

The process $\varepsilon_t X_{t-1}' \beta$ is a martingale difference sequence and hence

$$T^{-\frac{1}{2}} \sum_{t=1}^{T} \varepsilon_t X_{t-1}' \beta \xrightarrow{w} N(0, \Omega \otimes \Sigma_{\beta\beta})$$

since the average conditional variances satisfies

$$T^{-1} \sum_{t=1}^{T} \mathrm{Var}(\varepsilon_t X_{t-1}' \beta | X_1, \ldots, X_{t-1}) = \Omega \otimes T^{-1} \beta' \sum_{t=1}^{T} X_{t-1} X_{t-1}' \beta$$
$$\xrightarrow{P} \Omega \otimes \Sigma_{\beta\beta};$$

see Theorem B.3. Combining (1) and (2) we find that

$$T^{\frac{1}{2}}(\hat{\alpha} - \alpha) \xrightarrow{w} N(0, \Omega \otimes \Sigma_{\beta\beta}^{-1}).$$

2. The estimator for β can also be found by regression since it is a linear hypothesis on the parameter when α is known. We find it by differentiating the likelihood function.

We find (see SJ, p. 182) that the likelihood equation for determining $\hat{\beta}$ is given by

$$\alpha' \Omega^{-1} \sum_{t=1}^{T} (\Delta X_t - \alpha \beta' X_{t-1}) X_{t-1}' = 0,$$

and hence that

$$\hat{\beta} = \left(\sum_{t=1}^{T} X_{t-1}X'_{t-1}\right)^{-1} \sum_{t=1}^{T} X_{t-1}\Delta X'_t \Omega^{-1}\alpha(\alpha'\Omega^{-1}\alpha)^{-1},$$

such that

$$\begin{aligned}\hat{\beta} - \beta &= \left(\sum_{t=1}^{T} X_{t-1}X'_{t-1}\right)^{-1} \sum_{t=1}^{T} X_{t-1}\varepsilon'_t \Omega^{-1}\alpha(\alpha'\Omega^{-1}\alpha)^{-1} \\ &= S_{11}^{-1} S_{1\varepsilon}\Omega^{-1}\alpha(\alpha'\Omega^{-1}\alpha)^{-1}.\end{aligned}$$

Since $T^{-1}S_{11} \xrightarrow{w} C\int_0^1 WW'duC'$ is singular, where $C = \beta_\perp(\alpha'_\perp\beta_\perp)^{-1}\alpha'_\perp$, we consider instead

$$\begin{aligned}T^{-1}\beta'_\perp S_{11}\beta_\perp &= T^{-2}\sum_{t=1}^{T} \beta'_\perp X_{t-1}X'_{t-1}\beta_\perp \xrightarrow{w} \beta'_\perp C \int_0^1 WW'duC'\beta_\perp, \\ T^{-\frac{3}{2}}\beta' S_{11}\beta_\perp &= T^{-\frac{3}{2}}\sum_{t=1}^{T} \beta' X_{t-1}X'_{t-1}\beta_\perp \xrightarrow{P} 0, \\ \beta' S_{11}\beta &= T^{-1}\sum_{t=1}^{T} \beta' X_{t-1}X'_{t-1}\beta \xrightarrow{P} \Sigma_{\beta\beta},\end{aligned}$$

and therefore formulate the limit as

$$\begin{aligned}&(T^{-\frac{1}{2}}\beta, T^{-1}\beta_\perp)'\sum_{t=1}^{T} X_{t-1}X'_{t-1}(T^{-\frac{1}{2}}\beta, T^{-1}\beta_\perp) \\ &\xrightarrow{w} \begin{pmatrix} \Sigma_{\beta\beta} & 0 \\ 0 & \beta'_\perp C\int_0^1 WW'duC'\beta_\perp \end{pmatrix}.\end{aligned}$$

Thus by normalizing by the matrix $A_T = (T^{-\frac{1}{2}}\beta, T^{-1}\beta_\perp)$ we obtain a non-singular limit.

Since we have the results

$$T^{-\frac{1}{2}}\beta'\sum_{t=1}^{T} X_{t-1}\varepsilon'_t \xrightarrow{w} N(0, \Sigma_{\beta\beta}\otimes\Omega),$$

and

$$T^{-1}\beta'_\perp\sum_{t=1}^{T} X_{t-1}\varepsilon'_t \xrightarrow{w} \beta'_\perp C\int_0^1 W(dW)',$$

we can apply the same normalization to the product moments of ε_t and X_{t-1} to get

$$A'_T S_{1\varepsilon} = (T^{-\frac{1}{2}}\beta, T^{-1}\beta_\perp)'\sum_{t=1}^{T} X_{t-1}\varepsilon'_t \xrightarrow{w} \begin{pmatrix} N(0, \Sigma_{\beta\beta}\otimes\Omega) \\ \beta'_\perp C\int_0^1 W(dW)' \end{pmatrix}.$$

Combining these results, we find

$$\begin{aligned}
&(T^{\frac{1}{2}}\bar{\beta}, T\bar{\beta}_\perp)'(\hat{\beta}-\beta) \\
&= (T^{\frac{1}{2}}\bar{\beta}, T\bar{\beta}_\perp)'A_T\left(A_T'S_{11}A_T\right)^{-1}A_T'S_{1\varepsilon}\Omega^{-1}\alpha(\alpha'\Omega^{-1}\alpha)^{-1} \\
&\xrightarrow{w} \begin{pmatrix}\Sigma_{\beta\beta} & 0 \\ 0 & \beta_\perp'C\int_0^1 WW'duC'\beta_\perp\end{pmatrix}^{-1} \\
&\quad\times\begin{pmatrix}N(0,\Sigma_{\beta\beta}\otimes\Omega) \\ \beta_\perp'C\int_0^1 W(dW)'\end{pmatrix}\Omega^{-1}\alpha(\alpha'\Omega^{-1}\alpha)^{-1}.
\end{aligned}$$

Since we have

$$(T^{\frac{1}{2}}\bar{\beta}, T\bar{\beta}_\perp)'A_T = (T^{\frac{1}{2}}\bar{\beta}, T\bar{\beta}_\perp)'(T^{-\frac{1}{2}}\beta, T^{-1}\beta_\perp) = \begin{pmatrix}I & 0 \\ 0 & I\end{pmatrix},$$

the results can be separated as follows:

$$\begin{aligned}
&T^{\frac{1}{2}}\bar{\beta}'(\hat{\beta}-\beta) \xrightarrow{w} N(0, \Sigma_{\beta\beta}^{-1}\otimes(\alpha'\Omega^{-1}\alpha)^{-1}), \\
&T\bar{\beta}_\perp'(\hat{\beta}-\beta) \xrightarrow{w} \left(\beta_\perp'C\int_0^1 WW'duC'\beta_\perp\right)^{-1} \\
&\qquad\qquad\times\beta_\perp'C\int_0^1 W(dW)'\Omega^{-1}\alpha(\alpha'\Omega^{-1}\alpha)^{-1}.
\end{aligned}$$

Thus the asymptotic distribution of $\hat{\beta}$ has a strange distribution due to the fact that α is assumed known. Some linear combinations of the coefficient are just asymptotically Gaussian but others have the asymptotic mixed Gaussian distribution that is found from the unrestricted reduced rank estimator when α is also estimated.

13.4

In the univariate case the model is given by

$$\Delta X_t = \pi X_{t-1} + \varepsilon_t.$$

1. Show that

$$T^{\frac{1}{2}}(\hat{\pi}-\pi)$$

is asymptotically Gaussian when $-2 < \pi < 0$.

2. Find the asymptotic distribution of

$$T(\hat{\pi}-\pi),$$

for $\pi = 0$.

3. Discuss the above problems for the model

$$\Delta X_t = \pi X_{t-1} + \mu + \varepsilon_t.$$

Solution to exercise 13.4

1. The estimator for π is given by

$$\hat{\pi} = \frac{T^{-1}\sum_{t=1}^{T}\Delta X_t X_{t-1}}{T^{-1}\sum_{t=1}^{T}X_{t-1}^2} = \frac{S_{01}}{S_{11}} = \pi + \frac{S_{\varepsilon 1}}{S_{11}}.$$

For $-2 < \pi < 0$ the process X_t is stationary with mean zero, and the law of large numbers shows that

$$S_{11} \xrightarrow{P} \mathrm{Var}(X_t) = \frac{\sigma^2}{1-(1+\pi)^2}.$$

We next apply the central limit theorem (Theorem B.3) to the martingale difference sequence $T^{-\frac{1}{2}}\varepsilon_t X_{t-1}$. We therefore investigate the sum of the conditional variances

$$T^{-1}\sum_{t=1}^{T}\mathrm{Var}(\varepsilon_t X_{t-1}|X_1,\ldots,X_{t-1}) = T^{-1}\sum_{t=1}^{T}X_{t-1}^2\sigma^2 \xrightarrow{P} \frac{\sigma^4}{1-(1+\pi)^2}.$$

The central limit theorem now implies that

$$T^{\frac{1}{2}}S_{\varepsilon 1} \xrightarrow{w} N\left(0, \frac{\sigma^4}{1-(1+\pi)^2}\right).$$

Combining the results, we find that

$$T^{\frac{1}{2}}(\hat{\pi}-\pi) \xrightarrow{w} N(0, 1-(1+\pi)^2).$$

2. If $\pi = 0$ the process X_t is a random walk

$$X_t = X_0 + \sum_{i=1}^{t}\varepsilon_i,$$

such that (see (B.12))

$$T^{-\frac{1}{2}}X_{[Tu]} \xrightarrow{w} W(u),$$

where W is a Brownian motion with variance σ^2. It follows from the continuous mapping theorem (see (B.13)) that

$$T^{-1}S_{11} \xrightarrow{w} \int_0^1 W(u)^2 du.$$

We also find from (B.14) that

$$S_{\varepsilon 1} \xrightarrow{w} \int_0^1 (dW)W.$$

Combining these results, we find that

$$T(\hat{\pi} - \pi) = \frac{S_{\varepsilon 1}}{T^{-1}S_{11}} \xrightarrow{w} \frac{\int_0^1 W(dW)}{\int_0^1 W(u)^2 du}.$$

Substituting the standard Brownian motion $B = \sigma^{-1}W$, we see that the limit distribution, the Dickey-Fuller distribution (see Fuller, (1976)), does not contain any parameters.

3. When the model contains the constant, the product moments are based upon the process, where its mean has been subtracted, and its differences. Thus we find in this case

$$\hat{\pi} - \pi = \frac{S_{\varepsilon 1}}{S_{11}} = \frac{\sum_{i=1}^{T} \varepsilon_t (X_{t-1} - \bar{X})}{\sum_{i=1}^{T} (X_{t-1} - \bar{X})^2}.$$

If $-2 < \pi < 0$ the process is stationary and we can again apply the law of large numbers to show that

$$S_{11} \xrightarrow{P} \operatorname{Var}(X_t) = \frac{\sigma^2}{1 - (1+\pi)^2},$$

and the central limit theorem to see that

$$T^{\frac{1}{2}} S_{\varepsilon 1} \xrightarrow{P} N\left(0, \frac{\sigma^4}{1 - (1+\pi)^2}\right),$$

so that the same result holds for $\hat{\pi}$ in this case. In case $\pi = 0$, the process X_t is a random walk with a drift

$$X_t = X_0 + \mu t + \sum_{i=1}^{t} \varepsilon_i.$$

This shows that if $\mu \neq 0$ the process is dominated by the linear trend and

$$T^{-1}(X_{[Tu]} - \bar{X}) \xrightarrow{w} u - \frac{1}{2},$$

but if in fact $\mu = 0$ we apply the limit results from question 2 and the continuous mapping theorem to find that

$$T^{-\frac{1}{2}}(X_{[Tu]} - \bar{X}) \stackrel{w}{\rightarrow} W(u) - \bar{W}. \tag{1}$$

Consider first the case where $\mu \neq 0$. We find that

$$T^{-1}S_{11} \stackrel{P}{\rightarrow} \int_0^1 \left(u - \frac{1}{2}\right)^2 du = \frac{1}{12},$$

and

$$S_{\varepsilon 1} \stackrel{w}{\rightarrow} \int_0^1 \left(u - \frac{1}{2}\right)(dW) = N\left(0, \sigma^2 \int_0^1 \left(u - \frac{1}{2}\right)^2 du\right)$$

such that

$$T(\hat{\pi} - \pi) \stackrel{w}{\rightarrow} \frac{\int_0^1 (u - \frac{1}{2})(dW)}{\frac{1}{12}} = N(0, 12\sigma^2).$$

Thus the fact that the trend is dominating implies the usual Gaussian asymptotics, even if the process is $I(1)$ (West, (1988)).

If, however, the parameter $\mu = 0$, then there is no trend in the process and we find from (1) that

$$T^{-1}S_{11} \stackrel{P}{\rightarrow} \int_0^1 (W(u) - \bar{W})^2 du,$$

$$S_{\varepsilon 1} \stackrel{w}{\rightarrow} \int_0^1 (W(u) - \bar{W})(dW)$$

$$T(\hat{\pi} - \pi) \stackrel{w}{\rightarrow} \frac{\int_0^1 (W(u) - \bar{W})(dW)}{\int_0^1 (W(u) - \bar{W})^2 du}.$$

Again the limit distribution does not contain any parameters, since the variance σ^2 cancels.

The fact that the limit distribution depends on the presence of the trend is the cause of the difficulty in Chapter 6, where we gave the asymptotic distributions for the test for cointegrating rank, which depends on the various possibilities for the trend.

13.5**

1. Show that in the model

$$\Delta X_t = \alpha\beta' X_{t-1} + \mu + \varepsilon_t,$$

the likelihood equations for the parameters α, β and μ when Ω is known are given by

$$(\tilde{\alpha} - \alpha)\beta' S_{xx}\tilde{\beta} + \tilde{\alpha}(\tilde{\beta} - \beta)' S_{xx}\tilde{\beta} + (\hat{\mu} - \mu)\,\bar{X}'\tilde{\beta} = S_{\varepsilon x}\tilde{\beta},$$

$$\tilde{\alpha}'\Omega^{-1}(\tilde{\alpha}-\alpha)\beta' S_{xx} + \tilde{\alpha}'\Omega^{-1}\tilde{\alpha}(\tilde{\beta}-\beta)' S_{xx} + \tilde{\alpha}'\Omega^{-1}(\hat{\mu}-\mu)\bar{X}' = \tilde{\alpha}'\Omega^{-1} S_{\varepsilon x},$$
$$(\tilde{\alpha}-\alpha)\beta'\bar{X} + \tilde{\alpha}(\tilde{\beta}-\beta)'\bar{X} + (\hat{\mu}-\mu) = \bar{\varepsilon},$$

where $S_{xx} = T^{-1}\sum_{t=1}^{T} X_{t-1}X_{t-1}'$ and $\bar{X} = T^{-1}\sum_{t=1}^{T} X_{t-1}$.

We introduce the notation U_α, U_β and U_μ for the limit distributions, that is,

$$U_\alpha^T = T^{\frac{1}{2}}(\tilde{\alpha}-\alpha) \xrightarrow{w} U_\alpha,$$
$$U_\mu^T = T^{\frac{1}{2}}(\hat{\mu}-\mu) \xrightarrow{w} U_\mu,$$
$$TU_\beta^T = (T\gamma', T^{3/2}\tau')(\tilde{\beta}-\beta) \xrightarrow{w} U_\beta.$$

2. Show that in the limit we have the equations to determine the distributions U_α, U_β and U_μ:

$$U_\alpha E(\beta' X_t X_t'\beta) + \alpha U_\beta' \bar{G}_0 E(X_t'\beta) + U_\mu E(X_t'\beta) = W_0(1) + W(1)E(X_t'\beta),$$
$$\alpha'\Omega^{-1}U_\alpha E(\beta' X_t)\bar{G}_0 + \alpha'\Omega^{-1}\alpha U_\beta' \int_0^1 G_0 G_0' du$$
$$+\alpha'\Omega^{-1}U_\mu \bar{G}_0' = \alpha'\Omega^{-1}\int_0^1 (dW)G_0',$$
$$U_\alpha E(\beta' X_t) + \alpha U_\beta' \bar{G}_0 + U_\mu = W(1),$$

where $W(u)$ is the weak limit of $T^{-\frac{1}{2}}\sum_{t=1}^{[Tu]}\varepsilon_t$, $W_0(u)$ is the weak limit of the process $T^{-\frac{1}{2}}\sum_{t=1}^{[Tu]}\varepsilon_t(X_{t-1}'\beta - E(X_{t-1}'\beta))$ and

$$G_0(u) = \begin{pmatrix} \bar{\gamma}' C W(u) \\ u \end{pmatrix}.$$

3. Show by eliminating U_μ that U_α and U_β are given by the results from Lemma 13.2. Note that although the equations determining the limit distributions have to be solved simultaneously, the equations we get by eliminating U_μ are block diagonal, indicating that inference concerning α and β can be conducted as if the other were known.

Solution to exercise 13.5

1. First, we write down the first-order conditions. They are given in SJ, p. 182, equations (13.8) and (13.9), for the parameters α and β. We find

$$\tilde{\alpha}'\Omega^{-1}\sum_{t=1}^{T}\left(\Delta X_t - \tilde{\alpha}\tilde{\beta}' X_{t-1} - \hat{\mu}\right) X_{t-1}' = 0,$$
$$\sum_{t=1}^{T}(\Delta X_t - \tilde{\alpha}\tilde{\beta}' X_{t-1} - \hat{\mu}) X_{t-1}'\tilde{\beta} = 0.$$

We have defined the estimators as normed on the true value, that is, $\tilde{\beta} = \hat{\beta}(\bar{\beta}'\hat{\beta})^{-1}$ and $\tilde{\alpha} = \hat{\alpha}\hat{\beta}'\beta$, such that $\tilde{\alpha}\tilde{\beta}' = \hat{\alpha}\hat{\beta}' = \hat{\Pi}$. We similarly find the first-order condition for the parameter μ,

$$\sum_{t=1}^{T}(\Delta X_t - \tilde{\alpha}\tilde{\beta}'X_{t-1} - \hat{\mu}) = 0;$$

see SJ, p. 189. Next, we insert the expression for ΔX_t in all equations, and find the three equations

$$D_\alpha = 0 : \sum_{t=1}^{T}(\varepsilon_t - (\tilde{\alpha}\tilde{\beta}' - \alpha\beta')X_{t-1} - (\hat{\mu} - \mu))X'_{t-1}\tilde{\beta} = 0, \quad (1)$$

$$D_\beta = 0 : \tilde{\alpha}'\Omega^{-1}\sum_{t=1}^{T}(\varepsilon_t - (\tilde{\alpha}\tilde{\beta}' - \alpha\beta')X_{t-1} - (\hat{\mu} - \mu))X'_{t-1} = 0, \quad (2)$$

$$D_\mu = 0 : \sum_{t=1}^{T}(\varepsilon_t - (\tilde{\alpha}\tilde{\beta}' - \alpha\beta')X_{t-1} - (\hat{\mu} - \mu)) = 0. \quad (3)$$

Dividing these equations by T completes question 1.

2. We assume that we have already shown that the relevant limits exist, and concentrate on applying the equations to find these limits. Thus both $\tilde{\alpha}$, $\tilde{\beta}$ and $\hat{\mu}$ are consistent and the normalization needed for the asymptotic distributions is explicit in the assumptions about their limit distributions. See also SJ, p. 145, for the definition of γ and τ.

We find that

$$\begin{aligned}
&(\tilde{\alpha}\tilde{\beta}' - \alpha\beta')X_{t-1} \\
&= (\tilde{\alpha}\tilde{\beta}' - \alpha\beta')(\bar{\beta}\beta' + \tau\bar{\tau}' + \gamma\bar{\gamma}')X_{t-1} \\
&= (\tilde{\alpha}\tilde{\beta}' - \alpha\beta')\bar{\beta}\beta'X_{t-1} + (\tilde{\alpha}\tilde{\beta}' - \alpha\beta')\gamma\bar{\gamma}'X_{t-1} + (\tilde{\alpha}\tilde{\beta}' - \alpha\beta')\tau\bar{\tau}'X_{t-1} \\
&= (\tilde{\alpha} - \alpha)\beta'X_{t-1} + \tilde{\alpha}(\tilde{\beta} - \beta)'\gamma\bar{\gamma}'X_{t-1} + \tilde{\alpha}(\tilde{\beta} - \beta)'\tau\bar{\tau}'X_{t-1} \\
&= T^{\frac{1}{2}}(\tilde{\alpha} - \alpha)T^{-\frac{1}{2}}\beta'X_{t-1} + \tilde{\alpha}[T(\tilde{\beta} - \beta)'\gamma T^{-1}\bar{\gamma}'X_{t-1} \\
&\quad + T^{\frac{3}{2}}(\tilde{\beta} - \beta)'\tau T^{-\frac{3}{2}}\bar{\tau}'X_{t-1}] \\
&= U_\alpha^T T^{-\frac{1}{2}}\beta'X_{t-1} + \tilde{\alpha}U_\beta^{T\prime}(T^{-1}\bar{\gamma}'X_{t-1}, T^{-\frac{3}{2}}\bar{\tau}'X_{t-1}),
\end{aligned}$$

where we have introduced the non-stationary process $\bar{\tau}'X_t$ dominated by the trend t, the non-stationary process $\bar{\gamma}'X_t$ dominated by a random walk $\bar{\gamma}'C\sum_{i=1}^{t}\varepsilon_i$, and finally the stationary process $\beta'X_t$.

From equation (1) we find

$$U_\alpha^T\beta'S_{11}\tilde{\beta} + \tilde{\alpha}U_\beta^{T\prime}(T^{-\frac{1}{2}}\bar{\gamma}'S_{11}\tilde{\beta}, T^{-1}\bar{\tau}'S_{11}\tilde{\beta}) + U_\mu^T\bar{X}'_{-}\tilde{\beta} = T^{\frac{1}{2}}S_{\varepsilon 1}\tilde{\beta}, \quad (4)$$

where $\bar{X} = T^{-1}\sum_{t=1}^{T}X_{t-1}$.

We next go to the limit in this equation and apply the results

$$\tilde{\alpha} \xrightarrow{P} \alpha,\ \beta' S_{11}\beta \xrightarrow{P} E(\beta' X_t X_t' \beta),\ \beta' \bar{X} \xrightarrow{P} E(\beta' X_t),\ \tilde{\beta} \xrightarrow{P} \beta$$

and

$$(T^{-\frac{1}{2}}\bar{\gamma}, T^{-1}\bar{\tau})X_{[Tu]} \xrightarrow{P} G_0(u) = \begin{pmatrix} \bar{\gamma}' C W(u) \\ u \end{pmatrix}.$$

Let us consider the limits

$$\begin{aligned} T^{-1}\bar{\tau}' S_{11}\beta &= T^{-2}\sum_{t=1}^{T} \bar{\tau}' X_{t-1} X_{t-1}' \beta \\ &= T^{-2}\sum_{t=1}^{T} \bar{\tau}' X_{t-1}(X_{t-1}'\beta - E(X_{t-1}'\beta)) \\ &\quad + \left(T^{-2}\sum_{t=1}^{T} \bar{\tau}' X_{t-1}\right) E(X_{t-1}'\beta). \end{aligned}$$

In the first term we replace $\bar{\tau}' X_{t-1}$ by t and find that the factor T^{-2} makes it tend to zero, while the second term becomes

$$\left(T^{-2}\sum_{t=1}^{T} \bar{\tau}' X_{t-1}\right) E(X_{t-1}'\beta) \sim \left(T^{-2}\sum_{t=1}^{T} t\right) E(X_{t-1}'\beta) \rightarrow \frac{1}{2} E(X_{t-1}'\beta).$$

Next consider, from (4),

$$\begin{aligned} T^{-\frac{1}{2}}\bar{\gamma}' S_{11}\beta &= T^{-\frac{3}{2}}\sum_{t=1}^{T} \bar{\gamma}' X_{t-1} X_{t-1}' \beta \\ &= T^{-\frac{3}{2}}\sum_{t=1}^{T} \bar{\gamma}' X_{t-1}(X_{t-1}'\beta - E(X_{t-1}'\beta)) \\ &\quad + \left(T^{-\frac{3}{2}}\sum_{t=1}^{T} \bar{\gamma}' X_{t-1}\right) E(X_{t-1}'\beta). \end{aligned}$$

The first term has a factor $T^{-\frac{3}{2}}$ which makes it tend to zero, and the second is normalized to converge:

$$\left(T^{-\frac{3}{2}}\sum_{t=1}^{T} \bar{\gamma}' X_{t-1}\right) E(X_{t-1}'\beta) \xrightarrow{w} \int_0^1 \bar{\gamma}' C W(u) du E(X_{t-1}'\beta).$$

Similarly we can prove

$$T^{-\frac{1}{2}}\bar{\gamma}' S_{11}\tilde{\beta} \xrightarrow{w} \int_0^1 \bar{\gamma}' C W(u) du E(X_{t-1}'\beta).$$

Finally we find for the right hand side

$$T^{\frac{1}{2}} S_{\varepsilon 1}\beta = T^{-\frac{1}{2}} \sum_{t=1}^{T} \varepsilon_t (X'_{t-1}\beta - E(X'_{t-1}\beta)) + \left(T^{-\frac{1}{2}} \sum_{t=1}^{T} \varepsilon_t \right) E(X'_{t-1}\beta)$$
$$\xrightarrow{w} W_0(1) + W(1) E(X'_{t-1}\beta).$$

Again we get the same limit when we replace β by $\tilde{\beta}$.

Thus by going to the limit in (4) we obtain the first result

$$U_\alpha E(\beta' X_t X'_t \beta) + \alpha U'_\beta \bar{G}_0 E(X'_t\beta) + U_\mu E(X'_t\beta) = W_0(1) + W(1) E(X'_t\beta). \tag{5}$$

Note that $W_0(1)$ is distributed as $N(0, \Omega \otimes \Sigma_{\beta\beta})$.

Equation (2) is treated similarly, and by multiplying from the right by $(T^{-\frac{1}{2}}\bar{\gamma}, T^{-1}\bar{\tau})$ we find

$$\alpha'\Omega^{-1}[U_\alpha^T \beta' S_{11} + \tilde{\alpha} U_\beta^{T\prime} (T^{-\frac{1}{2}} \bar{\gamma}' S_{11}, T^{-1}\bar{\tau}' S_{11})$$
$$+ U_\mu^T \bar{X}'](T^{-\frac{1}{2}}\bar{\gamma}, T^{-1}\bar{\tau}) = \alpha'\Omega^{-1} S_{\varepsilon 1}(\bar{\gamma}, T^{-\frac{1}{2}}\bar{\tau}).$$

We find the various contributions

$$\alpha'\Omega^{-1} S_{\varepsilon 1}(\bar{\gamma}, T^{-\frac{1}{2}}\bar{\tau}) \xrightarrow{w} \alpha'\Omega^{-1} \int_0^1 (dW) G'_0,$$
$$\bar{X}'(T^{-\frac{1}{2}}\bar{\gamma}, T^{-1}\bar{\tau}) \xrightarrow{w} \int_0^1 G_0(u)' du$$
$$(T^{-\frac{1}{2}}\bar{\gamma}' S_{11}, T^{-1}\bar{\tau}' S_{11})(T^{-\frac{1}{2}}\bar{\gamma}, T^{-1}\bar{\tau}) \xrightarrow{w} \int_0^1 G_0(u) G_0(u)' du,$$
$$\beta' S_{11}(T^{-\frac{1}{2}}\bar{\gamma}, T^{-1}\bar{\tau}) \xrightarrow{w} E(\beta' X_t) \int_0^1 G_0(u)' du.$$

Combining these, we get the second result

$$\alpha'\Omega^{-1} U_\alpha E(\beta' X_t) \bar{G}'_0 + \alpha'\Omega^{-1} \alpha U'_\beta \int_0^1 G_0 G'_0 du$$
$$+ \alpha'\Omega^{-1} U_\mu \bar{G}'_0 = \alpha'\Omega^{-1} \int_0^1 (dW) G'_0. \tag{6}$$

Finally we find, by normalizing equation (3) by $T^{-\frac{1}{2}}$, that

$$U_\alpha^T \beta' \bar{X}_- + \tilde{\alpha} U_\beta^{T\prime} (T^{-1}\bar{\tau}' X'_-, T^{-\frac{1}{2}}\bar{\gamma}' X'_-) + U_\mu^T = T^{\frac{1}{2}}\bar{\varepsilon},$$

which converges towards

$$U_\alpha E(\beta' X_t) + \alpha U_\beta' \bar{G}_0 + U_\mu = W(1). \tag{7}$$

3. Next we solve equations (5), (6) and (7) by eliminating U_μ. Multiplying (7) by $E(\beta' X_t)$ and subtracting from (5) gives us

$$U_\alpha \Sigma_{\beta\beta} = W_0(1),$$

where $\Sigma_{\beta\beta} = E(\beta' X_t X_t' \beta) - E(\beta' X_t) E(X_t' \beta)$. This can be solved for U_α and we find

$$U_\alpha = W_0(1)\Sigma_{\beta\beta}^{-1} = N(0, \Omega \otimes \Sigma_{\beta\beta}^{-1}).$$

Next we multiply (7) by $\alpha'\Omega^{-1}$ and $\bar{G}_0'$ and subtract from (6), and find

$$\alpha'\Omega^{-1}\alpha U_\beta' \int_0^1 GG' du = \alpha'\Omega^{-1} \int_0^1 (dW)G'.$$

where $G = G_0 - \bar{G}_0$. Solving this equation for U_β gives us

$$U_\beta = \left(\int_0^1 GG' du \right)^{-1} \int_0^1 G(dW)'\Omega^{-1}\alpha \left(\alpha'\Omega^{-1}\alpha\right)^{-1}.$$

These results are the same as those proved in Lemma 13.2.

Finally equation (7) gives an asymptotic expression for the distribution for U_μ as follows:

$$\begin{aligned} U_\mu &= W(1) - U_\alpha E(\beta' X_t) - \alpha U_\beta' \bar{G}_0 \\ &= W(1) - W_0(1)\Sigma_{\beta\beta}^{-1} E(\beta' X_t) \\ &\quad -\alpha \left(\alpha'\Omega^{-1}\alpha\right)^{-1} \alpha'\Omega^{-1} \int_0^1 (dW)G' \left(\int_0^1 GG' du \right)^{-1} \bar{G}_0, \end{aligned}$$

from which the various results for μ in Theorem 13.6 can be derived.

13.6**

1. Find in the model described by (4.1) the maximum likelihood estimator of

$$E(\beta' X_t) = \bar{\alpha}' (\Gamma C - I)\mu.$$

2. Find its asymptotic distribution.
3. Show that an efficient estimator is $\hat{\beta}'\bar{X}$.

Solution to exercise 13.6

1. We consider the model with the constant term μ,

$$\Delta X_t = \alpha\beta' X_{t-1} + \sum_{i=1}^{k-1} \Gamma_i \Delta X_{t-i} + \mu + \varepsilon_t,$$

and can answer this part of the question quite easily, since the maximum likelihood estimator of $\kappa = E(\beta' X_t) = \bar{\alpha}'(\Gamma C - I)\mu$ is simply given by

$$\hat{\kappa} = (\hat{\alpha}'\hat{\alpha})^{-1}\hat{\alpha}'(\hat{\Gamma}\hat{C} - I)\hat{\mu}. \tag{1}$$

2. The equation to determine the estimator of μ is given in SJ, p. 189, and can be written as

$$T^{-1}(X_T - X_0) - \sum_{i=1}^{k-1} \hat{\Gamma}_i T^{-1}(X_{T-i} - X_{-i}) = \hat{\alpha}\hat{\beta}'\bar{X} + \hat{\mu}.$$

Multiplying on the left by $T^{\frac{1}{2}}(\hat{\alpha}'\hat{\alpha})^{-1}\hat{\alpha}'(\hat{\Gamma}\hat{C} - I)$ and using the fact that $\hat{C}\hat{\alpha} = 0$, we find

$$(\hat{\alpha}'\hat{\alpha})^{-1}\hat{\alpha}'(\hat{\Gamma}\hat{C} - I)\left(T^{-\frac{1}{2}}(X_T - X_0) - \sum_{i=1}^{k-1} \hat{\Gamma}_i T^{-\frac{1}{2}}(X_{T-i} - X_{-i})\right)$$
$$= -T^{\frac{1}{2}}(\hat{\beta}'\bar{X} - \hat{\kappa}). \tag{2}$$

We will now show that many of the terms on the left hand side are $o_P(1)$ and are therefore of no consequence for the limit distribution.

We have that the initial values are normalized by $T^{-\frac{1}{2}}$ and will therefore be left out. Next consider the Granger representation theorem,

$$X_t = C\sum_{i=1}^{t} \varepsilon_i + C\mu t + Y_t + \phi + A,$$

where Y_t is stationary with mean zero, ϕ is a constant and A depends on initial values such that $\beta' A = 0$. Obviously the term $Y_t + \phi + A$ will not play any role in the limit distribution because of the factor $T^{-\frac{1}{2}}$. Next consider the contribution from $C\mu t$. We see that X_{T-i} contains a term of the order of T, and that the coefficient contains the factor

$$(\hat{\Gamma}\hat{C} - I)\left(I - \sum_{i=1}^{k-1} \hat{\Gamma}_i\right) C = (\hat{\Gamma}\hat{C} - I)\hat{\Gamma} C = \hat{\Gamma}\hat{C}\hat{\Gamma} C - \hat{\Gamma} C.$$

In these expressions we can replace $\hat{\beta}_\perp$ by $\beta_\perp$ and make an error of only $O_P(T^{-1})$. We then find

$$\begin{aligned}\hat{C}\hat{\Gamma}C &= \hat{\beta}_\perp(\hat{\alpha}'_\perp\hat{\Gamma}\hat{\beta}_\perp)^{-1}\hat{\alpha}'_\perp\hat{\Gamma}\beta_\perp(\alpha'_\perp\Gamma\beta_\perp)^{-1}\alpha'_\perp \\ &= \beta_\perp(\hat{\alpha}'_\perp\hat{\Gamma}\beta_\perp)^{-1}\hat{\alpha}'_\perp\hat{\Gamma}\beta_\perp(\alpha'_\perp\Gamma\beta_\perp)^{-1}\alpha'_\perp + O_P(T^{-1}) \\ &= C + O_P(T^{-1});\end{aligned}$$

see SJ, p. 192. Hence $\hat{\Gamma}\hat{C}\hat{\Gamma}C - \hat{\Gamma}C \in O_P(T^{-1})$ and, multiplying by $T^{\frac{1}{2}}$, the terms from the trend in X_{T-i} tend to zero in (2).

Hence we are left with the random walk component, but exactly the same argument shows that the contribution from these vanishes because of the relation $\hat{\Gamma}\hat{C}\hat{\Gamma}C - \hat{\Gamma}C \in O_P(T^{-1})$. This shows that the left hand side is $o_P(1)$ and that

$$T^{\frac{1}{2}}(\hat{\kappa} - \kappa) = T^{\frac{1}{2}}(\hat{\beta}'\bar{X} - \kappa) + o_P(1). \tag{3}$$

Next we want to find the limit distribution. We decompose as follows:

$$T^{\frac{1}{2}}(\hat{\beta}'\bar{X} - \kappa) = T^{\frac{1}{2}}(\hat{\beta} - \beta)'\bar{X} + T^{\frac{1}{2}}(\beta'\bar{X} - \kappa).$$

We define $B_T = (\bar{\gamma}, T^{-\frac{1}{2}}\bar{\tau})$, such that

$$T^{-\frac{1}{2}}B'_T\bar{X} \xrightarrow{w} \begin{pmatrix} \bar{\gamma}'C\int_0^1 W(u)du \\ \int_0^1 udu \end{pmatrix} = \bar{G}_0$$

and $\hat{\beta} - \beta = B_T U_T = B_T(\gamma, T^{\frac{1}{2}}\tau)'(\hat{\beta} - \beta)$. Then

$$T^{\frac{1}{2}}(\hat{\beta} - \beta)'\bar{X} = TU'_T T^{-\frac{1}{2}}B'_T\bar{X} \xrightarrow{w} \int_0^1 (dV_\alpha)G'\left(\int_0^1 GG'du\right)^{-1}\bar{G}_0,$$

where $V_\alpha = (\alpha'\Omega^{-1}\alpha)^{-1}\alpha'\Omega^{-1}W$. Finally we have

$$T^{\frac{1}{2}}(\beta'\bar{X}_T - \kappa) \xrightarrow{w} N(0, \mathrm{Var}(\beta' X_t)).$$

3. Equation (3) shows that the estimator $\hat{\beta}'\bar{X}$ is consistent for κ and efficient, in the sense that the limit distribution is the same as that of the maximum likelihood estimator.

13.7**

Consider the model

$$\Delta X_t = \alpha\beta' X_{t-1} + \varepsilon_t, \tag{13.20}$$

where β is identified by the restrictions

$$\beta = (H_1\varphi_1, \ldots,\ H_r\varphi_r).$$

This means that $\mathrm{rank}(H'_{i\perp}\beta) = r - 1$, since $H'_{i\perp}\beta_i = 0$ and the remaining columns are linearly independent. We normalize β_i as $\beta_i = h_i + H^i\psi_i$.

1. Show that the identification condition implies that there is no vector $\eta \neq 0$, such that $H^{i}\eta \in \mathrm{sp}(\beta)$.

2. Show that

$$T^{-1}H^{i\prime}S_{11}H^{j} \xrightarrow{w} H^{i\prime}\int_0^1 CWW'C'duH^{j}.$$

3. Show that the likelihood equation for ψ_i is given by

$$\hat{\alpha}_i'\hat{\Omega}^{-1}(S_{01} - \hat{\alpha}\hat{\beta}'S_{11})H^{i} = 0, \quad i = 1, \dots, r.$$

4. Show by going through the proof of Lemma 13.2 that Theorem 13.4 holds.

Next consider model (13.20) with a constant term μ in the equation. From Granger's representation theorem we have

$$H^{i\prime}X_t = H^{i\prime}C\sum_{i=1}^{t}\varepsilon_i + H^{i\prime}C\mu t + \text{stationary process}.$$

This gives rise to the directions $\tau_i = H^{i\prime}C\mu$ and $\gamma_i = \tau_{i\perp}$, such that in the direction τ_i the process $H^{i\prime}X_t$ is dominated by the linear trends and in the directions γ_i the trends are eliminated, and the process converges towards a Brownian motion.

5. Find the proper normalization of the matrix $H^{i\prime}S_{11}H^{i}$ and determine the limit.

6. Show that the results of Theorem 13.4 hold in this case.

Solution to exercise 13.7

1. Assume that there is a vector η such that $H^1\eta = \beta a$ for some a. The idea of the identification condition is that there should not be two linear combinations of the columns of β that satisfy the constraints imposed. We show that η can be applied to construct a linear combination that also satisfies the constraints.

Consider therefore the vectors

$$(H_1\varphi_1 + \beta a, H_2\varphi_2, \dots, H_r\varphi_r).$$

We want to show that these vectors satisfy the constraints of the conditions, and in particular we consider the condition

$$H_{1\perp}'(H_1\varphi_1 + \beta a) = 0,$$

since $H_1 = (h_1, H^1)$ implies that $H_{1\perp}'H^1 = 0$. Thus we also have that $H_{1\perp}'\beta a = H_{1\perp}'H^1\eta = 0$. Thus, the new vectors satisfy the constraints and since only one set of vectors has this property, we have that

$$H_1\varphi_1 + \beta a = \lambda H_1\varphi_1$$

or, with $H_1\varphi_1 = h_1 + H^1\psi_1$,

$$h_1 + H^1(\psi_1 + \eta) = \lambda h_1 + \lambda H^1\psi_1,$$

which implies that $h_1 = \lambda h_1$ and hence that $\lambda = 1$, and further that $H^1(\psi_1 + \eta) = H^1\psi_1$ such that $H^1\eta = 0$. Since the columns of H^1 are linearly independent, this implies that $\eta = 0$.

2. From Granger's representation theorem we have

$$H^{i\prime}X_t = H^{i\prime}C\sum_{i=1}^{t}\varepsilon_i + H^{i\prime}Y_t + H^{i\prime}A.$$

Note that $H^{i\prime}X_t$, apart from being non-stationary, is not cointegrating since there is no vector η such that $H^i\eta \in \mathrm{sp}(\beta)$, in other words there is no linear combination of the process $H^{i\prime}X_t$ that is stationary.

We find that

$$T^{-\frac{1}{2}}H^{i\prime}X_{[Tu]} \xrightarrow{w} H^{i\prime}CW(u), \tag{1}$$

such that the continuous mapping theorem gives

$$T^{-1}H^{j\prime}S_{11}H^i \xrightarrow{w} H^{j\prime}\int_0^1 CWW'C'duH^i. \tag{2}$$

Similarly we find that

$$H^{j\prime}S_{1\varepsilon} \xrightarrow{w} H^{j\prime}\int_0^1 CW(dW)'. \tag{3}$$

3. The derivative of the log likelihood function in the direction b is given by

$$D_\beta \log L(b) = -tr\{\alpha'\Omega^{-1}(S_{01} - \alpha\beta'S_{11})b\}.$$

If we consider an increment of the form

$$b = (H^1b_1, 0, \ldots, 0) = H^1b_1(1, 0, \ldots, 0),$$

we get the equation

$$tr\{(1, 0, \ldots, 0)\alpha'\Omega^{-1}(S_{01} - \alpha\beta'S_{11})H^1b_1\} = 0,$$

for all b_1, which is the same as

$$\hat{\alpha}_1'\Omega^{-1}(S_{01} - \hat{\alpha}\hat{\beta}'S_{11})H^1 = 0,$$

which we write as

$$\hat{\alpha}_1'\Omega^{-1}S_{\varepsilon 1}H^1 = \hat{\alpha}_1'\Omega^{-1}\hat{\alpha}(\hat{\beta}-\beta)'S_{11}H^1 + \hat{\alpha}_1'\Omega^{-1}(\hat{\alpha}-\alpha)\beta'S_{11}H^1 = 0; \quad (4)$$

see SJ, p. 182.

The derivative with respect to α gives the equation

$$(S_{01} - \hat{\alpha}\hat{\beta}'S_{11})\hat{\beta} = 0,$$

which we write as

$$S_{\varepsilon 1}\hat{\beta} = \hat{\alpha}(\hat{\beta}-\beta)'S_{11}\hat{\beta} + (\hat{\alpha}-\alpha)\beta'S_{11}\hat{\beta} = 0. \quad (5)$$

4. Results (1), (2) and (3) are the basic limit results on the behaviour of the process and its product moments, and we just apply these to discuss the limit of the equations (4) and (5).

Note that

$$\hat{\beta} - \beta = (H^1(\hat{\psi}_1 - \psi_1), \ldots, H^r(\hat{\psi}_r - \psi_r)),$$

such that by replacing 1 by i, (4) becomes

$$\hat{\alpha}_i'\Omega^{-1}S_{\varepsilon 1}H^i = \sum_{j=1}^{r} \hat{\alpha}_i'\Omega^{-1}\hat{\alpha}_j T(\hat{\psi}_j - \psi_j)'H^{j\prime}T^{-1}S_{11}H^i + O_P(T^{-\frac{1}{2}}) = 0.$$

Now let $(T(\hat{\psi}_1 - \psi_1)', \ldots, T(\hat{\psi}_r - \psi_r)')' \xrightarrow{w} D$, and $\hat{\alpha}_i'\Omega^{-1}\hat{\alpha}_j \xrightarrow{P} \rho_{ij}$; then we get the limit equation

$$\sum_{j=1}^{r} D_j'\rho_{ij}H^{j\prime}\int_0^1 CWW'C'du H^i = \alpha_i'\Omega^{-1}\int_0^1 (dW)W'C'H^i,$$

which can be solved for D. This shows that the distribution of D is mixed Gaussian with a mixing parameter given by

$$\left\{\rho_{ij}H^{j\prime}\int_0^1 CWW'C'du H^i\right\}^{-1},$$

and hence that the result of Theorem 13.4 holds.

5. For the model with a constant term, the product moments are based upon the process (corrected for its mean) and its difference. We have the representation

$$H^{i\prime}X_t = H^{i\prime}C\sum_{i=1}^{t}\varepsilon_i + H^{i\prime}C\mu t + H^{i\prime}Y_t + H^{i\prime}A.$$

We let $\tau_i = H^{i\prime}C\mu$, such that

$$T^{-1}\bar{\tau}_i' H^{i\prime} X_{[Tu]} = u + O_P(T^{-\frac{1}{2}}).$$

It follows that

$$\begin{aligned} T^{-3}\bar{\tau}_i' H^{i\prime} S_{11} H^i \bar{\tau}_i &= T^{-1}\bar{\tau}_i' H^{i\prime} \sum_{t=1}^{T} (X_{t-1} - \bar{X}_-)(X_{t-1} - \bar{X}_-)' H^i \bar{\tau}_i \\ &\xrightarrow{P} \int_0^1 \left(u - \frac{1}{2}\right)^2 du. \end{aligned}$$

Similarly we find that in the direction γ_i, chosen orthogonal to τ_i, we have

$$\bar{\gamma}_i' H^{i\prime} X_t = \bar{\gamma}_i' H^{i\prime} C \sum_{i=1}^{t} \varepsilon_i + O_P(1),$$

which implies that we get the normalizations and limits

$$T^{-1}\bar{\gamma}_i' H^{i\prime} S_{11} H^j \bar{\gamma}_j \xrightarrow{w} \bar{\gamma}_i' H^{i\prime} C \int_0^1 (W - \bar{W})(W - \bar{W})' du C' H^j \bar{\gamma}_j$$

and

$$T^{-\frac{3}{2}}\bar{\gamma}_i' H^{i\prime} S_{11} H^j \bar{\tau}_j \xrightarrow{w} \bar{\gamma}_i' H^{i\prime} C \int_0^1 (W - \bar{W}) \left(u - \frac{1}{2}\right)' du.$$

Thus, defining $B_{iT} = (\bar{\gamma}_i, T^{-\frac{1}{2}}\bar{\tau}_i)$, we have

$$T^{-1} B_{iT}' H^{i\prime} S_{11} H^j B_{jT} \xrightarrow{w} \int_0^1 G_i G_j' du,$$

with

$$G_i(u) = \begin{pmatrix} \bar{\gamma}_i' H^{i\prime} C (W(u) - \bar{W}) \\ u - \frac{1}{2} \end{pmatrix}.$$

6. The likelihood equation for the parameters ψ_i is in this case given by

$$\hat{\alpha}_i' \Omega^{-1} S_{\varepsilon 1} H^i = \sum_{j=1}^{r} \hat{\alpha}_i' \Omega^{-1} \hat{\alpha}_j T(\hat{\psi}_j - \psi_j)' H^{j\prime} T^{-1} S_{11} H^i + O_P(T^{-\frac{1}{2}}),$$

where the parameter μ has been eliminated from the equations. Thus exactly the same proof can be given as above, by replacing $\bar{\gamma}_i$ with the matrix B_{iT}.

14

The Power Function of the Test for Cointegrating Rank under Local Alternatives

It is shown in this chapter that the power function under local alternatives can be expressed in term of an Ornstein–Uhlenbeck process. In model $H_2(r)$ without deterministic terms the local alternative considered is

$$\Pi_T = \alpha\beta' + T^{-1}\alpha_1\beta_1'.$$

It is shown in Theorem 14.1 that

$$T^{-\frac{1}{2}}\alpha_\perp' X_{[Tu]} \xrightarrow{w} K(u),$$

where the process $K(u)$ is defined by the equation

$$K(u) = \alpha_\perp' W(u) + \alpha_\perp'\alpha_1\beta_1'\beta_\perp(\alpha_\perp'\beta_\perp)^{-1}\int_0^u K(s)ds, \qquad u \in [0,1],$$

or by the solution

$$K(u) = \alpha_\perp' \int_0^u \exp(\alpha_1\beta_1' C(u-s))dW(s), \qquad u \in [0,1].$$

Various results on the product moments are then derived from this result, and it is shown in Theorem 14.4 that the trace statistic converges under the local alternative to the random variable

$$tr\left\{\int_0^1 (dK^*)K^{*\prime}\left(\int_0^1 K^*K^{*\prime}du\right)^{-1}\int_0^1 K^*(dK^*)'\right\},$$

where $K^*(u)$ is given by the equation

$$K^*(u) = B(u) + ab'\int_0^u K^*(s)ds, \qquad u \in [0,1],$$

in which a and b depend on the parameters of the model and the alternative. The exercise extends these results via the companion form to hold for models with more than one lag.

14.1**

In the model

$$\Delta X_t = \left(\alpha\beta' + T^{-1}\alpha_1\beta_1'\right) X_{t-1} + \sum_{i=1}^{k-1} \Gamma_i \Delta X_{t-i} + \varepsilon_t, \tag{14.19}$$

define $\tilde{X}_t' = (X_t', \ldots, X_{t-k+1}')$, and $\tilde{\varepsilon}_t = (\varepsilon_t, 0, \ldots, 0)$.

1. Show that $\tilde{X}_t$ satisfies the equation

$$\Delta\tilde{X}_t = \tilde{\Pi}_T \tilde{X}_{t-1} + \tilde{\varepsilon}_t,$$

and find an expression for $\tilde{\Pi}_T$ in terms of the other parameters.

2. Show that $\tilde{\beta}_\perp' = \beta_\perp'(I, \ldots, I)$, and $\tilde{\alpha}_\perp' = \alpha_\perp'(I, -\Gamma_1, \ldots, -\Gamma_{k-1})$, and hence that

$$\tilde{C} = \tilde{\beta}_\perp\left(\tilde{\alpha}_\perp'\tilde{\beta}_\perp\right)^{-1}\tilde{\alpha}_\perp' = (I, I, \ldots, I)'C(I, -\Gamma_1, \ldots, -\Gamma_{k-1}).$$

Find expressions for $\tilde{\alpha}$, $\tilde{\beta}$, $\tilde{\alpha}_1$ and $\tilde{\beta}_1$.

3. Next apply Theorem 14.1 to the process $\tilde{X}_t^{(T)}$, and express the results for the process $\tilde{\beta}'\tilde{X}_t^{(T)} - \tilde{\beta}'\tilde{X}_t$ and $\tilde{\alpha}_\perp'\tilde{X}_{[Tu]}^{(T)}$ in terms of the original parameters and processes. Find the equation for the process K_t, and show that the results of Theorem 14.4 still hold with the same definition of a provided b is defined as $b = (\alpha_\perp'\Omega\alpha_\perp)^{\frac{1}{2}}(\beta_\perp'\Gamma'\alpha_\perp)^{-1}\beta_\perp'\beta_1$. Thus the limit result for the power function does not depend on the short-term dynamics.

Solution to exercise 14.1

1. For notational convenience we let $k = 4$.

We find

$$\tilde{\Pi}_T = \begin{pmatrix} \Pi_T + \Gamma_1 & \Gamma_2 - \Gamma_1 & \Gamma_3 - \Gamma_2 & -\Gamma_3 \\ I & -I & 0 & 0 \\ 0 & I & -I & 0 \\ 0 & 0 & I & -I \end{pmatrix}.$$

Let $\tilde{\Pi} = \lim_{T\to\infty}\tilde{\Pi}_T$ and define $\tilde{\alpha}$ and $\tilde{\beta}$ by $\tilde{\Pi} = \tilde{\alpha}\tilde{\beta}'$.

2. A vector $v = (v_1', \ldots, v_4')'$ which satisfies $\tilde{\Pi}v = 0$ must satisfy the equations

$$\begin{aligned} (\Pi + \Gamma_1)v_1 + (\Gamma_2 - \Gamma_1)v_2 + (\Gamma_3 - \Gamma_2)v_3 - \Gamma_3 v_4 &= 0, \\ v_1 - v_2 &= 0, \\ v_2 - v_3 &= 0, \\ v_3 - v_4 &= 0 \end{aligned}$$

(see exercise 4.7), which show that $v_1 = \cdots = v_4$ and that the common value satisfies $\Pi v_1 = \alpha\beta' v_1 = 0$, such that $v_1 = \beta_\perp$, and $\tilde{\beta}_\perp' = v' = \beta_\perp'(I,\, I,\, I,\, I)$.

Similarly a vector that satisfies $v'\tilde{\Pi} = 0$ must satisfy the relations

$$\begin{aligned} v_1'(\Pi + \Gamma_1) + v_2' &= 0, \\ v_1'(\Gamma_2 - \Gamma_1) - v_2' + v_3' &= 0, \\ v_1'(\Gamma_3 - \Gamma_2) - v_3' + v_4' &= 0, \\ -v_1'\Gamma_3 - v_4' &= 0. \end{aligned}$$

Adding these equations we find that v_1 must satisfy $v_1'\Pi = 0$, and that $v_1 = \alpha_\perp$, such that $v_2 = -\Gamma_1' v_1$, $v_3 = -\Gamma_2' v_1$ and $v_4 = -\Gamma_3' v_1$, which shows that $\tilde{\alpha}_\perp' = \alpha_\perp'(I, -\Gamma_1, -\Gamma_2, -\Gamma_3)$. In particular we find that

$$\tilde{\alpha}_\perp'\tilde{\beta}_\perp = \alpha_\perp'\left(I - \sum_{i=1}^{3}\Gamma_i\right)\beta_\perp = \alpha_\perp'\Gamma\beta_\perp,$$

and

$$\tilde{C} = \tilde{\beta}_\perp\left(\tilde{\alpha}_\perp'\tilde{\beta}_\perp\right)^{-1}\tilde{\alpha}_\perp' = (I, I, I, I)'C(I, -\Gamma_1, -\Gamma_2, -\Gamma_3).$$

We also find that

$$\tilde{\alpha} = \begin{pmatrix} \alpha & \Gamma_1 & \Gamma_2 & \Gamma_3 \\ 0 & I & 0 & 0 \\ 0 & 0 & I & 0 \\ 0 & 0 & 0 & I \end{pmatrix}, \quad \tilde{\beta} = \begin{pmatrix} \beta & I & 0 & 0 \\ 0 & -I & I & 0 \\ 0 & 0 & -I & I \\ 0 & 0 & 0 & -I \end{pmatrix}$$

and that

$$\tilde{\alpha}_1 = (\alpha_1', 0, 0, 0, 0)', \quad \tilde{\beta}_1 = (\beta_1', 0, 0, 0, 0)'$$

satisfy

$$\tilde{\Pi}_T = \tilde{\Pi} + T^{-1}\tilde{\alpha}_1\tilde{\beta}_1'.$$

3. We calculate the process

$$\tilde{\beta}'\tilde{X}_t = \begin{pmatrix} \beta & I & 0 & 0 \\ 0 & -I & I & 0 \\ 0 & 0 & -I & I \\ 0 & 0 & 0 & -I \end{pmatrix}' \begin{pmatrix} X_t \\ X_{t-1} \\ X_{t-2} \\ X_{t-3} \end{pmatrix} = \begin{pmatrix} \beta' X_t \\ \Delta X_t \\ \Delta X_{t-1} \\ \Delta X_{t-2} \end{pmatrix}$$

such that

$$\tilde{\beta}'\tilde{X}_t^{(T)} - \tilde{\beta}'\tilde{X}_t = \begin{pmatrix} \beta' X_t^{(T)} - \beta' X_t \\ \Delta X_t^{(T)} - \Delta X_t \\ \Delta X_{t-1}^{(T)} - \Delta X_{t-1} \\ \Delta X_{t-2}^{(T)} - \Delta X_{t-2} \end{pmatrix},$$

and

$$\begin{aligned} \tilde{\alpha}_\perp'\tilde{X}_t^{(T)} &= \alpha_\perp'(X_t^{(T)} - \Gamma_1 X_{t-1}^{(T)} - \Gamma_2 X_{t-2}^{(T)} - \Gamma_3 X_{t-3}^{(T)}) \\ &= \alpha_\perp'\Gamma X_t^{(T)} - \sum_{i=1}^{3}\Gamma_i(X_{t-i}^{(T)} - X_t^{(T)}). \end{aligned}$$

The first result (14.1) of Theorem 14.1, applied to the process $\tilde{X}_t^T$, implies that

$$\max_t \operatorname{Var}(\beta' X_t^{(T)} - \beta' X_t) \in O(T^{-1}), \tag{1}$$

$$\max_t \operatorname{Var}(\Delta X_t^{(T)} - \Delta X_t) \in O(T^{-1}). \tag{2}$$

The second result (14.5) implies

$$T^{-\frac{1}{2}}\tilde{\alpha}'_\perp \tilde{X}^{(T)}_{[Tu]} \tag{3}$$

$$= T^{-\frac{1}{2}}\alpha'_\perp \Gamma X^{(T)}_{[Tu]} - T^{-\frac{1}{2}}\sum_{i=1}^{3}\Gamma_i(X^{(T)}_{[Tu]-i} - X^{(T)}_{[Tu]}) \xrightarrow{w} \tilde{K}(u),$$

where $\tilde{K}$ is an Ornstein–Uhlenbeck process defined by

$$\tilde{K}(u) = \tilde{\alpha}'_\perp \tilde{W}(u) + \tilde{\alpha}'_\perp \tilde{\alpha}_1 \tilde{\beta}'_1 \tilde{\beta}_\perp (\tilde{\alpha}'_\perp \tilde{\beta}_\perp)^{-1} \int_0^u \tilde{K}(s)ds, \tag{4}$$

where $\tilde{W} = (W', 0, 0, 0, 0)'$.

Applying (2) and replacing $X_t^{(T)}$ by X_t in the last term of (3), we see that all the differences are stationary, such that the factor $T^{-\frac{1}{2}}$ ensures that their contributions vanish in the limit, and have

$$T^{-\frac{1}{2}}\alpha'_\perp \Gamma X^{(T)}_{[Tu]} \xrightarrow{w} \tilde{K}(u).$$

Note that we have the results

$$\tilde{\alpha}'_\perp \tilde{W} = \alpha'_\perp W, \quad \tilde{\alpha}'_\perp \tilde{\alpha}_1 = \alpha'_\perp \alpha_1,$$
$$\tilde{\beta}'_1 \tilde{\beta}_\perp = \beta'_1 \beta_\perp, \quad \tilde{\alpha}'_\perp \tilde{\beta}_\perp = \alpha'_\perp \Gamma \beta_\perp.$$

Thus the process we find from the stacked problem is given by the equation

$$\tilde{K}(u) = \alpha'_\perp W(u) + \alpha'_\perp \alpha_1 \beta'_1 \beta_\perp (\alpha'_\perp \Gamma \beta_\perp)^{-1} \int_0^u \tilde{K}(s)ds.$$

In order to show that the results of Theorem 14.4 hold for the process with more than one lag, we need to go through the proof and see where it should be changed. Note that it is not a good idea to apply Theorem 14.4 to the stacked process, since the companion matrix has many zeros and other restrictions and hence the matrices $\tilde{\alpha}$ and $\tilde{\beta}$ are not freely varying. Thus estimating the stacked process unrestricted, we are estimating too many parameters and the final test statistic would not be the one we derive from the process by first correcting for the lagged differences.

We therefore have to investigate the behaviour of the basic equation

$$|\lambda S_{11}^{(T)} - S_{10}^{(T)} S_{00}^{(T)-1} S_{01}^{(T)}| = 0,$$

where for instance $S_{11}^{(T)}$ is the product moment of the process $X_{t-1}^{(T)}$ corrected for lagged differences. From the results of Theorem 14.1 applied to $X_t^{(T)}$ we see that, if we define the normalizing matrix as

$$A_T = (\beta, T^{-\frac{1}{2}}\Gamma'\alpha_\perp)$$

(see SJ, p. 207), then we find all the results, including that the $p-r$ smallest roots normalized by T converge towards those of

$$\left|\rho \int_0^1 \tilde{K}\tilde{K}'du - \int_0^1 \tilde{K}(d\tilde{K})'(\alpha_\perp'\Omega\alpha_\perp)^{-1} \int_0^1 (d\tilde{K})\tilde{K}'\right| = 0.$$

Hence we find that the main conclusion of Theorem 14.4 holds if we define

$$\begin{aligned}
B(u) &= (\alpha_\perp'\Omega\alpha_\perp)^{-\frac{1}{2}}\alpha_\perp' W(u), \\
K^* &= (\alpha_\perp'\Omega\alpha_\perp)^{-\frac{1}{2}} K(u), \\
a &= (\alpha_\perp'\Omega\alpha_\perp)^{-\frac{1}{2}}\alpha_\perp'\alpha_1, \\
b &= (\alpha_\perp'\Omega\alpha_\perp)^{\frac{1}{2}}(\beta_\perp'\Gamma'\alpha_\perp)^{-1}\beta_\perp'\beta_1.
\end{aligned}$$

References

ANDERSON T. W. (1951), 'Estimating linear restrictions on regression coefficients for multivariate normal distributions', *Annals of Mathematical Statistics*, 22: 327–51.

BARNDORFF-NIELSEN, O. E. (1978), *Information and Exponential Families in Statistical Theory*, John Wiley, New York.

BOX, G. E. P. and JENKINS, G. M. (1976), *Time Series Analysis: Forecasting and Control*, 2nd edn, Holden–Day, San Francisco.

ENGLE, R. F. and KOZICKI, S. (1993), 'Testing for common features', *Journal of Business and Economic Statistics*, 11: 369–80.

ENGSTED, T. and JOHANSEN, S. (1997), 'Granger's representation theorem and multicointegration', EUI Working Paper ECO No. 97/15.

FULLER, W. (1976), *Introduction to Statistical Time Series*, John Wiley, New York.

GRANGER, C. W. J. and KONISHI, T. (1993), 'Separation in cointegrating systems', Discussion paper, University of California, San Diego.

—— and LEE, T.-H. (1989), 'Multicointegration', *Advances in Econometrics*, 8: 71–84.

HARBO, I., JOHANSEN, S., NIELSEN, B. G. and RAHBEK A. C. (1998), 'Test for cointegrating rank in partial systems', forthcoming in *Journal of Business and Economic Statistics.*

HYLLEBERG, S., ENGLE R. F., GRANGER, C. W. J. and YOO, S. B. (1990), 'Seasonal integration and cointegration', *Journal of Econometrics*, 44: 215–38.

JOHANSEN, S. (1996), *Likelihood-Based Inference in Cointegrated Vector Autoregressive Models,* 2nd edn, Oxford University Press, Oxford.

—— (1997), 'Likelihood analysis of the $I(2)$ model', *Scandinavian Journal of Statistics,* 24: 433–62.

—— and SCHAUMBURG, E. (1998), 'Likelihood analysis of seasonal cointegration', forthcoming in *Journal of Econometrics.*

PANTULA, S. G. (1989), 'Testing for unit roots in time series data', *Econometric Theory*, 5: 256–71.

STOCK, J. H. and WATSON, M. W. (1988), 'Testing for common trends', *Journal of the American Statistical Association*, 83: 1097–107.

WEST, K. D. (1988), 'Asymptotic normality when the regressors have a unit root', *Econometrica,* 56: 1397–417.